# LEARNING FOR LIFE: POLITICS AND PROGRESS IN RECURRENT EDUCATION

RADICAL FORUM ON ADULT EDUCATION SERIES
*Edited by Jo Campling, Series Consultant: Colin Griffin*

# Learning for Life
## Politics and Progress in Recurrent Education

Edited by Frank Molyneux, George Low
and Gerry Fowler

CROOM HELM
London ● New York ● Sydney

© 1988 F. Molyneux, G. Low and G. Fowler
Croom Helm Ltd, Provident House, Burrell Row,
Beckenham, Kent, BR3 1AT
Croom Helm Australia, 44-50 Waterloo Road,
North Ryde, 2113, New South Wales

Published in the USA by
Croom Helm
in association with Methuen, Inc.
29 West 35th Street
New York, NY 10001

British Library Cataloguing in Publication Data

Learning for life: politics and progress
    in recurrent education.
    1. Continuing education
    I. Molyneux, F.H. II. Low, George
    III. Fowler, Gerry
    374      LC5215
    ISBN 0-7099-4646-5

**Library of Congress Cataloging-in-Publication Data**

Learning for life.

    (Radical forum on adult education series)
    1. Continuing education — Great Britain. 2. Adult
education — Great Britain. 3. Great Britain — Social
conditions — 1945- . I. Molyneux, Frank, 1932-
II. Low, George, 1940- . III. Fowler, Gerry.
IV. Series.
LC5256.G7L35    1987      374'.941      87-9173
ISBN 0-7099-4646-5

Printed and bound in Great Britain by
Biddles Ltd, Guildford and King's Lynn

# CONTENTS

Preface

Foreword by John Alderson,
          former Chief Constable of
          Devon and Cornwall

Abbreviations

## Section 1: Ten Years of Change

Contents

Contents

# PREFACE

by the Association for Recurrent Education

In 1974 the embryonic Association (ARE) collaborated with Ward Lock Educational to produce
'Recurrent Education - A Plea for Lifelong Learning'. In their editorial introduction Vincent
Houghton and Ken Richardson argued that Recurrent
Education was much more than a convenient shorthand
for various approaches to the expansion and elabo-
ration of traditional adult education in face of
changing circumstances. They noted that, even
then, continuing education was used to describe
developments primarily related to the retraining or
'topping up' of adults needing or wishing to find
new occupations. They stressed that the twelve
contributors had only a broadly convergent approach
but that they all believed that the 70s and 80s
would be a watershed in Britain's educational
development. They predicted a crisis in education
but saw in it more than the problems of quantity
and organisation which would accompany falling
rolls, rising unemployment, severe inflation and
continued economic underperformance. They talked
of a 'crisis of paradigm', arguing the need for a
'new way of seeing', for radically different per-
ceptions of and attitudes towards the provision of
education and training which would have 'consequences not only for adult education but for the
whole education system'. Thus their seminal work
on recurrent education, which formed a philosophical cornerstone for ARE's first decade, attempted a
theoretical underpinning of this paradigm shift.
It also launched the Association's continuing campaign to convince practitioners, politicians and
public that, in a painful period of adjustment in
education, Britain simply could not afford 'tinkering with what exists by those who have no clear
idea of what might ideally exist'.

# Preface

In many respects it might be said that what
follows in this ARE sponsored review of thought and
practice in recurrent education during the 1980s
bears out that warning from Gerry Fowler in 1974.
However, in one vital respect our position in commissioning this book in 1986 was radically different. Then, while insisting that the concept represented 'an inherent optimism about the future of
mankind, invested in the growth and availability of
knowledge resources and in the liberation of human
potentiality', we feared a fatal dichotomy in the
debate between those who felt the situation to be
hopeless in the face of political indifference and
those with faith and optimism about the changes
needed. In the 1980s, as several contributors
demonstrate, circumstances nationally have forced a
series of shifts towards a situation in which publicly financed opportunities for learning beyond
the compulsory school are increasing - some dramatically. It is precisely because we still await a
rational articulation in political terms of an
alternative recurrent based model that this book
could also be seminal.

It goes far beyond repetition of familiar
semantic argument. Nor is it dominated by statements of faith and hope and pleas for government
charity. In 1984 ARE chose to deploy its limited
funds but considerable collective energies to
mounting a public party-political debate on the
prospects for recurrent education. Its annual
conference brought Peter Brooke, the then Conservative Minister of State for Higher Education, to
Sheffield as keynote speaker. Andrew Bennett, MP
and Anne Sofer put the Labour and SDP views. Mr
Brooke, who has since departed from his responsibilities at the DES, did not consider his Sheffield
paper an appropriate representation of the Conservative Party view. Thus, this is expounded at some
length by Keith Hampson, MP, alongside the original
papers. Since these were written the 1987 general
election has brought the future of education into
sharper political focus and both Labour and the
Alliance have amplified their views.

The Labour Party policy document <u>Investing in
People</u> puts the emphasis on education and training
for young adults. There is also a commitment to
require employers to release workers for off-the-
job training and education without loss of pay. In
a previous policy statement the Labour Party
promised to expand higher education and provide

student grants for all those over 16 who want to take further education or training. The SDP are advocating increased part-time and modular study with credit transfer and accumulation. The Liberal Party has made a pledge to open up the Open University again by doubling the number of places and providing study grants for OU students.

On the Conservative side the new Secretary of State, Mr Kenneth Baker, quietly buried Sir Keith Joseph's cuts programme for higher education and has firmly declared that it is now government policy that as many young people as possible should continue their education after 16 and in later life. Meanwhile, from the positions of power and influence in the MSC there is now an insistent cry - the nation must update and upgrade its knowledge and skills base or plunge into a rapid decline.

John Alderson's excellent foreword not only extends our political perspective (he is a Liberal) but with his background as a radically innovative Chief Constable he reflects ARE's determination to be more than another talking shop for educationists. At Sheffield such wider views were vigorously exchanged - not least by Allan Ainsworth and Mike Cunningham representing industry and unions. We hope that John Alderson will follow in the immediate footsteps of Derek Ezra and Paddy Devlin in giving the Association's John Daniels Memorial Lecture - a platform barred to professional educators!

At its Belfast conference in September 1986, the Association voted to maintain its emphasis on political debate during election year. This book thus represents its policy of continuing to press the argument for political decisions which will signal the conclusive shift in thought and attitude away from the outmoded apprenticeship view of education. It presents the evolving debate from many important viewpoints against a background of current party-political belief. It shows that much good practice has been developed since 1974 and that political bridgeheads do exist in the long campaign to secure the citizens' full learning rights in a truly educative and democratic society.

Finally, we wish to express our gratitude to Helena Tennant and Pet Blanks, for secretarial help, and to Rory O'Hara, for compiling the glossary and index to this volume - all of them staff of North East London Polytechnic.

Frank Molyneux
President, ARE.

# FOREWORD

John Alderson CBE, QPM, LL.D(HC),
        D.Litt.(HC) barrister-at-law

Formerly Chief Constable of Devon and Cornwall

Visiting Professor of Police Studies
University of Strathclyde

Adult and continuing education have played such crucial roles in many of our lives and careers that the need for their improvement and expansion should be axiomatic. But we cannot afford to take this for granted.

Apart from the iconoclastic tendency, there exists the danger of under-valuing continuing education, and thus to starve it of necessary resources. There are no such tendencies or doubts in the minds of those who, like myself, owe both personal and professional success, however modest, to the second or even third opportunity to acquire an education which in early youth had evaded us but which adulthood had demanded if our lives were to be adequately fulfilled.

One is acutely aware of the importance of adult and continuing education to the enrichment of the lives of individuals, of organisations, and therefore of society. But as the technological revolution both advances and threatens the welfare of people, adult and continuing education become even more important. Bread and circuses will not do.

The social order of Britain both now and in the foreseeable future manifests increasing divisions between the successful people and places and those where success is elusive, and this in turn has implications for educational opportunities. There is little problem where people have a foot on the first rung of the ladder in a progressive organisation, but problems abound elsewhere.

Ignorance is a prime source of disorder, or at least that has been my experience. Its tendency to diminish self-regard and self-confidence can fuel violence in both individuals and groups. Inarticulateness can hasten recourse to expression through violence, as a visit to many of our criminal establishments will testify. The ill-educated often feel, and indeed are vulnerable to the dishonesty of the erudite in both public and private affairs, and the cynicism which protects them from this at the same time diminishes them.

Needless ignorance is not only a denial of human progress but it can be the source of injustice too. Since justice both in its substantive and formal roles is the most important claim on social institutions, (according to John Rawl's theory of justice with which I largely agree), then justice is the most important claim on institutions of education. Continuing education offers repeated opportunities to redress shortcomings and failure. It offers the means to compete in a sometimes brutally competitive society; it offers the means to secure human rights and civil liberties, and it offers the way to an understanding of the need to do justice to others. As the veil of ignorance concealing justice is lifted through knowledge then the view has to be available to all. The debilitating effect of class can best be dispelled through the confidence which knowledge brings. Class is a companion of that other socially disfiguring malaise born of ignorance, racism, and both are enemies of justice.

Next in line for some improvement from continuing education is democracy itself. In Britain the system of social democracy is still undeveloped. It serves us less well than it might. Ignorance, apathy and complacency, are its detractors. From the legislature to the neighbourhood community its rennaisance can only come from the greater knowledge and understanding of more and more of the population. To decant the young from school without adequate political awareness and to observe its perpetuation in the wider society is to inhibit the greater flowering of constitutional understanding and its beneficial effect on social affairs. Knowledge is power, therefore to spread knowledge is to create greater opportunity for power sharing.

If both justice and democracy are strengthened through the spread of knowledge then the social order itself is rendered more stable. Instead of drifting towards the kind of world in which the policeman's plastic bullet poses a more modern and lethal alternative to his wooden stave, in which our prison population like a gulag sees 'leaky civil servants' occupying cells with members of the underworld, in which more and more of the powerful and affluent have to live behind security systems and walk about flanked by guards, we may increase the chances of a better social order even if, or in spite of, becoming a less rich one in the material sense. That prospect alone should fire the continuing cause of continuing education. But clearly that is not all.

It is pointed out in the following pages much better than I am able to, how important to all our futures it is that those in our manufacturing and service industries need to keep pace with, and at times to lead, changes in the production and sale of commodities. As more and more people make demands to share management, to cooperate, to share the profits, (all of which I hope will develop), they too will need to have greater knowledge and understanding.

As for the so-called professions, both old and new, it has always been a source of wonderment to me that their continuing training and education has often been inadequate. This will not do and indeed is not fair to those who put their trust in them. As for the isolation of the education of professions, this in itself is often carried too far. Inter-professional training and joint education claim a greater place in policies so that each may enrich and enlighten the other.

We would all condemn the positive use of misinformation to excite or tranquilise the people, whilst perhaps overlooking the negative attitude of knowingly neglecting continuing educational policies. Both are on the same spectrum of socially damaging phenomena. If the only permanence in contemporary British society and its future is change, then continuting education is vital both for the quality of our existence as a civilised society, as well as for its commercial viability.

# ABBREVIATIONS

| | |
|---|---|
| **ABE** | Adult Basic Education |
| **ACACE** | Advisory Council for Adult and Continuing Education |
| **ACSET** | Advisory Committee on the Supply and Education of Teachers |
| **ALBSU** | Adult Literacy and Basic Skills Unit |
| **ALRA** | Adult Literacy Resource Agency |
| **ALU** | Adult Literacy Unit |
| **BAS** | British Association of Settlements |
| **BBC** | British Broadcasting Corporation |
| **BFI** | British Film Institute |
| **BIAI** | British Institute of Adult Education |
| **BTEC** | Business and Technician Education Council |
| **CATS** | Credit Accumulation and Transfer Scheme |
| **CBI** | Confederation of British Industry |
| **CCPR** | Central Council for Physical Recreation |
| **CNAA** | Council for National Academic Awards |
| **CP** | Community Programme |
| **CPVE** | Certificate of Pre-Vocational Education |

# Abbreviations

| | |
|---|---|
| **CSE** | Certificate of Secondary Education |
| **DoE** | Department of the Environment |
| **DES** | Department of Education and Science |
| **DHSS** | Department of Health and Social Security |
| **EBAE** | European Bureau of Adult E@ducation |
| **ECCTIS** | Educational Counselling and Credit Transfer Information Service |
| **EMA** | Educational Maintenance Awards |
| **ESG** | Education Support Grants |
| **ESL** | English as a Second Language |
| **FEU** | Further Education Unit |
| **FREE** | Forum on the Rights of Elderly People to Education |
| **GCE** | General Certificate of Education |
| **HEC** | Health Education Council |
| **HMI** | Her Majesty's Inspectorate |
| **ILEA** | Inner London Education Authority |
| **ILO** | International Labour Organisation |
| **IMS** | Institute of Manpower Studies |
| **IT** | Information Technology |
| **ITB** | Industrial Training Board |
| **MSC** | Manpower Services Commission |
| **NAB** | National Advisory Body for Public Sector Higher Education |
| **NAEGS** | National Association of Educational Guidance Services |
| **NEDC** | National Economic Development Council |

# Abbreviations

| | |
|---|---|
| **NIACE** | National Institute of Adult and Continuing Education |
| **NUPE** | National Union of Public Employees |
| **OCEA** | Oxford Certificate of Educational Achievement |
| **OECD** | Organisation for Economic Co-operation and Development |
| **OU** | Open University |
| **PEVE** | Post-Experience Vocational Education |
| **PICKUP** | Professional, Commercial and Industrial Updating |
| **REPALN** | Regional Staff Development Programme |
| **RSA** | Royal Society of Arts |
| **SCEO** | Society of Chief Education Officers |
| **SIACE** | Scottish Institute of Adult and Continuing Education |
| **TAP** | Training Access Point |
| **TOPS** | Training Opportunities Programme |
| **TUC** | Trade Union Congress |
| **TVEI** | Technical and Vocational Education Initiative |
| **U3A** | University of the Third Age |
| **UDACE** | Unit for the Development of Adult Continuing Education |
| **UGC** | University Grants Committee |
| **UNESCO** | United Nations Educational, Scientific and Cultural Organisation |
| **VPP** | Voluntary Projects Programme |
| **WEA** | Workers' Education Association |
| **WEEP** | Work Experience on Employers' Premises |
| **YTS** | Youth Training Scheme |

# SECTION 1: TEN YEARS OF CHANGE

# 1. EDUCATION, ECONOMICS AND SOCIAL CHANGE

Michael D. Stephens

In his book 'Three Men in a Boat', Jerome K. Jerome says of one of his characters:

> George goes to sleep at a bank from ten to four each day, except Saturdays, when they wake him up and put him outside at two.

Much of present day writing on social change suggests that the Age-of-George has now dawned. For example, Leisure Consultants in their 1981 publication 'Leisure and Work: the Choices for 1991 and 2001' pointed out that in the United Kingdom 9% of the population's available time was devoted to work, whilst 31% was taken up by leisure. They suggested that by the beginning of the 1970s already the average British worker was spending more time in leisure than work. In a seminal paper entitled 'Microelectronics: their Implications for Education and Training' as early as 1978, the Council for Educational Technology was cautiously predicting the following job losses due to the introduction of control devices:

i) replacement of assembly-line workers by robots (currently under way in the car industry);

ii) clerical operations (e.g. automatic cash dispensers and deposit-accepting machines directly linked to a bank's computer - currently available);

iii) electronic information provision (the Prestel service of the Post Office, the broadcast CEEFAX/ORACLE services, currently available);

iv) automatic (driverless) transport (operates on the London Victoria Line tube, and on air-

3

craft landing systems; feasible for road transport).

As clerical posts in the United Kingdom number several millions, the potential unemployment resulting from 'the chip' could be substantial in this area alone. However, the obvious does not necessarily happen. Those who have seen secretaries master a word processor will be struck by the fact that little extra time is created, but the range of jobs and productivity increases substantially. Those forced into that style of leisure normally called 'unemployment' often seem less the victims of development in technology than of government policies.

In 1981 the English Advisory Council for Adult and Continuing Education (ACACE) published their report 'Protecting the Future for Adult Education' which stated:

> Time is essential for effective education; with every year that passes more time is available to more adults, to the employed as well as the involuntary unemployed. The balance between work and non-work continues to change. The interludes between periods of employment, the incidence of shorter working weeks and working shifts, "flexi-time" working, and earlier retirement are all going to increase ... Not only work patterns are changing. It scarcely needs repeating that the nature of our society and the environment in which we live is undergoing constant and accelerating change. Technology changes the physical environment, the levels of noise, traffic, and pollution, the nature and variety of food, clothing and housing, and indirectly it changes the roles of the individual and the state, of employer and employee, of teacher and student, of man and woman, of parent and child, as well as the significance of family life and the interdependence of people.

Many of these themes were touched upon by Professor Robin Marris of Birkbeck College's Department of Economics in his Inaugural Lecture on March 6th 1985 ('The Exceptional Productivity of British Universities'). Professor Marris pointed out that '... we need to rid ourselves of the outdated idea that industrial activity is a sacred and wonderful thing, always and everywhere superior to all other kinds of economic activity'. He reminded a British audience 'We are of course now a net importer of manufactured goods and a net exporter of higher education'.

Marris saw a strong overall benefit to both society and to the individual in gaining a university degree or similar qualification, with an economic return of some 10%. This does not take into account such matters as 'consumer good' or the more effective utilisation of leisure.

The National Advisory Board for Local Authority Higher Education's Continuing Education Group's Report of July 1984 pointed out that, '... individual needs as expressed by student demand are paralleled by the continuing and growing needs of the (British) economy for a more highly skilled and adaptable labour force - economic needs which will be stronger than ever before the next decade'. Between 1982 and 1990 (University of Warwick's Institute of Employment figures) employment in manual occupations can expect to fall by 13%, whilst that in health and caring professions will grow by 9%, almost 13% in technical and related occupations, 14% in engineering and scientific occupations and approaching 12% in other professions.

Professor Tom Stonier's famous prediction to the Government's 'Think Tank' in the 1970s, that by early in the next century all of Britain's material needs would be produced by 10% of the present workforce, might not prove correct, but illustrated an economic trend which most people appear to take seriously. In their 1980 Paper 'Continuing Education: Post-Experience Vocational Provision for Those in Employment', the British Department of Education and Science (DES) stated:

> The Government believe strongly in the importance of mid-career courses of vocational education for those at work. This does not deny either initial education, which indeed is likely always to take a large share of education resources; retraining of the unemployed; or general continuing education for adults. But rapid social and technological changes underline the importance of continuing education to the full development of the individual, to the well-

being of the society in which he lives, and to the strength of the economy which underpins it. Therefore, we must develop the qualifications and skills needed in the country's workforce if managers and employees at all levels are to be able to meet successfully the complex challenges facing them and to promote economic growth.

The discussion paper went on to list the sort of programmes that might be offered, such as updating in specialist areas of theoretical knowledge or general advances in a field, acquisition of new employment skills, or qualifications, understanding of new technologies or processes, preparation for new responsibilities or for upgrading in a job, skills packages for the development of new processes or articles, commercial competence in foreign languages, and the development of enhanced communication skills.

With the creation of the Manpower Services Commission (MSC) in 1974, British governments acknowledged the key role of education and training within a fast changing modern society. The Department of Education and Science gave Her Majesty's Inspector (HMI) Samuel the MSC brief (the MSC being part of the Department of Employment). HMI Samuel wrote after some time in the post:

> There is growing acceptance of the view that education and training are complementary aspects of a single process. Although there is still some disagreement and misunderstanding, a lot of progress towards a unified approach has been made through the development and implementation of a common curriculum. There is a similar need to get acceptance of the view that work has also got complementary aspects. It is regarded at present as employment, that is as an activity primarily for the purpose of obtaining money. It may be related to career ambitions, it may be unpleasant, or it may be both. But there is also work which is not for gain, which is a pleasure to do and which is career-less. In order to convey the sense of this wider concept of work we need to use terms like usefully occupied instead of gainfully employed and constructive activities rather than careers. The

use of a vocabulary of this sort might influence the policy makers to think broadly
about these matters as happened when the
term unified vocational preparation was
introduced earlier. This wider concept of
work could provide the basis for a unified
"education and training" curriculum that
would serve the long-term future without
needing to predict it. Given this it becomes possible to develop a coherent
"national training system".

By 1977 the Manpower Services Commission was
publishing its priorities for the next five or so
years. These covered contributing to raise employment and reduce unemployment, assisting the development of manpower resources and a full contribution to economic wellbeing, to help those in employment to lead a satisfying working life, to
improve the quality of decisions affecting manpower, and to improve the effectiveness and efficiency of the MSC. Inevitably such elements as
that relating to satisfying working lives have
received low priority with the development of economic recession during the 1980s. Despite this,
the MSC objectives have attempted to give at least
some recognition to the two major strands to be
found in, notably, English education since the
Industrial Revolution. The first predates that
event and is largely reflected in our 'traditional'
adult education provision. This is the belief in
the 'well-rounded man' of the Ancient Greeks and
the Renaissance. Citizens should be broadly educated. The second resulted from the Industrial
Revolution's skilled manpower crisis. The economy
demonstrated an ever increasing appetite for more
highly trained workers (whether on the shopfloor or
in management). For the foreseeable future the
latter will have priority in the encouragement of
educational investment. 'Relevancy' would seem
likely to be the fashionable word in education
during the 1980s and 1990s. Education will be
favoured where it is seen as an investment good,
but rarely where it is defined as a consumer good.
Thurber stated 'she who goes unarmed in Para-
dise should first make sure that's where she is'.
There is much writing of future economic and educational scenarios in all industrialised countries,
but even the most careful of predictions may not
prove correct. The uncertainty has locked national

attitudes into often very traditional postures.
There can still be (at governmental level in particular) a belief that education is something that
happens between 5 and 16 years, or for a minority,
until 21 years. An idea which is developing in a
number of countries is that of a _right_ of _all_
citizens to education after 16 years. Such a
notion would seem unthinkable to many governments
at this time, or to perhaps most of the educational
institutions. It will come, but as a belated response to events (e.g. already we are seeing it
discussed to cover the political embarrassment
caused by the young unemployed). And yet if we do
acknowledge people as a country's greatest national
asset, there is a logic in such a right being
central to their well-being. Or are we in danger
of seeing people as the greatest liability?

A sure sign of the outdated attitudes to be
found in Britain is the directing of most resources
to school education and, since at least Premier
Callaghan's unfortunate Ruskin College speech of
the late 1970s, a rather old fashioned idea of
education. What schooling should be providing is a
good grasp of basic principles and school-leavers
with quick and adaptable minds. Greater independence will enable them to cope with increasing
leisure, changing technologies, and ever faster
social change. Alas, there still prevails a belief
that some rote learning and much information giving
is the need of 5 to 16 year olds on the assumption
that they are being stacked up with their total
education for the journey through life. At some
stage, school-teachers need to be trained who know
that they are part of a lifelong education system,
rather than providing the totality of a citizen's
education.

The Institute of Manpower Studies in Britain
in 1984 produced a report entitled 'Competence and
Competition. Training and Education in the Federal
Republic of Germany, the United States, and Japan'.
Despite all the limitations displayed by such attempts to generalise about very diverse countries,
it did illustrate well both trends and restrictions.

When dealing with West Germany the report
pointed to the fact that there was an underlying
'training for stock' philosophy. It was agreed
that it was better to have unemployed _skilled_ workers than unemployed _unskilled_ workers. This means
that almost 70% of those over 15 years old enter

apprenticeships and over 20% of the age cohort go onto higher education.
The report states of West Germany:

> The system is relatively simple. After a general education in a secondary modern (Hauptschule), an intermediate (Realschule) or a grammar school (Gymnasium) up to the age of 15 or 16, over 65 per cent enter VET (in the 'Dual System' or in full-time vocational schools); nearly 20 per cent study for 'A' levels (Abitur or similar); nearly 10 per cent go into various prevocational courses; and the remaining small percentage are lost to the system.
>
> In the Dual System employers provide training and the Länder Governments the day-release colleges (Berufsschulen). The training content of each of the 439 (1983) 'recognised training occupations' is sanctioned by the Federal Government after it has been established by employers and unions meeting in the Federal Institute of Vocational Training (BiBB). It is then implemented by 'competent authorities', ie the Chambers of Industry and Commerce and the 'Craft' (Handwerk) Chambers through vocational training committees.
>
> Employers bear 80 per cent of the total cost of apprentice training and hence play the key role in determining the content - the other 20 per cent of the cost being largely met by the Länder Governments. The commitment and participation of trade unions contribute much to the system.

The American element in the report is interesting in its attempt to summarise certain cultural characteristics such as the continuing belief that it is a land of opportunity, where each citizen is responsible for his or her own destiny, and with success largely measured in dollar terms. Such criteria, in the light of social change and personal experience, could be seen as either very old fashioned or as eternal verities.
Of the American system the report records:

> Education and training in the US is so complex as to make it difficult to summarise. American ET has been described as a 'vast

non-system'. Vast it certainly is, with VET offered to most secondary school students, and 1300 largely-public two-year colleges, 3000 public and private four-year colleges and universities, several thousand privately-run 'trade' schools, and extensive ET provided in-house by civilian employers and by the armed forces...

In terms of throughput the numbers in any year are impressive; over 15 million young people and adults are on vocational courses in secondary schools and vocational centres; over 7 million students in four-year colleges; about 1.6 million students in 'trade' schools; 0.5 million are undergoing skill training in the Armed Forces; and an estimated 6 million are engaged in off-the-job learning provided in-house by civilian employers...

The American ET system has delivered a broadly educated and trained workforce, willing to learn and adapt in order to compete. The country's continued success is now seen to depend both on the ability to extend these achievements and to provide sufficient relevant ET to meet the needs of the economy.

The major Japanese traits are seen as an emphasis on the long-term view, a clear national perspective, perfection in performance, and a striving for consensus decisions. This results in 94% of the relevant population staying on at school for the three-year upper secondary programme and 37% going on to higher education. Education absorbs a staggering 10% of national income. The report records:

Education does not abruptly cease upon entry to work. The national policy of 'lifetime education' is reinforced by the stress which firms' manpower policies place upon self-development. Workers' attendance at courses in their own time is a feature of Japanese life. Effective training begins upon entry to work...

The pervasiveness of various forms of Off-the-Job Training ... is the most striking feature of Japanese training, and their contribition to organisational flexibility is manifest. They include: group working, quality control circles and organised job rotation. Many of these might not be recognised as 'training' elsewhere, but they develop skills and competences. When added to training in technical skills to a level at least comparable with other nations, they explain much of Japan's ability to adjust to change in product markets.

Recession and technical change have revealed Japan's strengths in ET. In recession, the volume of training has increased. The state's direct training spend is being maintained and the private sector spending is increasing.

The report demonstrated remarkable contrasts between these three countries and Britain. Only in the latter do a majority of 16 year olds attempt to enter the job market. In the other countries the figure is about 5% or less. In these countries, education and training is much more extensive, both initially and regarding continuing adult needs. Continuous learning is assumed to lead to a workforce which is more adaptable, can function better as a team, and has more commitment to the job.

In 'A New Training Initiative. A Consultative Document' (1981), Britain's Manpower Services Commission considered, in a period of rapid technological and social change, that 'Training is not given sufficient priority. It is costly. The pay off may take a long time and people's perspectives are short. Not enough training is done and some that is done is mis-directed and wasted. As a result, many people are less productive and derive less satisfaction and reward from their work than they might'. In 1983 the MSC followed up their important consultative document with 'Towards an Adult Training Strategy. A Discussion Paper' which set clear objectives such as the extending and improving of skills to meet fast-changing needs ('to cope with the consequences of technological and structural change'), to provide continuing education opportunities to give people more confidence, more motivation, and to create a greater sense of responsibility.

In the list of recommendations for the United Kingdom at the end of the 1984 Institute of Manpower Studies Report, are the following:

4    In the UK, at least 85 per cent of 16 year olds should achieve acceptable standards in a core of subjects at school which includes the 3Rs.

5    The UK should aim to enable at least 80 per cent of young people to enter the labour market with a qualification relevant to their employment - this would mean withdrawing 16-and-17-year olds from the labour market, as is done in the other three countries.

6    A Youth Training Scheme (YTS) oriented towards occupational competence rather than non-directional foundation experience should become an important step towards Britain gaining a more competent workforce.

7    If employers consider that knowledge and skill are valuable, but not sufficient without the competence to apply them in working situations, they should use the opportunity presented by YTS to define more clearly and coherently what competence they want. A more purposeful YTS could recognise, assess and accredit competence in less tradition-bound ways.

9    The UK could not reasonably aspire to the rates of adult participation in work-related education and training which are found in Japan and the US. UK rates are not known but we should not be satisfied with less than the German rate of 12 per cent.

10   To remain competitive, British companies need to develop amongst their employees the ability to learn and the habit of learning, plus an ability to behave in a self-reliant way. More specifically, employees need to be able to:

- use acquired knowledge and skills in changing circumstances
- perform multi-task operations
- cross occupational boundaries and work in multi-occupational teams
- act in and help manage an integrated system, with an understanding of its wider purpose
- diagnose relevant problems and opportunities and take action to bring about results
- find out and acquire the knowledge and

skills needed to cope with unfamiliar circumstances.

11 To bring about an education and training system which consciously pursues these outcomes requires a substantial campaign. All institutions and organisations which influence managers, workers, trainers and teachers would need to play a part.
16 Employers should take the lead in proposing training outcomes and standards which will:

- assure employability for young people, and for adults who have lost their footing in the labour market
- raise productivity and occupational mobility. Employers should also take the lead in assessing and accrediting the achievement of trainees. In addition they must provide work experience and training designed to achieve performance objectives, thus implying close links with the education service, especially at local level.

17 Trade unions could be more active in helping members to keep their competence up to date, so as to match as closely as possible the requirements in external and internal labour markets.
19 The time has come for individuals to see that their desire for learning is relevant to their employment roles.

In the 1980s our educational objectives are clearly before us, but our abilities to move towards them are in doubt. There is a need to focus on educational recurrency, but only in certain areas of employment such as medicine has such need been matched by the will to achieve it. There is an inertia typified by a recent question at the end of a Royal Society of Arts lecture, 'Why cannot the status quo be the way forward?' This has been reinforced by the events of the contemporary recession in the world economy since the 1970s and the bruising monetarist response to it. The future does not look hopeful so why not cling to the familiar past?
After the eccentricity of the monetarist

experiment has been fully abandoned there will be a slow return of confidence in education which is always an investment in the future. Doubtless, the first sign of this will be far greater investment in the front-end model; the plea for better resourced schools and universities with better paid staff will then point up the more pressing dilemma of an adult population desperately ill educated in all aspects ranging from the needs of the economy, through social understanding and awareness, to political and social criticism.

Alas, such pressing developments in Britain may take longer than elsewhere because the cradle of the Industrial Revolution, that unique contribution in the story of humankind, has become educationally over-cautious and burdened by traditions which give education low standing. To take lifelong education as seriously as the Japanese do means that you must assume it holds the key to a better future. As suggested earlier Britain has lost much of its interest in the future. Britain, by far the most innovative of countries over the past 200 years, has settled for old themes like high defence spending and a rising crime rate (both so apparent in the pre-industrial era). Recurrent education will be extended, but using models from abroad and always with less investment than in comparable societies. The self-sufficient middle class professionals will fare well, but the bulk of the population will have to make do with the front-end model of education. Perhaps our first priority should be better educated politicians?

## References

Council for Educational Technology, 1978, Microelectronics: their implications for Education and training, London.

Institute of Manpower Studies, 1984, Competence and Competition: Training and Education in the Federal Republic of Germany, the United States, and Japan, London.

Leisure Consultants, 1981, Leisure and Work: the Choices for 1991 and 2001, London.

Manpower Services Commission, 1981, A New Training Initiative: A Consultative Document, London and Sheffield.

Manpower Services Commission, 1983, Towards a Training Strategy: a Discussion Paper, London and Sheffield.

## 2. TOWARDS RECURRENT AND CONTINUING EDUCATION - EDUCATION CYCLES OF FAILURE

T.R.P. Brighouse

There is a sense in which the notion of secondary education as such deserves to be still-born.
In the United Kingdom it has in any case enjoyed so
far a short life. The 1944 Act gave legitimacy to
the reform itself which had been advocated by the
Hadow Report and the progressives of the 1930s who
had been demanding secondary education for all
rather than just the privileged few in the grammar
schools and the independent sector. Nevertheless,
by the time the last of the all-age schools were
removed in the middle 1960s at least in the two
authorities - Monmouthshire and Buckinghamshire -
where I was working at that time, there had already
been an amendment to the 1944 Act to enable the
West Riding under the guidance of the influential
educationalist Sir Alec Clegg to introduce middle
schools with breaks at ages 9 and 13. Indeed the
Department of Education and Science Circular of
1965 requiring comprehensive reorganisation (10/65)
quickly embraced such variations on a theme for it
illustrated the many organisational options which
were legitimate in the pursuit of the greater good,
namely comprehensivisation of secondary schools.
Transfer therefore at ages 7, 8, 9, 10, 11, 12, 13
and 14 became commonplace. In at least one large
authority, Leicestershire, with which I am reasonably familiar, the schools and the system seem not
to mention 'secondary' very often at all. Junior
high or high schools and colleges often, but
secondary schools rarely are among the small change
and currency of the conversations as age-breaks at
10 or 11 and 14 rule Leicestershire thoughts.
Perhaps, too, as that was accompanied in the
Leicestershire Plan by a strong move towards community colleges or centres, initially in the high

schools and colleges, but ultimately in the primary
sector too, it is reasonable to point to their
comparative success in the league tables of educational outcomes whether in examination achievement
at 16 plus or 18 plus compared with the socio-
economic background (DES Statistical Bulletin
1983), or in the manifestation of music where the
authority properly has an acknowledged national
pre-eminence.

Indeed, although fanciful and certainly contentious, it is the thesis of this section that
'secondary' education is too closely linked with
the trappings of failure for it to deserve much
further life. It will be argued that it should be
buried forthwith. Words and their associations
matter and 'secondary' education has inevitably
acquired the hint of failure. It was inevitable
because the model was one of failure. Moreover I
think that in this matter, and for no other purpose, I side with those who demand a major new
consolidating Education Act. For notwithstanding
the flexibility afforded Clegg's West Riding and
his subsequent pale imitators, the establishment
betrayed its tell-tale adherence to the world of
Ptolemy rather than Copernicus when they determined
that middle schools must be 'deemed' either primary
or secondary. Small wonder that those deemed
'secondary', i.e. 9-13 as opposed to 8-12, led such
a schizophrenic life and were so unsure of their
own identity that they were ultimately swallowed up
in many places as a result of falling rolls - in
Hull, Stoke and other points north and south of the
Trent. Born out of convenience they have been
unceremoniously dumped. Where, however, the notion
was linked to primary education e.g. in Norfolk,
Buckinghamshire, Grimsby - significantly the same
LEA as Hull - they survive. Indeed so great now is
the association of success with primary education
that where in practice middle schools are linked to
failure with the retention of selection for secondary education (e.g. Buckinghamshire) they are even
so retained.

As I have already argued about the word
'secondary' the association of words matters enormously. It will be for this reason that 'continuing education' is a word that has more sublimal
chance of success than 'community' education. Community is seen by some as left-wing, socialist,
even bordering on the communist. Rightly or
wrongly that's how it appears. And, of course, for

some it is as welcome as for others it is not. The intrinsic worth of the idea however struggles, not in a neutral forum of argument and counter-argument, but in a heavily, even though suppressed and at times unrealised atmosphere of partisanship and inherited prejudice. As it happens, the word 'community' is imprecise in what it is trying to express in the sense that 'community' gives an idea of space rather than the important one of time which is implied by 'continuing'.

This is not to argue that all 9-13 middle, deemed secondary, schools are throttled soon after their birth as the decline in the birth-rate takes its toll. After all in Oxford City, faced with the most horrendous problems of falling rolls the middle school system holds up its head, and in other places, for example Hereford and Worcester and the Isle of Wight, its champions hold the floor - but it is to argue that they do so against the odds. 'Wouldn't it be better', the sirens argue with a smile, 'faced with intractable problems of falling rolls, to go back to a break at 11 like the rest of the county?' Well, no, it would not. It would simply do nothing to challenge the notion of secondary education with its inevitability of failure. Indeed, until there is an Education Act which changes the language of a system rooted in failure, the battle for improvement will be that much more difficult.

The problem with the British system of schooling in any case is that it has its roots steeped in the language of failure in a way unparalleled in other places, such as North America, with students' grades, their credits, their confidence (albeit somewhat misplaced) and their strong embrace of lifelong learning. Even their universities of 20-30,000 undergraduates boast as much as a third of their students over the age of 30. It is not so in Britain, and it will be the purpose of this section to illustrate the British pre-occupation with failure epitomised in the secondary school, and to postulate ways of overcoming it. As I have argued those ways will really be successful only when our conversations have expunged words associated with failure, and our legal framework ceases to sustain them in their pernicious effects.

Let us consider the origins of our state maintained system.

The first inspectors of schools were appointed, significantly not under education legislation,

but under the Factory Acts of 1833 - in the year
ironically of the abolition of slave trade. Two
such inspectors were appointed, and it was some
years before there was any educational legislation
as such, separate from that of the necessary framework surrounding an emerging industrial society.
Schooling arose not from any sense of belief but to
avoid the scandal of child labour in the mines and
factories. Schools, however, were erected and
established alongside factories, so that they
should be convenient for working parents and create
the expectation of factory employment for their
pupils. Indeed the first educational reformers
(for example, Robert Owen and his espousal and
enablement of infant and nursery practice) were
enlightened industrialists. In the 19th Century
however, with its contorted attempts to reconcile
parliamentary democracy and votes for all ('We must
educate our masters') with the need for millions
and millions of unskilled or semi-skilled, but
above all obedient workers, in the mines and factories, there was little doubt that to succeed in
life and to enjoy a reasonable degree of adult
autonomy you needed to obtain a charitable place in
one of the private schools or the small number of
tiny endowed grammar schools springing up around
the country. (The exception was, of course, that
you were born into the right family.) Doubtless
the close juxtaposition of church and school in the
rural areas and factory and school in their urban
counterparts explained the relative lawlessness of
urban living. The Church did its best, however, to
ensure by its involvement in the state system that
future citizens had a strong moral sense of duty
and of the natural order of a society which was
essentially deferential. Deference to the squire
in the village, to the factory owner in the town
and to the mine owner and his minders in South
Wales was embedded in .the early rhythms of life.
    The unruffled calm of this emerging industrial
world continued until, on the one hand, the 'do
gooders' of the early twentieth century attempted
to equalise life's chances and, on the other hand,
the rich man's table was threatened by the possible
exclusion of some few among the masses who might
contribute to its further wealth at best or the
preservation of the existing order of society at
worst. They - the 'do gooders' and the establishment - settled on a tacit compromise. There should
be a selective examination at age eleven and those

20-30% who passed would enjoy grammar school education, while the rest of the population would stay on - initially to 13 then bravely 14 and (ultimately and dangerously after the Second World War) 15 in all-age schools. They, of course, were still tucked up hard against factories in the town, or hard by the Church in the villages, so that those who did not pass were reminded of the inevitability of their destined role as future citizens. So it came to pass that many of our former grammar schools were established during the first thirty years of the twentieth century. And in the grammar school I attended in the 1950s the staff still attempted to persuade some from the C stream - not the awkward squad, of course - to stay the course for 'O' Level rather than leave as they might at 15. The waste of talent was impressive. The basis of selection was rooted in ambiguity and doubtful authenticity.

The administrators and educationalists, in order to make the selection for grammar school, settled on a view of ability which was at once monocular and ungenerously flawed.

It was monocular because it viewed - and still views to this day - ability and intelligence as general and inherited and, in practice heavily dominated by the cognitive ability to deal with the abstract. It did not recognise a wide range of talents, for example musical, motor, physical, numerical, literacy, the practical ability to solve problems which may or may not be understood theoretically, inter-personal ability or intra-personal ability. Significantly such multifaceted notions of ability have always had greater currency in the United States, but they were suffocated in the secondary schools of our own country with their streams, their bands and their sets, even in their talk of 'mixed ability' classes. The very progressives indeed who embrace what they consider to be an enabling process for all youngsters use in the 'mixed ability' terms of their argument the very notions that they apparently seek to expose to overthrow.

It was also flawed and ungenerous because such a monocular view of ability was differentiated at 11 plus by tests of ability or intelligence founded and justified by an educational psychologist who quite simply invented some of his results to support his theory. Cyril Burt was not only knighted for his efforts, he ran the British Psychological

19

Journal as part of an elaborate structure designed to underpin his impregnable formulation. It even seems he invented academics and aliases in order to refute the real research of academic challengers such as A.H. Halsey. His pervasive influence has so dominated our thinking, especially in his own domain, the old London County Council, that even today his successors in the Inner London Education Authority categorise children into Band I, Band II and Band III in allocating secondary places. Moreover they judge their secondary schools by performance measured by the same flawed notions of ability institutionalised in exams at General Certificate of Education (GCE 'O' Level) and Certificate of Secondary Education (C.S.E.), even if they moderate them for socio-economic background.

That brings us to the issue - examination at 16 plus - which turns out to be the next refinement of the process of failure which has been a common theme of the development of the schooling system in the United Kingdom. When the next set of do gooders - the successors to those who had demanded secondary education for all - urged a non-selective form of secondary schooling, the industrialists were still in need of very large numbers of unskilled or semi-skilled obedient workers. So did the establishment. By selling comprehensive education as 'grammar school education for everyone' - for such was Prime Minister Wilson's phrase in the course of the political debate which led to DES Circular 10/65 - and most importantly by ignoring the Beloe report's critique of examinations and instead accepting the illogical recommendation of a new examination namely C.S.E., the cycle of failure based on a monocular view of ability was reinforced. Primary schools, freed of tests which failed 75% of their pupils, have with difficulty thrown off their mantle of failure. The baton was passed to secondary colleagues who now within one comprehensive establishment just as secondary education for all became a reality, attempted to sort the academic wheat from the chaff. Whereas their predecessors, the secondary modern and grammar schools, could within their own portals have their own limited view of success which was accessible to most pupils the comprehensive school could not. With a prospectus to provide grammar school education for all and an examination system stretching from the mountain of G.C.E. Grade A to the molehill of C.S.E. Grade 5 they set about their task with a vengeance. The earlier vast comprehensive schools streamed their schools in code 1C, 1M, 1P, 1R, 1H 1N, 1S, 1V so that the children should not realise whether they were aiming at the mountain or the molehill. With devilish cunning in some schools in year 2 they reversed the process - 2V, 2S, 2N, 2R, 2P, 2M and 2C - confusing not so much the children, who quickly realised where they were in the value system of the school, but the staff.

By the end of the third year and the prize day, all was revealed as the recipients of honour turned out to be the G.C.E. '0' and 'A' Level candidates, and the oak walls of former grammar schools still carried the names of illustrious alumni who obtained degrees at Oxford and Cambridge. The assembled third year were asked to note those who were honoured, and encouraged to put play behind them and to work hard for the next two years so that they too might be honoured. There was an unspoken compromise with those for whom such aspirations were unreal ... 'You don't bother us and we won't bother you'.

What was and is unfair in all that endeavour is the habit the education system has perpetuated of norm referencing the outcome on a very narrow view of ability. The existence of examinations tied to age does not help, but to have those examinations inexorably limited to percentage success rates for each grade is calculated to reinforce an inclination to failure. Until more practical prominence can be given to criterion referencing - the notion of known and understood standards of performance for assessment of certain skills and activities - the expensive tinkering with the examination system represented by the General Certificate of Secondary Education (G.C.S.E.) is doomed to reinforce failure. At first G.C.S.E. will merely be a more effective failure system. Pupils at new speech days should truthfully be told (and doubtless will in code), that however hard they work, more than 50% will achieve Grades F and G only. Not exactly a keen motivator, especially when the remaining 45% will have the remaining five Grades spread to settle their academic fine tuning.

Criterion referencing and the schooling system will properly escape failure only when they escape the concept of age-related learning and a narrow view of human talent. The notion of life-long learning on a continuum of learning along which each individual is properly at a different stage

depending on the knowledge, the skill and the attitude that he or she is developing, might then be a
realisable ambition.

The real and sadly rare examples of 'schools
for success' in the primary sector have features
which deserve close examination. The abolition of
the 11 plus was a start, but the real successes in
primary schools occur where teachers have consciously eschewed horizontal patterns of age group-
ing for learning. Where age group teaching per-
sists how often do you find red, yellow, green and
blue tables even in reception classes? What chance
is there for pupils to have a wide view of talent
when in such classes early reading schemes for 6
and 7 year-olds have the title 'one, two, three and
away', and when you are 'away' you are on the gold
table and learn to enjoy comparative success not
just in reading but everything? Even musical
opportunities with recorders are thrust into your
hands whether you have musical ability or not.
What must it be like to be 'one, one, one and never
away'?

But if there are residual problems in the
primary schools, they are as nothing compared with
secondary schooling even when it has been freed by
a change in the examination system. The comprehensive school has not yet thought through its philosophy or principles sufficiently to question the
inherited characteristics of a deferential age. I
have mentioned the examination system, which even
in its latest G.C.S.E. reform has the trappings of
failure, at least until the coursework and the
grade related criteria are generally introduced in
the 1990s. The option system, however, with its
lingering headlines of the grammar school curriculum, the grades A-E for attainment only given to
pupils' work throughout the school, the prize days,
the language (e.g. 'Our least able pupils'), the
hut for special needs at the end of the playground
or the books over-stamped 'remedial', the pastoral
(secondary modern)/academic (grammar) split of
posts, the hierarchical culture of posts ... the
list is endless.

The 'lockstep' of the age group betrays those
schools 'Going community'. Schools will escape
from the inevitability of failure when they look at
the drip-feed timetable, and when they therefore
cease to treat their pupils as products rather than
clients or workers, when they change their assessment system and when they break the 'lockstep' of

age related learning. This they now can do. The Oxford Certificate of Educational Achievement (OCEA) is a comprehensive system of assessment designed to reflect a full range of human talent, the various means of assessment and to celebrate success and not failure. It has three components; the E component contains external examination results such as those represented by G.C.S.E., C.S.E., and vocational certificates (Business and Technician Education Council, City and Guilds and the like), and is information dominated; the G component is a cross curriculum means of assessing skills; and the P component attempts to record through the pupils' eyes and hands their actions as proxy to their attitudes. It is being developed by the Oxford Delegacy of Local Examinations and will accredit schools and the teachers in them. In short it is an attempt designed under the most rigorous conditions by teachers in schools in Oxfordshire, Leicestershire, Somerset and Coventry to throw off the shackles of failure and embrace new mechanisms for clear success.

Unlike their predecessors such teachers have a chance. They have a chance because the deferential society has largely passed away. There is no longer the need for those millions of unskilled and semi-skilled workers. The tasks such workers would have performed, whether in manufacturing or service sectors of the economy, on the shop floor or at the supermarket till or the bank, can be performed equally well by micro-technologically engineered machines. Our wealth as a society will be generated by confident and competent human beings who have autonomy. Our inter-dependence as a society will be sustained by notions of equal value of human talent. The industrial or perhaps the 'drone-dependent' industrial society is giving way to the technological industrial society.

It becomes important now to join in the eternal chorus of educationalists with some belief that its message might at least be accepted. That chorus has always been - to treat man not as he is but as he might become. When a decade or so before the First World War, Holmes, the 'Payment by Results' Inspector, wrote a retirement repentance, 'What is and what might be', and when Temple at the time of the Second World War emphasised moral, social and political justice for treating man as what he has it in him to become, they echoed what every good teacher has always known but which the

system has demanded should be ignored.    Holmes and
Temple,  however,  raised their voices in a desert.
The  climate  has now changed,  the  irrigation  has
begun and the desert can be reclaimed.

## 3. THE CONTINUING EDUCATION OF ADULTS: TRADITION AND CHANGE

Alan Charnley and Arthur Stock

### Trends from 1919 to 1944

Though we may point to the development of adult education in Britain during the nineteenth century, there is a case for starting our examination of tradition and change by referring to the '1919 Report' of the Adult Education Committee of the Ministry of Reconstruction. That report identified the bases of our tradition, namely, the importance of the individual, his or her educational potential as a person, and the 'large and important place in the development of adult education for local education authorities in cooperation with the voluntary organisations'.

Between 1919 and 1945, concern for liberating the individual was exemplified in a number of ways. William Emrys Williams, once Secretary of the British Institute of Adult Education, set out in 1935 as an experiment of 'Art for the People', a movement which led to the formation of the British Film Institute and the Arts Council of Great Britain (Hutchinson, 1971). The right of education for all members of the community on grounds of morality, democracy and a '... necessary corrective to the conditions of our present system of industrial production' was mentioned by Ernest Barker at the Institute's Cambridge conference in 1923 (ibid.). In that address, Barker considered the growth of leisure, and remarked that '... if leisure be largely for education, education is also largely for leisure'. His vision was of society in which each and every individual enjoyed reasonable periods of leisure, and in which education provided the knowledge and skills for the happy and fruitful deployment of that leisure. There was also concern

for the individual victims of society. Speaking
about the unemployed, A.D. Lindsay, in 1933, commented that what weighed most on those who had been
long unemployed was that they had no status or
function in the community (ibid.). But Richard
Livingstone, in 1937, said that '... one of the
most important tasks of education at the present
day is to study the victims, to have in our minds a
clear idea of what we think education should do and
to ask how far our present system actually achieves
that result...' (ibid.). In that speech to the
Institute we may discern a widening of view to take
into account not only the growth of each individual's personality, achievement and wisdom, but
also the positive assistance of groups of individuals, such as the unemployed, who were paying the
price of societal and technical change. The tradition for the special programme model was being
established.

Less impressive than the developments described above were the responses of the local education authorities. Their main concerns were for
schools and the pupils. It may be argued that
Morris in Cambridgeshire, in his development of the
village colleges, managed against great odds to
place the schools within a community context; but
making the community part of the schools is a
battle still to be completely won.

### 1944 onwards

The 1944 Education Act was not particularly
helpful to adults; its main concern was the education of children. True, it was a duty of the LEA
'... to contribute towards the spiritual, moral,
mental development of the community...' (our emphasis) but this and Section 41, with its duty '... to
secure the provision of adequate facilities for ...
leisure-time occupations in such organised cultural
training and recreative activities as are suited to
their requirements...' could, in the words of
Gordon Bessey, Director of Education in Cumberland,
'hardly be less precise' (Bessey, 1963). Bessey,
addressing the Society of Chief Education Officers
in 1963, commented that in operational terms,
Section 53 (on facilities and training) is permis-
sive; and the duty to provide 'adequate facilities'
is undefined. If anything flowed from the 1944
Act, so far as it affected adults, it was in spite
of this legislation rather than because of it.

Bessey ably describes progress up to 1963; on the credit side, nearly one million people were in adult education classes in 1961; on the debit side, there was a widespread impression that they were low-grade continuation classes, inferior in importance since their standards of achievement were different (again, our emphasis). He remarks on the support of local non-statutory organisations by the LEAs, but noted that these organisations were '... struggling against each other for help from limited public funds', sometimes engaging in '... damaging internecine criticism'. Clearly, in the early sixties, the traditional words, 'leisure', and 'recreation', which had their carefully defined and understood meanings in the context of the 1919 to 1939 period, were now perceived differently, possibly inaccurately, by the general public.

## The growth of further education establishments

A relatively fashionable phrase, 'non-vocational adult education', which gained in currency and in favour during the sixties, created an even worse impression. 'Non' meant something negative; 'vocational' meant following a calling. What on earth did this negative phrase mean other than something pursued by lucky people with time on their hands, namely the middle classes? The public image of adult education was further eroded by the spectacular growth in the vocational (or further) education sector of education for adults, for here appeared to be an activity with clear and easily understood objectives. From the early fifties, Britain's poor industrial performance, relative to Western Germany in particular, exercised the minds of various Governments. In the 1960s technical schools became technical colleges, or colleges of further education, and some of them burgeoned into Colleges of Advanced Technology. The pressure came from a series of reports, circulars and Acts of Parliament such as the 1965 White Paper on Technical Education, the DES Circular of 1962 and the Industrial Training Act of 1964. 'Day-release' from work, usually for young adult males, became the standard mode of continuing study. In 1920-21 there were in the day-release category 48,800 students in vocational classes and 3,200 in non-vocational classes; by 1950-51 the respective figures were 246,300 and 58,800. F. Jones, writing in his M.Ed. thesis (University of Nottingham

27

1954), remarked that the function of day-release in 1950 was to carry on the vocational work of the evening continuation classes. Writing in 1972, A. Shaw in his M.Ed. thesis (University of Manchester) noted that after the introduction of part-time General Certificate of Education Courses in the 1950s, part-time GCE students represented 6.5% of all part-time enrolments in 1970. Thus, evening classes in colleges of further education, as a form of continuing adult education courses, seemed to be more and more used for vocational studies; but in these colleges, although 'evening only' students increased in numbers between 1951 and 1961, the rate of increase was far below that experienced in the whole day-release category of students. From 1974 to 1983 'evening only' student registrations declined whereas 'day-release' numbers continued to increase.

Table 1  Total number and percentages full-time and part-time 1974/75 and 1983/84 in non-advanced further education in England

|  | 1974/75 | 1983/84 | % change 83/84 from 74/75 |
|---|---|---|---|
| Total number (000s) | 1583.4 | 1578.3 | -0.3 |
| Full-time (%) | 13.8 | 21.8 | +8.0 |
| Part-time (%) | 86.2 | 78.2 | -8.0 |

Source: Parliament, answers to question in 'Education', 5 July 1985, Vol. 166 No. 1, page 23.

From the early sixties a pattern emerged of a switch from evening to day-time study and towards vocational/examination courses, even in those courses that remained available for evening study. Within this trend a sexist bias could be discerned: in 1970 over half the 'evening only' part-time students were female, whereas only one quarter of part-time day students were female.

## The growth of adult education and the confirmation of basic principles

Nevertheless, the growth of local education authority provision in major further education establishments up to the mid-1970s was paralleled by the growth in adult education classes and in the influence of adult education methods and values.

Some of the traditional principles of adult education - for example, the concern for the individual's general culture and the contribution of each student's experience to group learning - percolated into the further education sector through the medium of the 'liberal studies' curriculum. At the same time subjects such as 'modern languages' would appear in the prospectus of either a college of further education or an adult centre. So far as student choice was concerned there was no doubt that by the middle of the 1970s local provision was wider based and offered more choice than ever before. — A major curriculum notion remained: that adult education should offer a stimulation of interests, a challenge to creative capability and an extension of trends of experience unfettered by the 'straight-jacket' of examinations. In seeking to extend their general culture, students would as a group and in equal negotiation with their tutor, determine the educational route they would take. From a generalised analysis of culture emerged the notion of the peculiar contribution of education to developing - through experiences of study and activity - the 'rounded individual' i.e. Renaissance man or woman.

It may by contrast be argued in the mid-1980s context that a series of special programme models and new emphases in main stream provision has extended educational opportunities for adults; and that change has not meant the rejection of traditional values but rather an increasing influence of that traditiion (i.e. the 'great tradition') which gave equal attention to both the process of learning and the acquisition of knowledge. Consequently the terms 'vocational' and 'non-vocational' are eschewed as being irrelevant to our consideration of tradition and change. Indeed it is interesting that in a paper of 1984, R.L. Corbridge, (Area Vice-Principal, Central Area of Community Education, Manchester) wrote, 'This (the activities of the Manchester Open College Federation) will yet further weaken the unreal and invidious distinction between vocational and non-vocational provision'.

## The growth of special programmes

The year 1973 was, using hindsight, a turning point in the education system for adults. It was, in a sense, the year of a nightingale which found a cuckoo's egg in its nest, and as is the habit of

29

nightingales it did not recognise the resultant chick until too late. The nightingale was, of course, the Russell Report, a document of lyrical vision. 'The value of Education', it argued, 'is not to be measured solely (our emphasis) by direct increases in earning power or productive capability or by any other materialistic yardstick, but by the quality of life it inspires in the individual and generates for the community at large' (HMSO, 1973).

Three points are worthy of selection from that extensive Report for the purposes of this chapter. First, it called for early clarification of what was meant by a 'varied and comprehensive service' (as written in the 1944 Act) in relation to adult education; that is, a clarification of those vague phrases questioned by Gordon Bessey ten years earlier. Second, it asked for the revision of Sections 41 and 42 of the Education Act of 1944, '... as soon as the opportunity arises'; and thirdly, it encouraged local education authorities in cooperation with other agencies to make special efforts to provide for the 'disadvantaged'. In the event, none of those three recommendations was carried out directly as a consequence of the Report. There was no policy statement clarifying terms; and of course, when 'the opportunity arises' is a gift to government intertia, so the law remained unchanged. The first essay into a large scale service for adult illiterates resulted more from pressure groups, particularly from the British Broadcasting Corporation (BBC) and the voluntary sector organised by the British Association of Settlements, than from local government initiatives.

In 1974, a million pounds was allocated for the financial year 1975/76 by central government to the Adult Literacy Resource Agency, (ALRA), a national agency set up and made responsible to the National Institute of Adult Education Council (NIAE), to advise and, through grants, help local authorities and voluntary organisations establish provision for adults with severe difficulties in reading and writing. A series of BBC prime-time television broadcasts from October 1975 paved the way in a drive to recruit students and volunteer tutors and to increase public awareness of the problems. There was no doubt that many local education authorities were worried at the prospect of a nationally led adult literacy campaign with its concomitant stimulation of local expectations, and

regarded ALRA as an unwelcome precedent of centralised influence. But the advisory role of ALRA,
extended through its metamorphoses into the Adult
Literacy Unit (ALU, 1978) and the Adult Literacy
and Basic Skills Unit (ALBSU, 1980), clearly left
the final decision making and provision in the
hands of the local authorities. The Unit is seen
as an essential specialist educational resource
upon which local authorities and voluntary organisations can draw. The result is that the education
service for adults has recruited, over the period
of ten years, some 350,000 adults whose previous
educational experience largely ended at the minimum
school-leaving age. It has proved to be a remarkably successful extension of educational opportunity to adults hitherto outside the service's horizons. But the characteristics of this special
programme are, first, the predominance of local
authority support and finance and second, through
research, an understanding of the criteria of success as being equally skill acquisition, self-
confidence and self-image improvement which create
the basis for motivation to further cognitive
effort. It should be noted that with the exception
of a few experienced specialists, such as Alan
Wells (current Director of ALBSU), it was thought
in 1974 that skill acquisition in literacy would be
the sole easily identifiable criterion of successful course completion. Thus the acceptance by NIAE
of the relatively narrow terms of reference of ALRA
was seen as a tactical necessity; the broader
strategy should be pursued once a successful initiative had been established. Nevertheless,
because of its breadth of vision, the Russell
Report remains a powerful influence for the
encouragement of general liberating education. The
Russell Report was in many ways unfortunate in its
timing; and this was in stark contrast to the adult
basic education 'cuckoo's egg' which, once hatched,
prospered.

The Employment and Training Act of 1973 set up
the Manpower Services Commission (MSC), which
started in 1974 to run many of the public employment and training services previously provided by
the Department of Employment and the Industrial
Training Boards. Ten years later, the Commission
handled a budget of £2 billion per annum and itself
employed some 22,000 officers. In Autumn 1984 it
issued a discussion paper called 'The Adult
Training Strategy'. Though there were ambiguities

31

in the paper, the main thrust of the argument was towards skill training and an education system which was primarily aimed at preparation for work and which reflected the changing needs of the market place. But just as the Russell Report did not wholly exempt market conditions from its criteria of desirable aims, <u>after ten years experience</u> the MSC did not wholly <u>dismiss general education</u>; for in its Adult Training Strategy proposals (Section 5(e)) it argues that 'the need for <u>education</u> (our emphasis) and training for any individual <u>will</u> not be once and for all, but <u>continuing</u>'. Thus, in spite of the turmoil resulting from a major Department of State (that of Education and Science), and a massively funded 'quango' (the MSC) accountable to the Secretary of State for Employment, being both involved in the education of adults, by 1984 a pattern of provision emerged which was not too far from the aims stated in the 1919 Report and not wholly inconsistent with the views of the Russell Report. What happened was that the Department of Education with its local education authorities and voluntary body partners, focused some of its activities on the needs of the economy and market; and the Manpower Services Commission, through experience, came to recognise - at least in part - the place of general education and the importance of 'building up self-confidence as a means of flexible response to conditions in a changing economy in which relevant skill training is a principal ingredient' (MSC, 1985). It is not surprising, therefore, to find that the following special programme models which take place within the ambience of DES/LEA/Voluntary Organisation management or the MSC/LEA/Volunatry Organisation systems have tended to converge.

The MSC courses originally started with the simplistic assumption of skill acquisition as the goal for success. The various schemes were directly funded and the syllabuses largely centrally devised by the MSC. A diversity of agencies, including the LEAs, could apply for financial support but the general understanding was that they had to meet the objectives, fairly strictly defined by the MSC. Such courses, schemes or activities were many and various and include, for example, Training Opportunities Programmes (TOPS), Preparatory Programmes (Pre-TOPS), and the Community Programme to which is currently linked training as part of the Adult Training Strategy, the Voluntary

Projects Programme, New Opportunities for Women and Wider Opportunities for Women schemes.

There were additional programmes funded by other Departments of State such as the Department of Health and Social Security's Opportunities for Volunteering, the Department of the Environment's Special Grants Programme and Urban Aid Fund and the Home Office Section 11 grants. Indirect sources of finance were also available from (for example) the Council for Small Industries in Rural Areas, the Health Education Council and the Sports Council. But together these resources are a tiny fraction of the MSC's budget.

It is interesting to note that in practice, general education has crept into many schemes. Certainly in some MSC Community Programmes, the criteria of success, such as self-confidence and self-image, are recognised to be as important to an individual seeking employment as the acquisition of the defined working skill itself. It is ironic that the DES and LEAs with their traditions do not wish to appear purely work-oriented other than in their long-standing concern to provide a preparation for employment; and that the MSC, largely because of its legal status, wishes to appear primarily if not exclusively work-oriented; hence the constant use of the term 'training' and avoidance of the term 'education'. But though the student or client probably has little or no concern about the source of the provision, the power structure and style of operation affect him or her in one principal way: if it is left completely to local authorities to determine, then as in the case of basic skills provision, there are differentials between one local geographical area and another and local conditions may well be taken into account. By contrast, a centralised organisation such as the MSC may direct the provision and thus equalise; but if the central body lacks vision and sensitivity a uniformly poor service prevails regardless of local circumstances and oportunities. The signs are that both DES and MSC recognise this dilemma and are attempting various mixtures of central and local cooperation; and it is perhaps because of these attempts that there has been such a growth in the number of schemes. Under the DES umbrella examples of recent additions are the Professional, Industrial and Commercial Updating (PICKUP) scheme, the REPLAN scheme of educational opportunities for the adult unemployed; also the direct funding of the

Unit for the Development of Adult Continuing Education scheme (UDACE), which is part of the National Institute of Adult Continuing Education (NIACE).

In March 1984, the government decided to make available some £2.5 million over the period 1984-87, for a programme to encourage the further development of educational opportunities for unemployed adults in England and Wales. This programme, funded by DES and the Welsh Office, is known as REPLAN; and principal features of the scheme, managed by NIACE, include the appointment of an advisory team of field officers, the funding of development projects, and regionally organised programmes of staff development. There is also a programme of curriculum development managed by the Further Education Unit (FEU). Additionally, Educational Support Grants (ESG) have been made available from 1985/86, to support projects by LEAs relating to the planning, coordination and development of educational provision for the unemployed (expenditure amounting to about £1.6 million was approved for ESG support in the first year) (Charnley, 1985).

Clearly this is a case of funding specifically or directly for education purposes in contrast to the Department of the Environment grant for Urban Renewal in which an educational input is regarded as a useful supportive or instrumental activity.

The Unit for the Development of Adult Continuing Education (UDACE) receives a separate grant from the Department of Education and Science, but is a unit of the National Institute of Adult Continuing Education. Its purpose is to examine areas of possible development in education for adults, to recommend strategies for development and to sponsor projects which will encourage development. The overall pattern of the Unit's work is decided by a Steering Committee, which sets up small development groups of experienced practitioners to examine particular topics and to steer enquiries and pilot projects. Ideas for development are received from a variety of sources, including the Department of Education and Science, the local authorities, universities, voluntary organisations and interested individuals. The Development Groups meetings and other activities such as seminars and conferences provide frameworks and ample opportunities for adult educators substantially to influence UDACE's activities. None the less, it is true that the purse strings are ultimately in the hands of a department of state; and this contrasts - for the most part - with previous systems of allocating grants where providers spent as they themselves determined (within the fiat of the overall grant purpose).

These are some examples - and there are others - to establish the argument that various systems of special programme funding have greatly modified the systems of finance and institutional management which pertained before 1973. What are the results of this phenomenon? How far has it affected the nature of adult education in England and Wales? Are there other factors which are responsible for more extensive and fundamental changes?

## Results and responses

There are certain features of the finance of education for adults that are worth rehearsing, as much of the following argument depends on these assumptions. The first important characteristic is that the adult education budget is a small marginal proportion of the total educational budget and it is not secured by precise legal obligation. Therefore, in any period of economic restriction adult education finance is at risk. Secondly, as adults pay a considerable proportion of their costs, if total costs are to be kept constant then free or low tuition fees for special target groups may lead to increases in the fees charged for other students, thus often reaching levels at which there is considerable consumer resistance. In periods of retrenchment, the concern of society as a whole for a specific group entails subsidy either from local rates or from the pockets of other adult students. The more concentrated geographically the target group, the greater the local financial burden unless central funds are made available. Moreover, special programmes and finance from the DES (and other departments of state) have tended to be short-term, so that local authorities have a continuing problem in arranging their finance over the long-term.

It is a feature of most special groups, particularly those designated as disadvantaged, that their educational problems are long-term. There immediately arises a local political concern, deriving partly from the short-term nature of the systems of locally disposable finance, to avoid accepting liabilities for the future; there is equally an educational concern based on the problems of retaining local expert staff, advisory services and other essential resources when the central funding ceases. Consequently, the response to 'pump-priming' may be muted. Something is usually done, but care may have to be taken to ensure that enthusiastic publicity does not recruit too many of those in need; and schemes which are seen by local educationalists as potentially important and worthwhile are not fully implemented. These criticisms also apply to the MSC courses which, for adults over twenty-one years, are usually limited to a maximum of one year. However, these special post-1973 programmes to redirect help to specific groups and to extend adult education to those previously not attracted, are largely a result of such innovations. It is impossible to prove that if all providers had been given an extra ten per cent in real terms that there would inevitably have been adult basic education provision and also educational opportunities for the unemployed. What is known is that in the period 1945 to 1973 the growth in adult education students tended to be from a restricted range of socio-economic and formally educated groups, whose demand was essentially for 'more of the same'. Extra money seemed to be used to keep fees down rather than to innovate. For these reasons, we expect in the foreseeable future, a continuing requirement for services to specific target groups for which some finance will be provided; but an unwillingness by central or local government, whatever the political complexion, to supply money on a long-term basis or to offer it unconditionally to providers to spend as they think fit. Nevertheless, we still believe that special funding for target groups will not exceed 50% of net (i.e. net fee income) expenditure. In 1984, in one of the most socially deprived areas, adult education enrolments by target groups was about 2,000, whereas enrolments in general class provision reached about 2,600. (These figures do not include the work of voluntary organisations in the area).

There are further reasons for believing that financial help will be directed to target groups and will be short-term. Demographically, the structure of our population, because of changing birthrate and terminal ages is very uneven, as can be seen from the demographic statistics below. Courses, schemes and activities for the 30-44 year

old age group will continue to be relatively important, but the relative and absolute growth in numbers of the over 60s, and indeed in the over 65s,
will clearly exert pressure for new developments in
the service in this direction.

The multi-racial nature of our society similarly points to a service tailored for specific
group interests and needs rather than to a service
which could take for granted cultural and social
homogeneity.

Technological changes in broadcasting and
information technology suggest opportunities for
more programmes and delivery systems appealing to
target audiences. If the present trend of adult
educational provision by the broadcasting authorities continues at the level of about one quarter of
local authority expenditure, we may predict that
new patterns of broadcasting (especially where
'recruiting' is a major emphasis) will place pressure on the local authority and voluntary organisation providers to seek out and service target
groups. But this change may result in an improvement in the service as a whole, if we are to retain
our tradition of courses, classes, groups, in which
individuals from differing backgrounds and experiences come together as equals to share in a common
interest, study or activity. It is in this respect
that we defend the 'great tradition' of adult
education; and it is in this area that our concern
for 'target groups' may reduce the civilising
vision of adult education. What we think is needed
is a sense of balance and this we do not think has
been maintained because there is evidence that
'mainstream' general education has been denied the
resources needed for 'natural' expansion, and to
meet the obvious needs and expectations stimulated
by many of the new 'target group' programmes themselves.

Enrolments in adult education since 1973
increased to 1976 and then decreased. But the
moving annual average trend is about that given for
1982/83 (see Table 2).

If this figure has remained fairly stable,
then because of the increase in enrolments on
special programmes and projects, 'general' adult
education has not expanded. But it should have
done so, as Table 3 shows.

In 1971, 1980 and 1981, the most numerous
cohort is the 16-29 years group; the second most
numerous cohort is the 30-44 age group and it is

Table 2    Enrolments in adult education 1982/83*

| | |
|---|---|
| Total | 2,770,000 |
| Men | 900,000 |
| Women | 1,870,000 |

(*Adult education defined as courses provided by adult education centres, community centres, youth clubs, residential colleges, maintained or assisted by local authorities, university extra-mural departments, and the Workers Education Association).
(Source: Parliament, answers to questions reprinted in 'Education' 29th February 1984, Volume 163, number 16, page 335).

this which will display the greatest percentage increase from 1991 to 1997. As it is this group which has in the past provided the typically modal users of the education service for adults, then the adult education service could be expected to expand in enrolments, and in expenditure. A further reason for expecting the growth in 'general' courses is the changing proportion of men and women over sixty-five years of age, normally with non-work related interests. This group increased proportionately from 13.1% in 1971 to 14.6% in 1980, and is estimated at 14.9% in 1991. The percentage of women over 60, as a proportion of all females is quite startling; 21.8% in 1971, 22.6% in 1980 and an estimated 22.6% in 1991. Thus about one out of five of all females are of an age when 'general' or non-work related education is relevant. This suggests that there should have been growth, not a standstill, in 'general' adult education services from 1971 onwards. The statistical evidence surely confirms the responses from the field which the NIACE research and survey team have been receiving from their continuing informal contacts with providers. Consequently, our policy considerations below must be read in the context of a need for an increase in total expenditure which allows for special projects for targeted groups plus the maintenance of 'natural' growth in general education for adults as indicated by demographic trends.

## Table 3
### Sex and age of UK population (millions): % changes in 1971/1991 and 1980/1991

| Age (years) | 1971 (mid years) | | | | 1980 (mid years) | | | | 1991 (est) | | | | % Change 1971/1991* | % Change 1980/1991* |
|---|---|---|---|---|---|---|---|---|---|---|---|---|---|---|
| | Male | Female | Total | % | Male | Female | Total | % | Male | Female | Total | % | | |
| 0-4 | 2.3 | 2.2 | 4.5 | 8.1 | 1.8 | 1.7 | 3.5 | 6.3 | 2.3 | 2.2 | 4.5 | 7.9 | +0.2 | +1.6 |
| 5-15 | 5.0 | 4.7 | 9.7 | 17.4 | 4.8 | 4.6 | 9.4 | 16.8 | 4.1 | 3.9 | 8.0 | 14.0 | -3.4 | -2.8 |
| 16-29 | 5.6 | 5.4 | 11.0 | 19.8 | 6.0 | 5.7 | 11.7 | 20.5 | 6.2 | 5.9 | 12.1 | 21.2 | +1.4 | +0.7 |
| 30-44 | 4.9 | 4.8 | 9.7 | 17.4 | 5.4 | 5.3 | 10.7 | 19.1 | 6.0 | 5.9 | 11.9 | 20.3 | +2.9 | +1.2 |
| 45-59 | 5.0 | 5.2 | 10.2 | 18.3 | 4.8 | 4.9 | 9.7 | 17.3 | 4.6 | 4.7 | 9.3 | 16.3 | -2.0 | -1.0 |
| 60-64 | 1.5 | 1.7 | 3.2 | 5.8 | 1.3 | 1.5 | 2.8 | 5.0 | 1.3 | 1.5 | 2.8 | 4.9 | -0.9 | -0.1 |
| 65-74 | 2.0 | 2.7 | 4.7 | 8.4 | 2.2 | 2.9 | 5.1 | 9.1 | 2.2 | 2.7 | 4.9 | 8.6 | +0.2 | -0.5 |
| 75-84 | 0.7 | 1.4 | 2.1 | 3.8 | 0.9 | 1.7 | 2.6 | 4.6 | 1.0 | 1.8 | 2.8 | 4.9 | +1.1 | +0.3 |
| 85+ | 0.1 | 0.4 | 0.5 | 0.9 | 0.1 | 0.4 | 0.5 | 0.9 | 0.2 | 0.6 | 0.8 | 1.4 | +0.5 | +0.5 |
| All Age Total | 27.1 | 28.5 | 55.6 | | 27.3 | 28.7 | 56.0 | | 27.9 | 29.2 | 57.1 | | +2.7 | +2.0 |

Source: Social Trends 13, Central Statistical Office, London, HMSO, 1983, CR1, P.12, Table 1.2.

* Own calculations + (increase), - (decrease).

## Policy conclusions

1.  Each local education authority, having the
    responsibility in law '... to secure the pro-
    vision for their area of adequate facilities
    for further education...' needs to be mapping
    and monitoring trends and effectiveness of
    provision and underwriting schemes from volun-
    tary organisations, to ensure that 'natural'
    expansion in enrolments takes place.
2.  At the same time, they have a special respon-
    sibility to ensure that the quality of the
    service is improved, specifically through
    staff training and development.
3.  In particular, the quality of the service
    depends both on the inclusion of proper
    'general' cognitive and affective elements in
    all programmes and on an offer of a wide
    variety of learning experiences which are able
    to be progressively pursued by participants in
    a continuous and coherent fashion.
4.  We see much of the above range of objectives
    being realised through greater linkages. At
    local levels, there should be a further growth
    in linkage encompassing all institutions/
    organisations offering educational courses
    and/or activities for adults. But this policy
    only makes sense if educational information
    and guidance services for adults become inte-
    gral features of all education and training
    efforts.
5.  We suggest a policy which does not either
    favour or diminish projects for specific
    groups but which encourages greater coopera-
    tion to create an educational service for
    adults which offers a multitude of means for
    learning, from a variety of providers. We
    could present specific detailed paradigms to
    achieve these ends but this is beyond the
    scope of this paper.

Here we have indicated the 'tradition' and the
inevitability of change. Our plea is for proper
overall resources to take up the challenges and
opportunities seen so clearly by Emrys Williams -
and Lindsay - more than fifty years ago, and by the
authors of the Russell Report over ten years ago,
and more recently by the several authors of the
Advisory Council for Adult and Continuing Education
(ACACE) reports, and very recently by discussion/

action documents emerging from UDACE.

We should suggest that unless these challenges are firmly and positively addressed then the nation state will be the poorer, both economically and socially. And above all, the people will not live as well, as fruitfully or as happily as they deserve.

## References

Barker, Sir E., 1923; address to the British Institute of Adult Education, reprinted in Hutchinson, E.M. (ed), 1971.

Bessey, G., 1963; Light on a Dark Patch, Presidential Address to the Association of Chief Education Officers.

Charnley, A.H., McGirney, V.K., and Sims, D.J., 1985; Educational Provision for the Adult Unemployed: some responses, NIACE, Leicester.

Education, Journal of the Society of Education Officers, Longmans, London -
- vol. 163, no. 16, 29 February 1984
- vol. 166, no. 1, 5 July 1985
- vol. 166, no. 5, 2 August 1985 (Collier, A.)

HMSO, 1973; Adult Education: A Plan for Development, Report by a Committee of Inquiry appointed by the Secretary of State for Education and Science under the Chairmanship of Sir Lionel Russell C.B.E. ('The Russell Report'), DES/HMSO, London.

Hutchinson, E.M. (ed.), 1971; Aims and Action in Adult Education 1921-71, NIAE, Leicester.

Jones, F., 1954; M.A. thesis, University of Nottingham, Nottingham.

Lindsay, A.D., 1933; Unemployment and Adult Education, Metcalfe Memorial Lecture, reprinted in Hutchinson, E.M. (ed), 1971.

Livingstone, Sir R., 1937; reprinted in Hutchinson, E.M. (ed), 1971.

MSC, 1985; Community Programme News, issue no. 13, Self start - building confidence, Manpower Services Commission, Sheffield.

Shaw, A., 1972; M.Ed. thesis, Victoria University of Manchester, Manchester.

Williams, W.E. 1935; The pre-history of the Arts Council, reprinted in Hutchinson, E.M. (ed), 1971.

# 4. ADULT AND CONTINUING EDUCATION: NATIONAL ADVISORY COUNCIL AND ALL

John Taylor

The Advisory Council for Adult and Continuing Education held its first meeting in October 1977 and Council members met formally for the last time in October 1983. For most of those six years I was the senior member of the Council's small secretariat. From that experience I want now to suggest what I personally regard as the issues which were then and continue to be critical to the growth of adult and continuing education.

To do that I will sketch in the Council's beginnings, recall something of what it was hoped it might achieve, describe some of the things which happened, note a few of the achievements, and then speculate briefly on the future consequences, or perhaps some are subsequences, for adult and continuing education.

First then the beginnings. From the start two issues were never far from the Council's thinking: the distinction, if any, to be made between adult and continuing education; and the difference between an advisory and a development responsibility.

Both were implicit in the name - Advisory Council for Adult and Continuing Education - and inherent in the Council's putative parentage. If we cite those parents, in the horse-world way, as by Russell out of Venables, the 1973 Russell Report (HMSO 1973), called for a national development council for adult education, while in 1976 the Open University's Venables Report (Open University 1976) recommended a similar council for what it saw as the wider scene of continuing education. Both reports emphasised the importance of the development function.

When the newcomer's arrival was announced by the then Secretary of State for Education, Shirley

42

Williams, it turned out of course to be Advisory with a dual remit for both Adult and Continuing Education. This suggests ministerial caution, fostered no doubt by the educational administrators' maxim that advice is cheap but action runs up the bills, and perhaps by some reluctance to play at Solomon in judgement over where the latest neologism should fit in any naming of educational parts. It was the Council therefore which had to devise the distinctions to help stake out its area of work.

This practical imperative led to the assumption that the 'Adult' and the 'Continuing' in the Council's polysyllabic title were not tautological. At least if they were synonymous one could have been jettisoned to lighten the title's load - although which one should have gone overboard would have brought us back to Solomon. In the event the Council took the hint from its double-barrelled remit drafted by the Department of Education and Science:

(a) to promote co-operation between the various bodies in adult education and review current practices, organisation and priorities, with a view to the most effective deployment of available resources; and

(b) to promote the development of future policies and priorities, with full regard to the concept of education as a process continuing throughout life.

Very neatly, function (a) was seen as standing for the organisationally defined trinity of local education authority, responsible body, and voluntary body provision, usually and inaccurately lumped together as non-vocational education. A sector which the Council thereafter sought to rename - with limited success - adult general education. While adult education did at least exist as a recognisable, if nearly always impoverished, sector of the education system, function (b) was by contrast seen by the Council as the educational world's unchartered continent, which had to be surveyed and assessed so that maps could be drawn and development plans written.

These two defined spheres, however, were not separable. Therein lies another aspect of the naming of educational parts - the relationship of those parts. Was the adult education sector to be

43

seen as the engine of the new continuing education machine? Or was it one of the wheels, and nonetheless important because the machine would not get far without it? Or put more starkly was the adult education sector central or peripheral to the development of continuing education?

Perhaps not surprisingly the Council's 'balanced' view was shaped by the make-up of its membership. Out of the twenty-three members, all appointed by the Department of Education and Science (DES), who served in the Council's first three years, perhaps a dozen could be regarded as professional 'adult educators', including Richard Hoggart, the Chairman, although his early university extra-mural career had been followed first by international work and then the directorship of a university college.

Presumably this balance in the membership was not mere chance. The Department had, certainly after a good deal of consultation, drawn up the Council's twin title and remit. From this negotiation perhaps stemmed the notion of an eleven-a-side membership. It must be said that this never led in any sense to two opposing teams, but there could occasionally be some hesitation about the precise direction in which to kick the ball.

In the Council's second three-year term, for which the membership was partly changed, there were perhaps eight adult education members. By then the Council's direction was set towards revealing the scope for continuing education while at the same time seeking to head off any further decline in the there-and-then of adult education provision.

Again this highlights another of the dichotomies in the Council's existence, and one still only too obvious today; a declining education budget having to be matched with a growing number of adults in the population and with a spreading conviction that they too had a right to education.

Against this confused background the Council was in business to give advice. It had no power, and no budget, to create, but it had authority to influence. Part of that authority lay in the Council's membership and part in the right they had to place their advice at the highest ministerial level. A further and unusual advantage was the openness of the Council's remit: it could advise whom it wished about whatever it chose - and it did.

It would be fair to argue that in choosing

where to exercise this authority the Council was
guided more by responding to real problems and the
practical world than by constructing any overall
philosophy. That after all is the way the British
- or at least the English - generally do things.

On the adult education side the job was seen
to be promoting confidence in the future by examining, reporting and exhorting on and about the
countless contributions that adult educators were
and could be making, and by drawing the lines of no
retreat.

With continuing education there had to be more
speculation, but even here it came down largely to
clarifying the practical aims and matching them to
the present and future resources of a re-orientated
adult, further and higher education system. The
post-colon part of the title of the Council's main
report on Continuing Education: from Policies to
Practice (ACACE 1982a) reflected where the Council
reckoned the emphasis had to be put.

Insofar as the Council consciously subscribed
as a body to some guiding belief beyond the imperative value of rapidly expanding the opportunities
for the education and training of adults, I always
felt this was contained in Richard Hoggart's rally-
ing cry, usually brought forth at the end of a long
toing and froing discussion, when he would quote
Bacon to the effect that we were all working for
'the love of God and the relief of Man's estate'.

The very fact that there was a national advisory council for adult education raised the confidence and expectations of the adult education sector. The very fact that this same council was also
to advise on continuing education made the further
and higher education world a little wary of some
kind of attempt at a take-over by the adult educators; and left the adult educators uneasy that any
grand design for continuing education could leave
them overlooked and overtaken by the big battalions
of tertiary education.

Nevertheless there was no shortage of goodwill
at the outset for the Council's work. This was
confirmed by the large and supportive response
received to the Council's two early discussion
papers, which rehearsed for public reaction the
Council's stance and broad intentions in relation
respectively to adult education and continuing
education under the self-explanatory titles Present
Imperfect (ACACE 1980a) and Towards Continuing Education (ACACE 1979a). These early publications

gave speedy evidence that the Council could spread its influence through the printed word. This was amply borne out later in the impressively large sales figures for many of its reports, some of which had to be reprinted.

This pursuit of influence had obviously to be at the heart of the Council's efforts. To help achieve this the Council made a very early decision to go for an open policy on circulating public information releases about its current deliberations and actions; nothing was confidential except the working drafts for its reports. By the end of six years there was a long list of the Council's papers which had been circulated in this way. For example thirty-seven formal responses were made to other organisations' invitations to comment on their proposed developments, including a half-dozen responses to the Manpower Services Commission on different initiatives, three to the Home Office, and three memoranda to the House of Commons Select Committee on Education (full list in ACACE 1984).

Similarly the Council reacted quickly to any retrograde proposals, wherever they might emanate from, by sending letters of protest and making counter-proposals, as for example when a local authority proposed to shut its short-term residential college or the Customs and Excise began to levy value added tax on adult education course fees. On each of these many occasions the Council could bring to bear the weight of its independent opinion made up of the collective views of its respected membership.

However the main weight of the Council's efforts was put into its full-scale published reports, the compilation of most of which was overseen by small steering groups. Forty-one printed publications appeared in this way; thirty reports, six discussion papers and five occasional papers (ACACE 1984).

The reports covered a remarkable range of concerns from particular aspects like training for management in adult education to distance learning and adult students. To the extent that these thirty reports can be classified as either 'adult education' or 'continuing education' orientated, my count comes out at eighteen for the former and twelve for the latter. But allowing that there has to be a lot of overlap between these categories, the division is more like half-and-half with perhaps an emphasis towards more specifically adult education concerns.

Only two of these reports - on adult basic education and on education for unemployed adults - were in response to direct commissions from the DES. The remainder were decided upon by the Council and thereby reflect its interests and concerns and its notion of the component parts and boundaries of the continuing education field.

That record leaves no doubt that the Council became a substantial publishing house in its own right; indeed for a few years it must have been the biggest publisher in its field.

One thing that was not foreseen in the setting up of the Council was that the national provision and take-up of education for and by adults was only sketchily measured and recorded. Hence, with only a few exceptions, every area that the Council decided to enquire into and report on, had first of all to be surveyed and as far as possible statistically assessed. Only then could the current state of play and thereby the starting point for any proposed developments be stated with any confidence. As a result the Council became the biggest research and survey body in its field.

To carry out these enquiries and draft the subsequent reports, the Council not only employed a steady succession of researchers, but it also called on the voluntary unpaid services of a large number of knowledgeable and experienced people to act as members of its steering groups. Beyond that the Council took part in several joint enquiry exercises with other bodies, for example the Arts Council of Great Britain and Birkbeck College. As a result the Council's deliberations and conclusions were most often shared by many more people in the field than just the Council's own membership.

In the final year of its work the Council's time was obviously much occupied by considerations of what its own future should be. With so much research done, so many reports published, and so much advice offered to so many, the Council was sceptical about recommending any continuation of its limited advisory remit. The feeling was that while there was some justification for going on with the sort of work done by the Council, it would nevertheless soon mean repeating and updating the work already done. This conjured up images of the educational equivalent of painting the Forth Bridge - important enough to the survival of the structure, but not getting the bridge widened or even bigger and better bridges built.

This line of thinking led the Council to advise the DES that it should be succeeded by a body with a substantial and free-ranging developmental remit (ACACE 1982b). After much reflection it was further decided that, in the event that the Department would not accept this development proposal, the Council would not recommend any such fall-back position as the continuance of a national advisory body. It was to be all or nothing. The Department first chose to do nothing. Sometime later it announced the setting up of the Unit for the Development of Adult Continuing Education (UDACE) and a separate Replan organisation for the education of unemployed adults.

The Council was of course no longer in existence to comment on these Departmental initiatives. Had it been, my guess is that the response would have been to welcome the gift horses, with a strongly worded regret that ministers were apparently not prepared to advance on the broad front needed to make a reality of a national system of continuing education. Instead progress was to be made piecemeal, and even the pieces were to be slenderly funded.

Any comparison of the initial hopes invested in the Council with the outcome of its six years of work is complicated by the difficulty of relating cause and effect in educational developments. We have to tread carefully near the trap of post hoc ergo propter hoc (i.e. what happens afterwards must be the direct result of what happened before).

It can certainly be claimed that UDACE and Replan (with the continuing education scope of its joint administration through the National Institute of Adult Continuing Education and the Further Education Unit - FEU) are reduced and limited versions of proposals made by the Council (ACACE 1982b and 1982c). Similarly the continued and flourishing existence of the Adult Literacy and Basic Skills Unit (ALBSU) may have been helped by the arguments in the Council's basic education report (ACACE 1979b). ALBSU's extension into literacy work was no doubt helped by the Council's pioneering surveys - with the Cockcroft Committee on the Teaching of Mathematics in Schools - of numeracy standards among the adult populaton (ACACE 1982d). Similar co-operative surveys with Birkbeck College and other bodies led to a report on the lack of part-time degree courses in Britain (ACACE 1982e). The steady growth in the provision of these courses since that report appeared may not be merely coincidence.

In the interval between the departure of ACSTT (Advisory Committee on the Supply and Training of Teachers) and the arrival of its successor ACSET (Advisory Committee on the Supply and Education of Teachers), the Council kept alive some national consideration of the original ACSTT proposals for the training of adult education staff (ACACE 1983). And in educational guidance work for adults the Council can claim to have published the first national report in Britain on this important subject (ACACE 1979c). This remains, seven years later, a basic text for the field, which was further described by the Council's annual publication of a directory of educational guidance services for adults, and then illuminated by a published collection of case studies about the practices and effectiveness of local guidance services (Butler 1983). Both the director and the case studies originated in joint enquiry work with the British Library's Research and Development Division. In 1979 the Council was able to list eighteen local guidance services operational or planned; the directory, which continues to be published elsewhere, shows that in 1986 that total has grown to seventy-four (ECCTIS 1986).

Adult guidance has more recently been taken up as one of UDACE's first areas of work. Its report on the subject (UDACE 1986) is a valuable successor to the Council's report, and demonstrates how particular strands of the Council's advisory activities are being carried forward at a national level.

The biggest single job undertaken by the Council was its attempt to draw a blueprint for the development of continuing education. The main outcome of this was the report on Continuing Education: from Policies to Practice (ACACE 1982a), which one of the Council's members, Naomi Sargant McIntosh, did so much to help bring to completion. It has proved to be the Council's biggest selling publication, with the National Institute for Adult and Continuing Education (NIACE) producing another reprint this year.

That report has provided educationalists with a check-list of the component parts of any continuing education system, and it has detailed advice on how those components can be developed into an inter-related system. Perhaps just as

49

importantly the report has helped to establish a definition of continuing education by comparison with inititial education:

> Initial education can be defined as the continuous preparatory period of formal study, to whatever level, completed before entering main employment. Continuing education covers anything which follows.

In a letter to Richard Hoggart, the Secretary of State for Education, Sir Keith Joseph, wrote 'I do not think you should underestimate the effect which the Council's work has had upon the terms of the debate about allocation of educational resources. Continuing education now has a "seat at the table"' (Chairman's Preface, in ACACE 1984). It is certainly true that continuing education as an idea now has a recognised and welcome currency that it did not have five or six years ago. The extent to which that would have happened anyway, without the intervention of a national advisory council, must be a matter of opinion. My concern now is how that 'acceptable currency' is going to affect the education and training of adults.

It seems to me that some of the particular areas of provision on which the Council anxiously advised are now tolerably secure, if still nowhere near as extensive as the Council had wanted to see. Thus Replan is in being to advance education for unemployed adults, and ALBSU is securely astride the national development of adult literacy and numeracy provision. As a personal note I can be confident that the Educational Counselling and Credit Transfer Information Service (ECCTIS) will give increasing support to guidance services and to credit transfer opportunities. UDACE has given educational guidance work a boost which may yet result in a national unit for its development; and in other areas, like the relationship of voluntary and statutory providers, the Unit can move in to advise and recommend.

There though is the nub of one of the still unresolved matters for the future. The Council advocated a successor body with developmental powers and a multi-million pound budget to itself make things happen (ACACE 1982b). UDACE has 'development' in its title and a very small budget. Can it move beyond its present essentially advisory and exhortatory function to doing these things itself? Or do we go on with a process that seems to offer no more than the chance of a developmental wing on an advisory prayer?

My second concern for the future is that since the Council's demise there has been no authoritative national focus for continuing education, excepting the work of interest groups, like the Association for Recurrent Education, which seek to maintain a synoptic view of what is needed. At worst this means drift, and maybe not even drifting forwards; at best it means largely unco-ordinated, and possibly contradictory, initiatives in separate educational sectors and institutions.

My third concern stems from the possibility of drift, which may be purposeful enough in some places, but could also be sporadic and unrelated to developments elsewhere. That in turn could breed a sense of sectoral and institutional competition, which may not in itself be a bad thing, except when it turns its back on co-operation and becomes opposition.

One of the few, but most persistent, charges laid against the Council was that in its proposals for the development of continuing education, it took little account of the adult education sector. This charge stemmed partly from the fact that the Council published a separate report on adult education (ACACE 1981) without making sufficiently clear its connection with the report on continuing education. For the Council it was a straightforward assumption that adult education was a fundamental part of continuing education. Perhaps the Council should have foreseen that that connection would not be so evident to others, like those who regarded the education of adults as the business of adult educators, to whom the influx of a new race of 'continuing educators' might do more harm than good.

Certainly the adult education sector is where the most professional experience and knowledge about the education of adults should be found, and where it should be actively pursued and improved. But the scale and variety of provision needed not just in the future but now, cannot be achieved by that sector alone. The much larger resources of further and higher education must be welcomed and harnessed.

Thus at the end I have come full circle. The definitional difficulties and the sectoral differences inherent in the title of the Advisory Council for Adult and Continuing Education are still with us. Equally the lead given by the Council in its six years of work is still there in its many published reports. Progress is being made piecemeal, but there is no machinery to lead and help integrate developments nationally. Worthwhile work will no doubt go on being done by such bodies as NIACE, UDACE and the FEU, but none can either fully represent the whole range of the providers, which together make up the continuing education field, nor are they adequately funded to do the work needed to launch new initiatives and encourage cross-linkages through the whole range of provision.

I submit that the Council's last publication outlining what was required of and by its successor body (22), modest as those proposals were, still represents the most effective way to move into the future on a broad enough front to make sense of the policies and practices needed for a system of continuing education.

## References

ACACE 1979a; Towards Continuing Education: from Policies to Practice: a report on the future development of a system of continuing education for adults in England and Wales, Advisory Committee for Adult and Continuing Education, Leicester.

ACACE 1979b; A Strategy for the Basic Education of Adults: report commissioned by the Secretary of State for Education and Science on national policy proposals, ACACE, Leicester.

ACACE 1979c; Links to Learning a report on Educational Information, ACACE, Leicester.

ACACE 1980a; Present Imperfect a discussion paper on the current trends in Adult Education and the issues to be met in the next few years, ACACE, Leicester.

ACACE 1980b; Regional Provision for the Training of Part-time Adult Education Staff, ACACE, Leicester.

ACACE 1981; Protecting the Future for Adult Education: a report on the issues affecting the present provision of Adult General Education, ACACE, Leicester.

ACACE 1982a; Towards Continuing Education: from Policies to Practice: a report on the future development of a system of continuing education for adults in England and Wales, ACACE, Leicester.

ACACE 1982b; The Case for a National Development Body for Continuing Education in England and Wales: proposals presented to the Secretary for Education and Science and the Secretary of State for Wales, ACACE, Leicester.

ACACE 1982c; Education for Unemployed Adults: report commissioned by the Secretaries of State for Education and for Wales on the role of the adult education service in providing for unemployed adults, ACACE, Leicester.

ACACE 1982d; Adults' Mathematical Ability and Performance, ACACE, Leicester.

ACACE 1982e; Tight, M., Part-time Degree Level Study in the United Kingdom, ACACE, Leicester.

ACACE 1983; Training for Education Management in Adult Education, ACACE, Leicester.

ACACE, 1984; Fifth Annual Report of the Advisory Council for Adult and Continuing Education, H M Stationery Office, London.

Butler, L. 1983, Case Studies in Educational Guidance for Adults, London.

ECCTIS 1986; Educational Counselling and Credit Transfer Information Service and the National Association of Educational Guidance Services, Director of Educational Guidance Services for Adults, Milton Keynes and Leicester.

HMSO 1973; Department of Education and Science, Adult Education: a Plan for Development (The Russell Report), HMSO, London; vide esp. para 160.4.

Open University 1976; Report of the Committee on Continuing Education (The Venables Report), Open University, Milton Keynes; vide esp. para 126.

UDACE 1986; The Challenge of Change: Developing Educational Guidance for Adults, Unit for the Development of Adult and Continuing Education, Leicester.

# 5. BROADCASTING AND RECURRENT EDUCATION

Naomi Sargant McIntosh

Both the terms in the suggested title of this chapter may well prove limiting if they are too strictly interpreted. The chapter is of necessity too short to engage in a philosophical discussion either about the validity of the concept of educational broadcasting or about the use of the term 'Recurrent Education'. And at any rate, terminology is frequently used by educators as an internal code for communication or to score points between themselves rather than to further the cause they pretend to espouse.

Others raise the specific merits and unique qualities of recurrent rather than continuing education, or of 'education permanente' (since 'permanent education' is even less appealing), lifelong learning (too emotional for the British), and others again have suggested that there is no need for a new term, since 'adult education', they say, has already been doing and is capable of doing all that needs to be done in the future. Since this last is patently not true and the other debates, being essentially sterile, merely feed into the hands of our enemies, this chapter starts from two premises, firstly that broadcasting <u>can</u> contribute to the education and training of adults and secondly, that we are concerned with 'education and training as a process continuing throughout life'. The terms of reference given to ACACE in 1977 'to advise generally on matters relevant to the provision of education for adults in England and Wales' and, in particular, its second charge 'to promote the development of future policies and priorities, with full regard to the concept of education as a process continuing throughout life' are still important guidelines for us. Distinc-

54

tions between education and training may be helpful to organisers and funders of education and training and also useful for politicians. They are not helpful for people who wish to learn.

Some will argue that educational 'broadcasting' in its original terrestrial sense has little role in the future: that video disc, cable, etc., should and will take over from it. In themselves, the new technologies are neutral, and are simply alternative distribution systems. None are intrinsically more suitable for 'public service' use or for educational and community broadcasting than others. The choices that need to be made revolve around peoples' needs, the type of content to be communicated and the question of who pays and at what stage in the process.

Broadcasting, in itself a term soon to become old-fashioned, is now at a moment of change when traditional monopolies, frequently developed in the public service tradition, are under threat of change from new satellite and cable technologies as well as video. Few people thought about the original meaning of the word 'broadcasting' until the term 'narrowcasting' was coined, and had indeed become a realistic proposition. Now a range of distribution possibilities are available for different purposes at different costs and for different sorts of people: choices therefore need to be made. In the past, the direction of far too many projects has been led by the newest technology and its arrival rather than by the needs of the user or the content of the educational programme.

There are however a number of assumptions currently being made both about education and broadcasting which it is worth arguing through. First, there is the assumption that new cable and satellite technologies will somehow render <u>broadcasting</u> as an educational tool obsolete. Second, there is the economic assumption that education and training are private goods and that investment in them adds only to private and personal capital and that therefore payment for them should also be private. Third, there is the assumption that training is in some way more intrinsically worthwhile and in some ways better than and different from education. These last two are principles that are held quite firmly by the current government. Let us discuss them in the reverse order.

The distinction between education and training is not clearly worked out or agreed. Nor indeed is there any reason why it should be. It is possible to argue that in almost all cases the distinction between education and training stems from the interests of the learners and their motivation rather than from any other formal distinctions. Education is a necessary precursor of most sorts of training. It is not sensible to look at them as if they are in opposition to each other. Identical content may constitute training for one person or education for another. Or it may constitute training at one stage of somebody's life and education at another stage. The same degree may be vocationally relevant for one person and not for another. Medicine needs elements of <u>both</u> training and education. An important example of this issue is basic education: it is necessary for everybody to have reached a minimum level of basic education and acquired a given level of basic skills to enter either further education or further training. To differentiate at this level between education and training is not helpful. Inevitably this raises the question of whose task it should be to provide this basic level. Is it the individual or the state? Is it the employer? We all agree that the state should provide it for the young and tend to accept that adult basic education and training should also be provided free to those adults who still need it, but we disagree about payment for the generality of education and training for adults. Sometimes we suggest adults should fund their own education or training. Sometimes we suggest the community should fund it, for example, if retraining of the unemployed is involved. Sometimes we believe it is the business of industry. An analysis of payment options currently in use (McIntosh, 1981) indicate no rational or agreed policy in place nationally. This lack of policy is relevant to this discussion since broadcasting has of course historically been free to the viewer at the point of use, while other technologies are likely to require direct payment by users.

Turning to the second question, we face the intractable problem that those who have most need of more education and training usually have least ability to pay for it at the point of use and also least motivation to participate in existing opportunities. Those who are already educated have more motivation to continue to learn and are therefore likely to pay more or to take more advantage of existing opportunities.

The economic view of education as a private
good thus becomes an argument for the continuation
of an elite in which those who have the ability
and/or the opportunity to know what they want and
can pay for it are the only ones who obtain it.
There is of course an underlying assumption that
the country can afford to continue only to educate
a small sector of the population. Many would argue
that the reverse is the case and that we need more
education for larger numbers of people. Most of
our industrial competitors have a significantly
higher investment in education and recognise its
importance, particularly in relation to the development of their economies.

Training, of course, provides a quicker pay
back to the investor than education, whose benefit
is likely to be more general and longer term. It
is perhaps not surprising that governments currently favour training at the expense of education.
They work on too short a time-scale to give education the matching priority it deserves.

So, what has this got to do with broadcasting?
Broadcasting is not, of course, free to the consumer, but it has been, heretofore, free at the
point of use. It is paid for in different countries in different ways through licence fees, progressive or regressive taxation, or revenue derived
from advertising. Viewers choosing to watch an
individual programme are making choices about the
use of their leisure time not about their money.
Moves to cable, satellite and pay TV , will change
the nature of the viewers' decisions to one which
includes elements of both the use of time and the
use of money and therefore will be affected more by
the alternative claims on that money both from the
individual and their family.

The importance of broadcasting to education is
that its message can reach freely into the homes of
practically everybody. It therefore overcomes the
two main barriers to access faced by all other
forms of education. The third barrier - the attitudinal or dispositional barrier is more complex.
It provides an important key to how we may need to
understand and best plan to use new resources
available. Those who know what they want, after
all, will find it and be prepared to pay for it
even if it means watching at unreasonable hours
e.g. the Open University (O.U.). Those who are
less well educated and do not know what they might
want or even where to find it are a much more

difficult problem with which to deal.

We then come to our second key distinction which is between what have been described as 'open' and 'closed' learning systems. When a closed or known group is using broadcast resources, with or without a teacher/mentor/facilitator it effectively creates a 'closed' learning situation. This is the predominant model in schools, in further education and may also become appropriate for sections of youth training. Individual motivation is less important here than the structure, organisation and control of the social and educational situation. However, in an open learning situation, with viewers choosing to learn on their own in their own way, individual motivation is of overriding importance. If people are not interested enough to turn the TV set on to watch the programme then all the carefully laid educational plans go astray. And if access to the technology requires an upfront payment then money may become a barrier to access in a way that it has not heretofore been.

We are moving to a time when people are increasingly aware of the cost of public service broadcasting and the assumption that the British Broadcasting Corporation (BBC) licence fee can be increased indefinitely has come under scrutiny. In a vertically integrated system such as the BBC where it is the cost overall which is looked at, and in which users pay a flat fee rather than in proportion to use, then it has not historically mattered if some parts of the system cost more or less than others, or make a profit or not. Cross subsidy between elements of the system is expected and is acceptable.

As systems are increasingly disaggregated and individual elements are organised separately, whether privatised or not, this flexibility cannot be sustained as each individual element must be profitable unless a new series of oligopolies are to be set up (McIntosh 1985). The National Consumer Council argued in relation to the advent of cable, that disaggregated systems would be more beneficial to consumers as power would be spread. The danger of much of the existing planning of cable is that 'more' will not necessarily mean 'different' but rather simply more of the same, only packaged up by intermediaries, i.e., cable franchise holders, into a set of commercially appealing packages which actually give consumers less choice, not more than they have before. It is

highly unlikely that cable coverage in the UK will
have any impact on educational provision at all
since its coverage will be too partial for any
general provision to be made. Exceptions may be
local projects in cabled areas and some motivated
sub-sections of people who may choose to use their
leisure time and money for personal purposes.
    Satellite technology is quite another matter,
however. When it is possible for people to have
individual dishes on their houses and receive programmes direct rather than through satellite feeds
into cable heads, then distinct new possibilities
start to arise. After all, new legislation and
technology will allow dishes under 2 ft. in size
very soon. There are effectively only two good
reasons for using new technologies. First, that
they do something better than before, either more
cheaply or more effectively, or secondly, that they
get to people who cannot be got to in other ways.
When the next generation of satellites with multiple channels arrives, then this will be the
obvious solution for many specialist purposes: to
schedule a training channel, for example, an O.U.
channel, or even a channel for the deaf. The cost
of putting dishes on the roofs of houses of O.U.
students or on the houses where there is somebody
who is deaf, compares very favourably with other
options in a caring society. Workplaces will be
able to provide on-site training as will local
government and further education. The examples are
numerous. Some of these are examples of closed,
known audiences who may be more efficiently dealt
with in that way in the future. There will be many
other examples of new special interest scattered
target groups where motivation is high and interest
is homogeneous, irrespective of income.
    The question of who pays and at what point in
the process remains acute. A satellite option
would not necessarily be popular for the O.U. as
even more of the cost would shift from the central
budget of the O.U. to the student, unless dishes
were also centrally provided, maybe for a hire
charge in the way that home experiment kits are
now. For socially needy groups like the deaf, the
cost of dishes could be subsidised, in the same way
that provision of gas and electricity meters for
those who need slot meters is now dealt with by the
Department of Health and Social Security (DHSS).
    So where does this leave open network terres-
trial broadcasting? The answer, confirmed by

others (Robinson, 1982) is that it will still remain in a very important position. It will still be the most accessible, both financial and geographical, form of broadcasting for the vast majority of people. It will have a key role in informing people, sensitising them to change, alerting them to new opportunities. It will still be the most important way to reach the under-educated, who are least likely, of their own accord, to be attracted into formal or traditional education. Once attracted people are more easily able to find their way to what they want.

In one sense broadcasting already engages in narrowcasting - by placing some programmes in times of the day which are virtually inaccessible to the majority of people, or by placing some special interest programmes where that category of people forms a large proportion of the available audience. Or again, programmes which are expected only to interest a minority of people are put out when people are physically available, but almost certainly needing to do other things, e.g., Saturday morning shopping. The O.U. is the extreme example of the first, having been forced into less and less acceptable times of day. Programmes for women at home, pre-school children, older people, are examples of the second. Educational programming, religion, cultural, minority programmes, the third.

Let us add into this discussion an additional dimension - a differentiation between three broad categories of education/training: that designed for enrichment or personal development, that for up-dating of knowledge and thirdly, that for retraining, recyclage. We noted earlier that the country has no clear policy about the financing of education and training, either at the institutional or personal level. Generally, individuals expect to make a contribution to the first of these categories but so does the community. Costs are shared. Employer involvement is clearest with the second, as is the individual's personal benefit with the third. Here, individual employers have no role and the state holds the major responsibility. How does this analysis effect our assessment of the likely future role of different technologies in relation to different sorts of learning?

Following a method of analysis developed by the same author (McIntosh, 1978) we can identify target audiences for whom existing terrestrial broadcasting will and must continue to be of critical importance. We need to identify separately existing audiences whose needs are met in existing ways, and consider which audience needs might be better met through new ways.

| | |
|---|---|
| Existing audiences<br>Existing ways | New audiences<br>Existing ways |
| Existing audiences<br>New Ways | New audiences<br>New ways |

Existing audiences include, among others, such groups as schools, colleges, trainees, home learners, O.U. students. These groups until now have mainly been using a limited number of existing 'ways'/delivery systems: live broadcasting, closed-circuit, video - including copying off air.

Which audience needs will continue to be met in existing ways? Which new needs can be met in existing ways?

Mapping existing and new audiences speculatively against existing and new ways shows a number of possibilities which are listed here. Sometimes new technologies will clearly allow us to meet new audience needs. Sometimes this will however involve a shift of expenditure from the community of groups or individuals, which may well raise financial barriers to access just when other barriers to access are being reduced.

## Existing audiences

schools
colleges
trainees
home learners
O.U. students

## Existing ways

live broadcasting
closed circuit
non-theatric use
video inc. copying
    off air

## New audiences

the unemployed
the over 60s
youth out of school
children out of school
the less well-educated
the deaf
ethnic minorities
special interest groups

## New ways

cable
satellite into homes
video disc
interactive systems
teletext

Just looking at these lists shows some of the many new and continuing audiences for live broadcasting, particularly the large categories of social need such as the unemployed, youth and over 60s. At the same time some existing users may be better served by the additional air-time of a satellite channel when it arrives, for example the O.U. or trainees nationally. And some new needs could also be met on a satellite channel, e.g. the deaf or ethnic minorities.

Of course, all forms of broadcasting and narrowcasting are subject to other controls. Choices are made by planners and producers, and educators both in the media and in the educational system, need to place media education high on their list of priorities as the government has already done with micro-technology. However, just introducing such education into schools, though an important step, is not enough - since it ignores the needs of by far the largest group, those currently adults, who are after all those who are now in a position directly to make decisions which affect us all.

At the end of the day broadcasting and its newer siblings are only a means to an end and not ends in themselves. It will be up to educators to use these means and to raise the level of educational expectation and demand for them, from the whole population, both of children and adults. This means changing attitudes, not only amongst those with a vested interest in initial education, but also among politicians and within the media themselves. We cannot any longer afford an undereducated nation of adults, and adults must be educated to demand and make optimum use of all the new technologies.

## References

McIntosh N. (1978); Development and diversification in post-school education: a view from across the Atlantic, in mimeograph, Virginia USA, 1978.
McIntosh N. (1981); Demand and supply in the education of adults in Educational Analysis Vol. 3, No. 3., The Falmer Press, 1981.
Robinson J. (1982); Learning over the air, BBC London, 1982.
Sargant (McIntosh) (1985); Coping with change in communications: the experience of Channel Four Television in the UK in 'Coping with Communication', Department of Extra Mural Studies, University of London, London, 1985.

6.  WHAT WORKERS, WHAT LEAVE?  CHANGING PATTERNS
    OF EMPLOYMENT AND THE PROSPECTS FOR PAID
    EDUCATIONAL LEAVE

John Field

     In the 1970s, Paid Educational Leave (PEL) was
an exciting concept.  Often inspired by broader
philosophies of recurrent education or lifelong
learning, PEL was an attractive campaigning focus
in Britain and elsewhere for those who were fed up
with the inability of conventional adult education
to break out of its narrow curriculum and middle
class clientele, and who sought to overturn the
sterile barrier separating 'education' and 'training'.  A lot of educational water has flowed under
the bridge since then, and with it has floated much
of the optimism that surrounded the notion of PEL.
     Whether as practice, policy or aspiration, PEL
was very much a creation of the 1970s.  While
British practitioners could point convincingly to a
body of existing experience [for example, Barratt
Brown, 1969], discussion increasingly drew on
international thought and policy debates.  There
was the Organisation for Economic Cooperation and
Development, for instance, whose 1973 report on
Recurrent Education was followed four years later
by the major policy study of educational leave,
Alternation Between Work and Education.  Convention
140 of the International Labour Organisation, adopted in 1974, urged member states to grant workers
leave 'for educational purposes for a specified
period during working hours, with adequate financial entitlements'.  The Italian '150 Hours' agreement was promoted as a model, while at home debates
on workplace democracy and trade union representation were raising other, but related, questions
about opportunities for PEL [DES, 1973; SIT, 1977].
In 1976 the Department of Education and Science and
the Manpower Services Commission provided funds for
a pioneering survey of PEL in England and Wales,

raising new questions and new hopes [Killeen and Bird, 1981].

How relevant is PEL - as practice or policy - today? Since the mid-seventies, and especially since 1979, a number of significant changes have altered profoundly the context in which any discussion of PEL must be placed. Most substantially, there has been a dramatic deindustrialisation of the British economy, reducing the size of the workforce and changing the balance between different sectors within it. Second, the organisation of employment has started to change; the labour market is markedly more fragmented, the labour force more diverse. Third, education and training have also changed drastically as a result of public debate over the relationship between education and economic development. The changes, cumulatively, may not undermine our belief in the importance of PEL; but they should cause us to rethink how we define it, what we see it as including, what forces might bring it into being, what broader goals we wish it to fulfil.

## 1.  The scope and pace of change

Deindustrialisation is a global term. As description of experience it conceals almost as much as it reveals; as explanation, it is too often tied to apocalyptic slogans such as the 'death of the working class', 'post-industrial society'. Nevertheless, it highlights the quickening pace with which Britain, like much of the western world, is shifting away from its nineteenth century manufacturing base into an economy rooted more in the service sector.

Some illustrations: from 1971 - 1984, manufacturing employment in Britain fell by 3.3 million jobs, almost three-quarters of them lost since 1979; the service sector put on an extra 2.3 million jobs between 1971 and 1984, most of them coming before 1979 [Central Statistical Office, 1986]. In manufacturing, the great losses came in metals, vehicles and engineering; in services, the great gains were in retail, catering and (before 1979) public sector employment. Geographically, employment has moved out of the metropolitan areas, and from north to south [Massey and Miles, 1984]. The total numbers working are, of course, fewer than in 1971, while working life itself has been shortening at both ends. Young men and women find their entry onto the labour market delayed, often spent in the car park known as the Youth Training Scheme; at the other end of the life cycle, whereas eight out of ten men in their sixties worked in 1971, by 1984 almost half had dropped out of the labour market entirely (not including the registered unemployed) and increasingly men in their fifties were affected by the same process [Central Statistical Office, 1986]. Among women, on the other hand, economic activity rates have risen for almost every age group as the importance of the service sector - a traditional source of female employment - has grown.

There has also been a more general reorganisation of the labour process for those who are in work. In its nature uneven, it is often associated with the introduction of new technologies into both the manufacturing and service sectors. John Atkinson and Denis Gregory [1986] suggest that employment in the late twentieth century is increasingly characterised by one of two distinctive forms of flexibility: functional flexibility, or the development of a core of workers who are adaptable and mobile, possessing general competences as well as plant-specific skills; and numerical flexibility, where more or fewer workers are taken on and worked for longer or shorter hours to match fluctuations in output. Numerical flexibility may involve increasing amounts of part-time working, temporary employment, domestic labour or sub-contracting - all of which appear from Labour Force Survey data to be growing quite substantially [MSC, 1985; Huws, 1984]. The consequences are to segment and fragment further a labour market which is already undergoing the process of reorganisation away from manufacturing towards service employment.

We are used, often, to speaking of a particularly dramatic change as something that has 'happened in my lifetime'. The present set of changes, though, are moving much faster than that: within the first half of the 1980s, rapid socio-economic changes effectively transformed much of the world from which workers might or might not be granted educational leave of absence. Nor will they simply stop, or be readily reversed, so as to allow us to digest their implications while the next set of changes - the full introduction of information technology into the service sector - gets under way.

## 2. Education/Training and Employment

The turning point in the relationship between education and training and economic performance is usually dated from Jim Callaghan's 1976 speech at Ruskin College. But the displacement of 'human capital' approaches to investment in public education by an insistence upon targeted training for occupational competence has been international: throughout north America and much of western Europe, in education the 'romantic fifties and sixties were replaced by the cynical seventies' [Rubenson, 1985]. Governments everywhere argue that investment in education - more schooling - has generated neither continued economic growth nor greater social equality.

The British public education system is faced at every level with demands and inducements to 'meet industry's needs'. What is left of industry is not, as it happens, entirely clear as to what those needs are: two recent MSC surveys of British firms revealed a high degree of verbal commitment to the importance of training combined with virtual indifference towards their own training policy [Coopers and Lybrand Associates, 1985; MSC, 1986a]. Nevertheless, both public rhetoric and recent changes in funding arrangements for public education have confirmed the high policy profile of training and education for economic renewal and growth. Have philosophies of recurrent and life-long learning anything to contribute to this debate?

In so far as the high profile given to training recognises the needs of adult workers, and marks a break with the belief that significant learning only occurs in youth, it is consistent with the principles of lifelong learning and recurrent education. It also implies, as has been made explicit in the Review of Vocational Qualifications and other changes in the certification of learning, that there should be a coherent approach linking what are at present three disparate sectors (further/higher education, adult and continuing education, and vocational training). However, proponents of lifelong or recurrent education strategies have made little contribution to policy discussion and decision-making over training; as a result, there has been remarkably little debate over the contribution of training to social and economic equality.

Far from contributing to greater equalities in our society, current training initiatives are greatly reinforcing existing inequalities. Almost all education is a positional as well as a consumer good, helping to locate individuals at particular levels within the labour market. Where training is free-market led, it will tend to favour those who are already in the most favoured positions, and so it appears to be turning out at present.

Data from the 1984 Labour Force Survey confirm the extremely patchy nature and coverage of existing training [MSC, 1985; 1986b]. The Survey showed that on average 8.8% of the British workforce were likely to have undertaken some training within a given four-week period. The vast majority were young workers, for whom 'training' was a mixture of car park and continued initial education: 40% of 16 - 17 year olds had received some training, compared with 3% among 50 - 64 year olds. Those who possessed a previous qualification were ten times more likely to receive training than those without qualifications. Training levels were highest in areas with low unemployment and a high share of private and public sector service and high-tech manufacturing employment, and lowest of all in older industrial or agricultural areas. Women were far less likely to be trained than men, and when in training were less likely to have their fees paid by the employer. Hardly any took place among self-employed or part-time workers. Finally, those in work were less likely to have to pay their fees themselves than were trainees who were unemployed!

The disparities, then, are extremely marked. A crude ideal type of the worker most likely to receive training would be a skilled or professional (white) male, in permanent work in the south-east, and possessing relatively advanced qualifications already. Workers who receive little or no training are part-time or temporary, unskilled, lacking prior qualifications, female, and living in Wales. The O.E.C.D. study warned in 1977 that

when training is defined as vocational if it is relevant to the individual's current or immediately foreseeable occupational position its scope will broaden according to the interest of the job, with the consequence that those who already occupy the most interesting positions will be able to benefit from a far wider range of opportunities than the unskilled workers in dead-end jobs.

Since 1977, we have seen the steady emergence on a scale that could not have been predicted in the O.E.C.D. report of the dispensable worker; the worker who is excluded from the workforce in his fifties, or employed on a temporary basis, or is a part-timer with limited statutory rights. The employer is loath to invest in the training of such workers, while their own identification of training needs and desire to train reflects a lack of iden-tification with the job itself as a source of personal identity and material support over the longer term [Downs, 1986; Grigg, 1984]. In other words, current training policies reinforce fragmen-tation in the labour market, and are likely to constitute an increasingly important source of social and economic inequality.

## 3.    Support for PEL

The distribution, nature and quality of train-ing, in Britain, are generally not trade union issues. Even in the field of educational employ-ment, the flawed professionalism of the unions is at its weakest over the issues of staff development and in-service training. By default, workplace training policy is being left to the decisions of individual employers and the play of market forces. Yet of all the variables which can lead to greater or lesser action over PEL, trade union involvement is almost certainly far and away the most signifi-cant [Schuller, 1986].

So far, the trade union movement has been slow to recognise either the scale or pace of change, despite the impact on its own membership struc-tures. Union membership patterns have followed employment in becoming more dispersed, both geo-graphically and by sector; older manufacturing unions have declined much faster than public sec-tor, general and white collar unions; a growing proportion of trade unionists are women. At the same time, union membership is becoming more con-centrated in terms of age, with densities of around two-thirds among 45 - 65 year old workers, falling to less than one half among 20 - 24 year olds and just one fifth among teenagers [Central Statistical Office, 1985 and 1986; Massey and Miles, 1984]. So trade union membership is becoming more disparate in terms of its geography and occupational back-ground, and it is aging.

More difficult to establish is the effect of

changing employment patterns upon the collective
bargaining climate. While almost all agree that
these are tough times for the unions, there is less
agreement on whether we can discern changing styles
of management that have significantly shifted the
balance of power within the workplace. There is
some evidence that changes in working practices now
tend to go unresisted even by organised workers,
and that some managers are seeking to bypass established methods of communicating and reaching agreements with the workforce. Marginalisation of shop
stewards, a taste for single union agreements, and
a new willingness at plant level on the part of
unions and management jointly to promote the continued survival of the firm may not add up to a new
era of 'macho management', but they do represent a
considerable shift away from the attempts to extend
industrial democracy which reached their peak in
the Bullock report [Edwards, 1985; Terry, 1986].
    Trade unions are a considerably weaker force
on behalf of PEL than they were in the 1970s.
Under the impact of the recession, participation in
TUC regional day release courses fell by around
one-third between 1979 and 1983, and the educational programmes of many trade unions have suffered equally [Field, 1986]; even the long-estab-
lished mineworkers' day release courses have been
under threat in several areas since the 1984/85
dispute, while other industrial sectors in which
broad-based day release schemes operated in the
past - docks, railways, printing - read like a
casualty list of the 1980s. Only in the health
service and local government has broad-based PEL -
if extremely patchy and localised - survived, or
even occasionally grown [Bond, 1986]. If trade
unions constitute the most effective point of pressure for workers in negotiating PEL at workplace
level, or in implementing statutory rights to PEL,
then the prospects at present for any further
growth are weak. Even on the most generous interpretation of the Labour Party's programme, which
includes provision for a universal adult education
entitlement [Labour Party, 1986], educational leave
of absence from the workplace, with adequate financial support, remains a distant aspiration.

## 4.  Rethinking PEL

    The original debate on PEL in the 1970s re-
vealed considerable confusion about what precisely

the term was intended to cover. Killeen and Bird, at one end of the spectrum, included in their survey any education or training, on the job or away from it, for which financial support was available to workers; as a result, they collapsed into one category a range of educational and training activities, each of which may be differently affected by changing employment patterns.

The most liberal forms of PEL are clearly in decline. Lengthy two- and three-year programmes of industrial day release for manual workers, organised through university extra-mural departments and following a broad and entirely non-vocational curriculum, were negotiated in a political and economic context which reflected wider concerns for social equity and smooth adaptation to change among adult educators together with a willingness among government and employers, largely in newly-nationalised industries often with a poor industrial relations record, during a post-war period of reconstruction and debate over citizenship and welfare [Barratt Brown, 1969; Mee, 1984]. Deindustrialisation, greater use by employers of education/training as a screening device, change in the state-owned industries and - we have to admit - shifting political priorities within adult education institutions, including the university extra-mural departments, are combining to turn traditional liberal day release programmes into a largely residual category.

At the other end of the spectrum, it is likely that for many 'core' workers, especially those in supervisory or technician roles, there will be continued expansion of vocationally-oriented training which is supported by the employer. It is already assuming new, flexible forms: concerns for cost-effectiveness and quality are encouraging some employers to offer support for home- or free-time study, to develop distance learning techniques, and to expect the employee to share some of the costs. Given the unregulated market which governs such training in private industry, inequality of opportunity is not only probable: it is systematic and inevitable. Even in local authorities whose training programmes form part of a labour-oriented employment policy, anti-discriminatory training is directed towards initial rather than recurrent opportunities. Resources are concentrated on, for example, courses attracting women or girls into engineering and construction trades rather than conversion or upgrading courses for the authority's own female employees who are locked into deskilled and routine tasks at the periphery of the labour market (part-time cleaners, data-processing operators, and so on). And at all levels, other than senior management - often already possessing third-level qualifications - education for broader skills and general knowledge is rare.

What policy options are available to those wishing, at a time of severe recession and rapid change, to defend and promote PEL as a means of extending learning opportunities throughout the lifespan? Contextual changes need to be taken into account in framing arguments on behalf of PEL that are appropriate to the labour market from which release will be taken.

First, the priority given to vocational training, by government and employers, is an accomplished fact. Participation in such training is a vital part of the individual worker's conditions of employment, affecting his or her future employment prospects as well as his capacity to cope with a greater amount of time spent away from paid employment or her capacity to remain for a greater amount of time in paid employment. Training policy might constitute part of a wider strategy for tackling low pay, the balance between numerical and functional flexibility, and even overall employment levels: the more workers that are away from the job, the more replacements will be required [International Federation of Workers' Educational Associations, 1981]. The content and organisation of training will also determine the degree to which it acts as a consumer as well as a positional good.

Because they are not, at present, a collective bargaining issue, training decisions are made entirely by management (and usually fairly junior management at that). They are therefore taken in terms of management's definitions of organisational goals and as part of management's forward planning, including its planning of job content, labour force deployment, and employment levels; management is thus increasingly able to define the nature of skill and knowledge, and to control access to their possession.

In the ultimate analysis, the crucial question will be whether work is organised in such a way as to facilitate a more even distribution of knowledge within the workforce... Swedish labour unions regard the matter of education and training of their members as one of the most crucial issues in their struggle for industrial democracy and successful and equitable adjustment to the information technology [Rubenson, 1985].

Without the formulation of trade union policies on training, it is hard to see how any movement could be made towards greater opportunities for PEL. Yet in their absence, especially as new technologies are introduced, employers' ability to use training policy to define job content, skill and knowledge will be vital.

Second, the organisation of PEL must be adapted to the new needs created by changing employment patterns. New flexible forms of employment, growing economic activity among women, and the shortening of the working life among men, all pose new problems. These could be met by the adoption of equally flexible forms of PEL, together with demands that they receive employer support; participation in distance learning, or in own-time education, can involve far greater numbers of workers than the 'purest' forms of PEL and there is no reason why workers undertaking them should not receive support from the employer and the state.

Third, the content of PEL should reflect the needs of new constituencies and new contexts. In many ways, the difficulties shared by many adult workers in non-management posts, whether 'core' or 'periphery', are closely tied up with the difficulties of 'learning to learn'. Those employees who get most from currently available training opportunities are those who have got the most credentials out of initial learning; what PEL is not doing is challenging that gross disparity. Where available to shop-floor or office workers, PEL is either strongly instrumental and role-specific (whether employer-led or union-led) or if more general and broad-based it is forced, by virtue of the small numbers of places made available, to be deeply exclusive. In neither case does it address the real difficulties and problems of that vast majority of adult workers who possess neither academic credentials nor the skills and knowledge required to make best use of further learning opportunities.

Just as mass unemployment has caused many in the WEA to question inherited definitions of 'liberal adult education' [see WEA, 1985], so drastic change in employment patterns should cause us to rethink the content of PEL.  If it is to have a progressive and egalitarian influence, it may well be that the most important curriculum will be one which offers a path back into learning, building confidence, developing control over knowledge, and encouraging an ability to take responsibility for one's own learning, as in the many Second Chance to Learn programmes that have been developed for unemployed adults.  Such curricular approaches, flexibly operated, could develop in ways that would meet the distinctive needs of older workers approaching an ever-longer period of 'retirement', surely ill-met by existing gestures towards 'pre-retirement education'; or of women seeking longer and more continuous periods of paid employment of a more rewarding kind; or of workers threatened by deskilling or displacement through the implementation of information technologies; or of those in part-time and temporary employment.  It would be directed most towards the needs of those who had benefited least from initial education and training.  But it is - partly for these reasons - a curriculum that depends upon direct intervention in the labour market, and not upon the free play of market forces.

This is precisely why PEL remains such an attractive and necessary part of the recurrent education agenda.  By definition, PEL is oriented towards the labour market; as practice and as policy, it can only advance across a broad front where it is linked to wider strategies for intervention in the labour market, as at local government level where authorities like Derbyshire, Sheffield or the Greater London Enterprise Board have started the process of questioning free market definitions of education and training.  This involves taking training seriously - perhaps to the extent of framing a new acronym, PETL, standing for Paid Educational and Training Leave - and having confidence that recurrent education philosophies can transform training policy as well as educational practice.

## References

Atkinson, J. and Gregory, D. [1986], 'A Flexible Future: Britain's Dual Labour Force', Marxism Today, April.

Barratt Brown, M. [1969], Adult Education for Industrial Workers, Leicester.

Bond, S. et al. [1986], 'The Origins of Take Ten', Association for Recurrent Education Conference on PEL, University of Warwick, June.

Bryant, I. [1984], 'Paid Educational Leave', in D. Cosgrove and C. McConnell (eds), Post-16: Development in Continuing Education in Scotland in the 1980s, Dundee.

Central Statistical Office [1985], Social Trends, vol. 15.

Central Statistical Office [1986], Social Trends, vol. 16.

Coopers and Lybrand Associates [1985], A Challenge to Complacency: Changing attitudes towards training, Sheffield/London.

Department of Education and Science [1973], Adult Education: A Plan For Development, London.

Downs, S. [1986], 'Can trainers learn to take a back seat?', Personnel Management, March.

Edwards, P.K. [1985], 'Myth of the macho manager', Personnel Management, April.

Field, J. [1986], 'Adult education and the trade union movement', in T. Lovett (ed), Radical Approaches to Adult Education, London.

Grigg, C. [1984], Women and Technical Training: The West Midlands Situation, Birmingham.

Huws, U. [1984], The New Homeworkers, London.

International Federation of Workers' Educational Associations [1981], Paid Educational Leave: A New Social Right, London.

Killeen, J. and Bird, M. [1981], Education and Work: A Study of Paid Educational Leave in England and Wales, London.

Labour Party [1986], Education Throughout Life: a statement on continuing and higher education, London.

Manpower Services Commission [1985], Labour Market Quarterly Report, November.

Manpower Services Commission [1986a], Small Firms Survey, Sheffield.

Manpower Services Commission [1986b], Labour Market Quarterly Report, February.

Massey, D. and Miles, N. [1984], 'Mapping Out the Unions', Marxism Today, May.

Mee, G. [1984], Miners, Adult Education, and Community Service, 1920-1984, Nottingham.

O.E.C.D. [1977], Alternation Between Work and Education: A Study of Educational Leave of Absence at the Enterprise Level, Paris.

Rubenson, K. [1985], 'Adult Education: The Economic Context', Paper prepared for the 50th Anniversary of the Canadian Association for Adult Education, February.

Schuller, T. [1986], 'Perspectives from Europe', Association for Recurrent Education Conference on PEL, University of Warwick, June.

Society of Industrial Tutors [1977], 'Industrial Democracy: evidence presented to the Bullock Committee', Industrial Tutor, March.

Terry, M. [1986], 'How Do We Know If Shop Stewards Are Getting Weaker?', British Journal of Industrial Relations, July.

Workers' Educational Association [1985], Working with the Unemployed: A Manifesto, London.

# 7. ECONOMIC AND FINANCIAL IMPLICATIONS OF RECURRENT AND CONTINUING EDUCATION

Maureen Woodhall

Advocates of recurrent or continuing education have, in some cases argued, for a radical shift of resources from traditional 'front-end' patterns of education, which concentrate both opportunities and resources on formal education and initial training for young people, in favour of a system of 'life-long education', which would provide opportunities for adults to participate in formal or non-formal education or training at any time in their lives, and to combine or alternate periods of education, work and other activities, including the care of children and leisure. For example, an OECD report in 1973 called for 'a comprehensive educational strategy for all post-compulsory or post-basic education, the essential characteristic of which is the distribution of education in a recurring way, i.e. in alternation with other activities, principally with work, but also with leisure and retirement', which would lead to 'a continuing in learning through one's entire lifetime'. (OECD 1973, p.24). In 1974 the ARE compendium on recurrent education was subtitled 'A Plea for Lifelong Learning' (Houghton & Richardson 1974). More recently the Advisory Council for Adult and Continuing Education (ACACE) called for 'a radical shift of emphasis by the whole post-school education system towards the educational needs of adults' (ACACE 1982, p.v).

In order to promote such a shift, some writers have proposed new financing mechanisms involving 'individual entitlements' or 'drawing rights' (Levin and Schütze 1983) which would guarantee subsidies for a period of post-compulsory education or training for everyone, regardless of age. Faced with the financial implications of such a system, however, many economists have argued that the cost would be prohibitive and the benefits questionable. The opportunity costs of education in terms of the loss of output or earnings to society and the individual, are much greater for an older, experienced worker, than for a young person. At the same time such workers can look forward to a shorter working life, which means that the expected lifetime benefits will be lower than in the case of a young entrant to the labour force. Thus, the OECD, in first putting forward the case for recurrent education in 1973, argued that 'a cost-benefit analysis, based on classical economic considerations is bound to turn out to the disfavour of recurrent education', but argued that 'social goals such as equality, participation and benefit to the individual ... may outweigh the higher costs in purely economic terms'. (OECD 1973, p.69). Similarly, Williams (1977) acknowledged that 'judged by orthodox criteria of evaluation, lifelong education based on conventional methods of educational provision is likely to prove very expensive in the use of resources in relation to the benefits obtained' (Williams 1977, p.109), and indeed, an early attempt to apply cost-benefit techniques to the concept of recurrent education, concluded that the cost would outweigh the benefits (Gannicott 1971).

Some economists have gone further, and argued that the concept of recurrent education lacks any economic justification:

> if the recurrent education movement were to succeed, it would prove to be the most expansionary education proposal that the world has ever seen. Fortunately, there is very little danger that it will succeed.
>
> (Blaug and Mace 1977, p.227)

On the other hand, advocates of recurrent education argue that a more flexible pattern of education and training opportunities for adults would result in a more highly skilled and adaptable work-force, able to respond to changing economic conditions; that the pace of technological change requires a system of continuing education which would allow workers to update and upgrade their skills, preventing technical obsolescence of skills, and overcoming shortages of new skills which might threaten economic growth. Thus recurrent education is often justified on efficiency as well as equity grounds.

One reason why there has been disagreement about the economic costs and benefits of shifting the balance of educational resources away from youth and initial training, in favour of adults, is that there are widely different definitions and concepts of recurrent, or continuing education. Stoikov (1973 and 1975) pointed out that proposals for recurrent education fall into two categories with very different economic implications. Some proposals involve a 'paradigm shift' of resources away from initial vocational education and training, and suggest that young people should be encouraged to postpone post-secondary education until after they have had some work experience, and that thereafter, 'educational opportunities should be spread out over the individual's life-time' (OECD 1973). This would result in an increase in opportunity costs, combined with a shorter working life for those acquiring education or training, which could lead to a loss, rather than a gain in human capital. On the other hand, others simply argue for a development of opportunities for adults to participate in further or higher education, either because they missed the chance to pursue their education at an earlier age or because they wish to extend or update their earlier education and training in order to acquire new skills, take a refresher course to keep up with the latest technical developments, or retrain for a new job.

However, there have been few attempts to analyse the economic and financial implications of proposals to shift resources in favour of adults, and establish a truly 'recurrent' or 'life-long' system of education.

In this chapter we consider the economic and financial implications of moving towards a more flexible system of recurrent and continuing education which would supplement, rather than replace, post-school education and initial training. Not only would the costs and the risks of such a policy be much less than in the case of the 'paradigm shift' sometimes advocated by the most enthusiastic proponents of recurrent education, but the advantages, in terms of flexibility, would be greater. The economic feasibility of such a system depends on how much it would be likely to cost and also on the magnitude and distribution of both costs and benefits. How the costs and the benefits of continuing education are shared between individuals, employers, institutions and taxpayers is, of course, crucial to the question of how recurrent and continuing education should be financed, which we consider in the last part of the chapter.

1. The Benefits of Recurrent and Continuing Education

Education can be regarded as both consumption and investment. Human capital theory suggests that investment in knowledge and skills can make workers more productive in the future and that the rate of return can be measured for both the individual and society as a whole. But adults attend courses in higher education for a variety of motives, and many derive immediate pleasure and satisfaction from learning as well as developing new skills which may or may not be useful in the present or future jobs.

The trends towards increased leisure and early retirement are likely to lead to increased demand for continuing education opportunities for reasons of personal development, interest and satisfaction. However, the National Advisory Body for Public Sector Higher Education (NAB) Continuing Education Group quotes recent research which 'suggests that most who seek this additional education experience do so with a vocational purpose in mind' (NAB 1984).

There are many reasons why demand for continuing vocational education can be expected to grow:

a) The rapid pace of technological change means that a single 'dose' of initial education and training is insufficient to provide the skills necessary for a whole working lifetime; without up-dating and renewal, technical and professional knowledge and skills will become obsolescent.

b) Changing labour market conditions, the decline of traditional industries and the growth of new occupations mean that workers may need to retrain for new jobs, requiring new skills. Continuing education may therefore help to reduce unemployment caused by changes in the demand for traditional skills.

c) Continuing education also helps create an adaptable, flexible workforce, and to overcome skill shortages. Demographic trends mean that the supply of young entrants to the labour force will decline in the late 1980s and

1990s, so that employers will increasingly have to rely on older workers acquiring new skills, and married women returning to the labour force in order to meet new demands.

d) Providing continuing education for workers who already have practical work experience means that skills may be learned more quickly and efficiently, and relevant knowledge and skills can be identified more readily, since theoretical and practical knowledge can complement each other.

These represent direct benefits to the individual, in terms of higher lifetime earnings and increased probability of finding employment, to employers, in terms of higher levels of output, which in turn will lead to higher levels of national income and economic growth, and lower unemployment, which will benefit the whole economy. In addition to these direct benefits, however, it is often suggested that continuing education for adults may bring indirect benefits to the community and to the institutions providing continuing education, and that these 'spill-over' benefits will ultimately benefit all participants of higher education, and society as a whole. For example, Continuing Education Working Party of the University Grants Committee (UGC) lists a number of indirect benefits to universities themselves:

a) Relationships with the wider community will be improved by the recognition that universities are an important source of relevant continuing education for society at large.

b) Continuing education will broaden the perspectives of academic staff and bring them into close contact with the needs of industry and society generally, which will mean that new lines of research and consultancy may be identified, new sources of funding tapped and the ability of universities to give practical advice on national and industrial problems enhanced.

c) The knowledge and experience gained by university teachers from their continuing education activities will feed back into regular undergraduate and postgraduate teaching.

Thus, it is often argued that increased investment in continuing education would lead to a more efficient use of resources in the education sector and in industry, but there are no actual estimates of the returns to such investments.

In addition to these efficiency gains, there may be equity gains from providing continuing education opportunities which widen access to education and reduce disparities between social classes and between generations. However, evidence suggests that participants in continuing education are most likely to be those who already have formal educational qualifications, and even 'second-chance' opportunities, such as the Open University, frequently benefit those who already have higher than average levels of education. Thus, the redistributive role of continuing education can be in question. For example, a recent American study concluded that 'Today's adult learners are disproportionately young, white, well-educated and earning salaries above the national family income' (Christoffel 1983, p.27).

— The question of who benefits from continuing education is very relevant for decisions about who should bear the costs. If the benefits accrue mainly to the individual, then a policy of cost recovery through fees, supplemented where necessary by grants or loans, can be justified. On the other hand, if the 'spill over' benefits are substantial, then there is a strong case for government subsidy to prevent under investment in continuing education and training. Before considering the advantages and disadvantages of alternative ways of financing continuing educatiion, however, we must first examine the costs and try to assess their magnitude, in order to judge the financial implications of advocating a shift towards recurrent patterns of education.

## The Costs of Continuing Education

The opportunity cost of education, in the form of output or earnings foregone, is much higher for adults than for young people. Even if they lack formal education their work experience means that the average earnings of adult workers are higher than the foregone earnings of young people who continue their education immediately after school. The opportunity cost of full-time further or higher education for adults is therefore substantial, which is why many economists, such as Stoikov, have been skeptical of the wisdom of postponing it, in favour of 'lifelong learning'. The opportunity cost of students' time, measured in terms of foregone earnings, increases the private costs to the individual, who must sacrifice paid employment, in order to undertake continuing education, and also the costs to employers and to the economy as a whole, since production is reduced if an experienced worker leaves employment for full-time education.

On the other hand, when unemployment is high, the opportunity costs of continuing education for the unemployed are reduced. If the alternative to full-time education is not productive work but unemployment, then there is no loss of production (or earnings), and both the private and social costs of retraining an unemployed worker are therefore lower than the costs of providing further training for the employed.

This has led to the suggestion that government funds currently used to finance unemployment benefit could, at no extra cost to society, be more productively used to finance continuing education. Emmerij (1983) estimated that in the Netherlands there are approximately 370,000 unemployed adults who could benefit from recurrent education or retraining, and he proposed that money now allocated to social security payments should be used to finance education and training opportunities, with training allowances for the unemployed. This would represent no greater drain on public funds than the present system of unemployment benefit; 'Instead of spending for negative reasons ... the same amount of money could be used for positive reasons.' (Emmerij in Levin and Schütze, 1983, p.307). More recently the NAB Continuing Education Group pointed out that an increase in the number of workers 'released to undergo necessary updating would provide some vacancies in the labour market, and thus contribute to the reduction in unemployment. The net fiscal cost of providing these opportunities is relatively small, when the cost of financial support to the unemployed is taken into account'. (NAB 1984, p.27). Similarly, Drake (1983) argues that 'In the United Kingdom alone, the fiscal cost (benefit payments plus tax revenues foregone) of each unemployed person by the end of 1982 was averaging about £4,500 a year. So for the 3.3 million registered unemployed were costing the national exchequer some £14.85 billion a year, which was far in excess of public spending on the education and training of adults'. (Drake 1983, p.117).

Another factor which may reduce the costs of continuing education at a time of declining birth rate, is the existence of spare capacity in further and higher education due to demographic fluctuations. The size of the traditional age group for higher education will fall in the next decade, which will create spare capacity that could be utilised for continuing education. The marginal cost of providing courses for adults would therefore be lower than average costs at present, provided that existing facilities or staff could be re-allocated to continuing education.

Continuing education for adults often takes the form of part-time, rather than full time, courses. This also reduces both the private and the social opportunity costs. However, it also means that it is often very difficult to obtain realistic estimates of the direct costs of continuing education, since it is notoriously difficult to calculate the costs of part-time courses. Both the UGC and NAB reports on continuing education recognise that current financing mechanisms do not adequately reflect the true resource costs of part-time courses, but very little accurate information is available.

Clearly, more accurate estimates of the true costs of continuing education are needed in order to assess the financial implications of a shift towards more flexible systems of recurrent and continuing education. Attempts have been made to compare the costs of education and training for adults with expenditure on formal education for children and young people. An OECD study estimated the total costs of education and learning for adults in 1970, including expenditure by employers, the armed services, and on all forms of professional and vocational retraining and part-time further and higher education, to be roughly half the total expenditure on all forms of full-time formal education (Woodhall in OECD 1977). An attempt to update this figure in 1980 showed that it was still very difficult to get accurate information on costs, but suggested that vocational training for adults probably cost about £3,000 million, compared with public expenditure on formal education of about £9,000 million (Woodhall 1981).

These figures are no more than rough estimates of orders of magnitude but they show that already there is substantial investment in education and training for adults. Proposals to extend recurrent and continuing education opportunities therefore need not imply a massive increase in funds, so much as a reallocation of existing resources and a relaxation of rigid age restrictions in order to ensure that systems of further and higher education and vocational and professional training become more open and more flexible, and therefore better able to cater for the needs of adults.

Another possibility is to try to seek new ways of developing low-cost, informal learning opportunities. For example, there have been proposals to develop informal 'learning networks' in the community which draw upon the experience and expertise of the unemployed or early retired, but there have been no attempts to cost such proposals. What is clear, however, is that the conclusion that recurrent education would have wholly unacceptable cost implications often rests on the mistaken assumption that recurrent or continuing education would simply extend <u>existing</u> patterns of provision to adults, throughout their working and non-working lives. Once this restrictive assumption is relaxed, the cost implications of recurrent education are less daunting. The question remains, however, who will pay?

## Financing Recurrent and Continuing Education

The question of who should pay for continuing education, i.e. whether the financing burden should fall on the individual, the employer or the taxpayer, depends crucially on the magnitude and the distribution of costs and benefits, but as we have seen it is not easy to answer this question with any precision.

In his classic formulation of the theory of human capital, Becker (1964) made a crucial distinction between <u>general</u> education or training, which increased a worker's productivity in a wide range of jobs and <u>specific</u>, work-related training, which increased a worker's productivity only in a single job, and argued that the way education or training is financed depends on whether it is general or specific. Employers will be willing to bear the cost of specific training, since they will reap the benefits, in the form of higher levels of output from more skilled workers. On the other hand, employers will not be willing to finance general education or training since they have no guarantee that they will benefit. Instead, the costs of general education or training are likely to fall on the individual, who must accept lower wages while receiving training, but subsequently will enjoy financial returns, in the form of higher earnings. Alternatively, if there are substantial spillover benefits, there is a case for public sub- sidy of general education. Thus the UGC Working Party on Continuing Education looking particularly at post-experience vocational courses (PEVE) con- cluded: 'We acknowledge that PEVE benefits both employers and participants and that they should bear most of the costs. But there are benefits to society above and beyond those to individual employers and participants for which they cannot be expected to foot the bill. We believe that a significant contribution from the public purse is both justified and essential if post-experience vocational education is to develop to meet the nation's needs'.

Contributions from the public purse may either take the form of subsidies to institutions, to enable them to develop new courses or to offer them at less than full cost, subsidies or for incentives to employers, to encourage them to spend more on training, or subsidies to individuals, in the form of grants, training allowances or subsidised loans. The 1964 Industrial Training Act and the 1973 Employment and Training Act created a system of financial incentives, through levies and grants, designed to encourage employers to devote more resources to training. In other countries, such as France with its vocational training tax or Norway, with a compulsory employer/employee training insur- ance fund, employers are required to contribute to the costs of publicly provided training through the tax system. In the UK the present government's policy, set out in the White Paper Training for Jobs, is to shift more of the financial burden from the taxpayer to employers and individual trainees.

At present, individuals wishing to undertake continuing education or training may be financed by their employers through paid education leave (PEL), or must finance themselves, with or without finan- cial support from their local education authority (LEA). A study of PEL (Killeen and Bird, 1981) estimated that in 1976-77, between 3 and 4 million

people (15 to 20% of the work-force) benefited from
PEL, and about 40% of all PEL-involved courses in
higher or further education. The UK, along with
many other countries, ratified the 1974 Resolution
of the International Labour Organization (ILO)
which called upon countries to promote PEL, but a
recent survey of PEL provision in Europe presented
a 'fairly gloomy picture' (CEDEFOP, 1984, p.194)
and concluded that in the current economic climate
in Europe, the scope for significant expansion of
PEL is limited, although expansion is desirable on
both social and economic grounds. The study quotes
the Confederation of British Industry (CBI) view in
the UK, that 'the only criterion' which could be
applied in deciding whether employees should be
released for PEL is 'the needs of the firm in
question' (CEDEFOP 1984, p.114). This underlines
the point that even if PEL provisions were to be
expanded it would still leave many adults unable to
benefit, particularly the unemployed, those outside
the labour market, and those wanting to pursue non-
vocational courses. Even within the work-force,
Killeen and Bird showed that at present, PEL is
very unevenly distributed between different occupations, with more than 50% of all PEL going to
managers, professional, scientific and technical
employees.

    The present pattern of student support favours
the traditional, full-time student entering higher
education straight from school, at the expense of
mature students and those studying part-time (Woodhall 1982). The mandatory grant system does not
extend to part-time students or to those who already have a qualification. Thus, although mature
students following a full-time course receive
higher grants than those under 25, many adults
taking continuing education courses do not qualify
for any financial support.

    What is needed is a comprehensive system of
financial support, involving both grants and loans,
covering both students in full time higher and
further eduation and adults wishing to pursue
recurrent and continuing education. Such a system
exists in Sweden, where full-time students receive
most of their financial support as a loan, but
grants are available for adults taking part-time
courses, including non-vocational as well as vocational courses. A combined system of loans and
grants in Britain would free resources which could
be used to provide subsidies for those who

currently receive no grant from public funds, including adults taking part-time courses.

A combined loan and grant system would also be more flexible and more equitable than the present system of student support which concentrates financial aid on a small minority (Woodhall 1982). A recent comparison of student aid in Britain, France, Germany, Sweden and the USA (Johnstone forthcoming) shows that at the undergraduate level British students bear a smaller proportion of total costs than their American, German, Swedish counterparts, who must rely heavily on loans. However, the result of this is that less financial aid is available for the non-traditional students, including adults in continuing education.

However, there will always be students for whom loans - even if backed by a government guarantee and offered at subsidised interest rates - would be insufficient. There have been a number of proposals in recent years, for radical new forms of support for adults in continuing education, including individual 'entitlements' or 'drawing rights' which would entitle all adults to a period of subsidised education, to be taken at a time of their choice. The costs of such a scheme are likely to be prohibitive, however. It is sometimes suggested that such a system could be financed by means of a pay-roll tax, or compulsory contributions to a 'training fund' such as exists in Sweden or France, but it is unlikely that this would be feasible for all types of recurrent education. Recent reviews of actual and proposed methods for financing recurrent education (Levin and Schütze 1983, and Drake 1983) summarise experience in France, Denmark, Sweden, Germany, the Netherlands and the USA but conclude that no country has yet devised a fully comprehensive, flexible and efficient system for financing recurrent education and training.

Proposals which attempt to cover all forms of recurrent education, including both recreational courses and vocational training or retraining are likely to prove so ambitious and to have such massive financial consequences for the taxpayer, that they could damage, rather than promote the case for a shift in resources towards a recurrent model. The NAB Continuing Education Group, reviewing the present pattern of finance for continuing education concluded that 'the emphasis of existing funding arrangements reflects an almost total concern with initial education', and recommended a shift in the balance of funding, in order to give greater priority to part-time and post-experience education. NAB cautions against the assumption that 'finance is the panacea for all problems', but argues, more modestly that 'The importance of finance is that when applied at points of most pressure, it can be the most effective lubricant for oiling the wheels of change, while lack of it can sometimes be the most effective brake'. (NAB 1984, pp.42-43).

Future proposals on the financing of recurrent and continuing education should, therefore, focus on ways of identifying these 'points of pressure', and ways of making existing financial mechanisms more flexible, in order to encourage a shift in resources. In this case the economic and financial implications of recurrent education would be less daunting, and the economic advantages of a system of provision and finance which would encourage individuals, employers and taxpayers to share the costs of continuing education and training, and ensure a flexible and mobile labour force with adequate and up-to-date skills, should be obvious to politicians and policy makers.

## References

ACACE (1982) Continuing Education: From Policies to Practice. Leicester: Advisory Council for Adult and Continuing Education (ACACE), 1982.

Blaug, M. (1973) Education and the Employment Problems in Developing Countries. Geneva: International Labour Office (ILO).

Blaug, M. and Mace, J. (1977) "Recurrent Education: The New Jersualem" Higher Education, Vol.6.

CEDEFOP (9184) (European Centre for the Development of Vocational Training) Educational Leave and the Labour Market in Europe. Berlin: CEDEFOP, 1984.

Christoffel, P. (1983) "An Opportunity Deferred: Lifelong Learning in the U.S." in Levin and Schütze (1983) pp.225-234.

Drake, K. (1983) Financing Adult Education and Training. Manchester Monographs No. 21. Manchester: Department of Adult and Higher Education (1983)

Emmerij, L. (1983) "Paid Educational Leave: A Proposal Based on the Dutch Case" in Levin and Schütze (1983) pp.297-316.

Johnstone, B. (1986 forthcoming) Showing the Costs of College: Student Financial Assistance in the U.S., U.K.,

Federal Republic of Germany, France and Sweden.
Killeen, J. and Bird, M. (1981) Education and Work:
A Study of Paid Educational Leave in England and Wales
1976/7. Leicester: National Institute of Adult Education
1981.
Levin, H.M. and Schütze, H.G. (eds, 1983) Financing Recur-
rent Education: Strategies for Increasing Employment, Job
Opportunities and Productivity. London: Sage, 1983.
National Advisory Body (NAB, 1984) Report of the Continuing
Education Group. London: NAB, August 1984.
OECD (1973) Recurrent Education: A Strategy for Lifelong
Learning. Paris: OECD, 1973.
Stoikov, V. (1973) "Recurrent Education: Some Neglected
Economic issues". International Labour Review, Vol. 108,
August-September 1973.
Stoikov, V. (1975) The Economics of Recurrent Education and
Training. Geneva: International Labour Office (ILO) 1975.
University Grants Committee (UGC, 1984) Report of the
Continuing Eucation Working Party, London: UGC, January,
1984.
Williams, G. (1977) Towards Lifelong Education: A New
Role for Higher Education Institutions, Paris: UNESCO,
1977.
Woodhall, M. (1977) "Adult Education and Training:
An Estimate of the Volume and Costs" in OECD, Learning
Opportunities for Adults, Vol.IV. Paris: OECD.
Woodhall, M. (1980) Scope and Costs of the Education and
Training of Adults in Britain. Leicester: ACACE.
Woodhall, M. (1982a) "Financial Support for Students" in
Morris, A. and Sizer, J. (eds) Resources and Higher Educa-
tion. Leverhulme Programme of Study into the Future of
Higher Education, Vol. 8. Guildford: SRHE pp.81-111.
Woodhall, M. (1982b) Student Loans: Lessons from Recent
International Experience. London: Policy Studies
Institute.

# 8. RECURRENT EDUCATION AND SOCIAL WELFARE POLICY

Colin Griffin

Broadly speaking, the argument to be pursued here is that recurrent education should be thought about in terms of social welfare policy rather than theorised about as another form of provision for adult learning. As anyone working in the field is likely to know, recurrent education tends to be included in a rag-bag of ideas describing new, alternative or just synonymous forms of adult education. Sometimes they catch on, sometimes they do not. In Britain, the term 'continuing' education has caught on whereas 'recurrent' has not. But beneath the often superficial level of terminology significant social and political issues remain to divide advocates of continuing, recurrent, lifelong and adult education. Their derivation as concepts, from UNESCO, OECD, educational reports and so on could be endlessly pursued and sometimes is in the development of adult education theory as a field of knowledge.

It has to be said that in Britain and the United States prevailing ways of thinking (the 'paradigms' and 'discourses' of theory) have tended to remove adult education from the policy process and 'de-politicise' its concerns. As a result, adult education tends to remain divided in its so-called 'liberal' and 'vocational' forms and increasingly reactive to government economic policies. As a form of social policy adult education is largely absorbed in its response to cuts in public expenditure. In the current economic and political climate the historic claims made for the social significance of adult learning are being put to the test. Historically, the origins of adult education lay in diverse social movements associated with the industrial revolution. Out of the struggles of sects, parties and social classes the state subsequently incorporated forms of adult learning as social welfare policy, whilst the professionalisation of adult education practice has shaped its theories. There is no reason to think that changes of government would send these processes into reverse; rather it is to be expected that the logic of history will continue to be worked out.

Before considering the issues raised by recurrent education as a form of social welfare policy, it may be useful to reflect upon adult education as a form of theory (of adult learning and the provision of adult education) and to trace some of the elements which have tended to remove it from the orbit of social policy analysis. In short, what has 'de-politicised' the discourse of adult education? Some elements constitute a conscious attempt to distance it from social and political policies whereas others, described beguilingly as 'radical' adult education, represent often a naive and utopian attempt to elevate a romantic individualism to the status of a revolutionary class politics.

The predominance of sociological functionalism and a psychology of adult learning which relates learning needs to the developmental life cycles of individuals is immediately apparent in the growing theoretical literature of adult education. In effect, this assumes a harmony of social and individual purposes, and a model of adult education according to which the reconciliation of the diversity of individual and social need is a primary function. Society itself - projected as a system - changes over time, as do individuals, and therefore the process of integration is continually at the heart of the adult learning enterprise. In this way, adult education fulfils a vital purpose of helping individuals and society to adjust to new conditions whilst essentially maintaining the same relationships and structures. The advantages of thinking about adult education in this way are obvious: it contributes both to the contentment of individuals and the smooth running of society. In a way it is difficult to see how anyone could possibly object to thinking about adult education in functional terms. One problem is that any conceivable political regime could happily embrace such an idea: under the name 'lifelong education' a whole range of ideologically diverse societies may advocate functional adult learning for purposes of democratic citizenship. Much depends upon what democratic citizenship entails.

Of course, sociological functionalism and developmental psychology, although sometimes associated with scientific methods, are not really neutral in a moral, philosophical or political sense, but reflect fundamental presumptions about the nature of individuals and society. Such presumptions may be correct, but presumptions they remain nevertheless. The adoption of a humanistic individualism as the fundamental paradigm of adult education theory has tended to make social policy analysis rather residual. After all, the supposition is that, given good will, there is no fundamental opposition between individual fulfilment and social change, and that once everyone has embraced the idea and translated it into 'political will', a harmony of individual and social purposes will spontaneously re-assert itself. The blandness of many reports stems from these ways of thinking about adult education - functional, humanistic and integrative ways. It is difficult to deny in principle but difficult to square with the realities of conflict and scarce resources and downright opposition, the conditions out of which the early adult education movements began but out of which adult education has not really grown.

The dominance of the 'psychology of individual growth' paradigm in adult education theory culminated in the teaching and learning technique called andragogy, which currently serves both to consolidate the professionalism of adult education (by distancing it from that of school-teaching) and to remove adult learning from social and political policy considerations. After all, whatever happens, adults will continue to learn, with or without professional facilitation.

Whilst one strand of writing about adult education focuses upon the development of professional theory as a body of knowledge and technique, apparently indifferent to the intrusion of politics into individual and social need, another appears to go to the opposite extreme in connecting adult learning with economic, social and political change, and in ascribing an important role to such learning. Thus adult education becomes connected with social change in a reactive and proactive way, helping individuals and societies to cope with the effects of change and also to intitiate it. We find adult education for the liberation of peasants in Third World countries or women and communities in industrialised ones, for combatting poverty, for learning about democratic citizenship in countries apparently lacking such a tradition, for strengthening international relations, and so on.

Large claims are sometimes made for adult education in bringing about social and political change, and few would doubt its capacity in this respect. Nevertheless, it seems significant that 'radical' adult education has come to stand for any political conception of adult learning whatever, reflecting the fact that, like social work, where a similar process has occurred, adult education has historically been subjected to conceptual and professional, 'de-politicisation': public monies become available for what was deemed to be non-sectarian and non-political education, wherever these boundaries are located in practice. An air of unreality pervades the existential, idealistic and utopian radicalism of some influential writers on adult education, and it also seems significant that their work, although often acclaimed by adult educationists, has for long been heavily criticised by education theorists and, by many, long dismissed. In fact there are few recognisable social or political policy proposals for analysis available in the work of Illich, Freire or Gelpi: they offer more or less persuasive critiques of the varieties of oppression to be discovered in the work, and have done a great deal to stimulate debate about knowledge, learning and power. It is doubtful, however, whether policy makers feel the need to take this much into account. It would be naive in the extreme to suppose that those in power are unaware of the potential of lifelong education for dealing with tricky situations. Gelpi, at least, has analysed the capacity of lifelong education as a potential for <u>either</u> liberation <u>or</u> repression, and he does not make the simple-minded assumption that knowledge is power regardless of who gains it. But even he has tentatively defined lifelong education as 'at once a concept, a policy, a practice, a process, a goal and an ideal', so it remains elusive and Procrustean to say the least.

With regard to social policies for adult education, therefore, the theoretical literature is polarised between an apolitical and professional technology of adult learning and a utopian radicalism, neither of which give much purchase on a social policy analysis of adult learning provision

in a society such as Britain. Perhaps this literature has failed to bridge precisely the gap between
adult learning and adult education which opened up
with the onset of state provided education in the
nineteenth century. Adult learning and the provision for its development are objects of much
theorising by now, but the issues raised by adult
education as a provision by the state at public
expense to achieve social as well as individual
purposes can hardly be said to have been a matter
of much analysis: the assumption has simply been
that any extension of provision for adult learning
is a good thing and anything that obstructs this is
a bad thing. Such prescriptions are totally
unobjectionable but hardly a basis for policy
analysis and decision-making. The bland language
of official reports elevates everything to a priority; in practice, as the fate of such reports tends
to bear out, priorities are determined by the
availability of public funding, in which process
professionals cannot do other than connive.

Recurrent education must establish itself on
other grounds than these. It must avoid the
perennial 'liberal-vocational', 'practice-theory',
'radical-mainstream' antitheses which have sent so
much adult education running for cover under the
name of 'continuing' education or the not-so-subtle
'education of adults' idea. The fact is that adult
education theory and practice has now become
straightjacketed by its own ideologies and traditions, partly obsessed by the concept of adulthood
itself and lacking adequate reflection of the ideo-
logical struggles over schooling which have been so
vigorously conducted at the level of theory and
practice since publicly-funded education began.
(See Brighouse, Ch. 2).

In establishing itself as a social welfare
policy rather than as an adult education paradigm,
recurrent education needs itself to be distanced
from sterile conceptual debates. For example, it
is not very illuminating to 'define' recurrent
education in abstract terms, such as in comparing
and contrasting it with 'continuing', 'lifelong' or
any other 'adult' ideas of education, since clearly
the same practice can fall under any name you care
to give it. This is not to say we should eschew
theoretical and conceptual work with recurrent
education, but only to do so upon its own terms
rather than in terms of other education ideas. The
argument that it does not matter what recurrent

education is, all we need to do is practise it, is clearly one to avoid like the plague. For one thing, it is deeply conservative in the effect it has of removing recurrent education from the public policy arena, with all the inevitable and desirable disagreements and conflict this implies. As with local government, the slogan 'let's keep politics out of this' delivers people into the hands of professionals however well-intentioned, as well as of conservatives pursuing their politics under the guise of neutrality. A rigid separation of theory and practice reflects a certain cultural style, perhaps even the possibilities of the English language, but it is to be avoided in a concept of recurrent education which reflects the dialectical relationship of theory and practice: each without the other is sterile, whilst at the same time they inevitably come into contradiction.

So it is not a good thing to define recurrent education in terms of other and similar terms. It is particularly not a good thing to construct tautological or circular definitions, or to seek for rhetorical substitutions such as that of 'life-long learning' for 'lifelong education'. The policy issue is that of education, not learning as such: publicly provided opportunities for people to learn more effectively than they would have learned anyway. Thus recurrent education is sometimes defined as 'a strategy for lifelong learning', but it is very questionable whether this is a defini-tion at all, not only because there is little if any conceptual differentiation between learning and education here, but because 'lifelong learning' and 'lifelong education' are themselves such imprecise terms. In the face of all these different but similar expressions, and especially when their definitions are apparently circular, widespread impatience and indifference to the whole lot of them is, to say the least, understandable.

The emptiness of defining recurrent education as a 'strategy for lifelong learning' (OECD) can be demonstrated by looking at it in relation to two different definitions of lifelong education, both of which emanate from UNESCO. There are, presum-ably, several possible ways of defining lifelong education, and they need not be incompatible with one another, but there is no possibility of con-structing a definition of recurrent education by defining it in terms of other concepts, particu-larly that of lifelong education, which seems at

95

least to be the most obvious.

One concept of lifelong education makes it stand for the functional integration of education systems so as to make possible the provision of learning opportunities during the whole of an individual's lifetime. According to this view, lifelong education is simply a new 'delivery system' in response to the kinds of change and crisis which affect all societies today: as society's needs change so the education system must change to meet them. Quite a lot of lifelong education is in place, since many existing institutions are flexible, either by choice or from necessity. But in order to become more systematised, such provision needs to be rationalised and integrated. Thus criticism of existing provision is implicit: in so far as they constitute an obstacle, through authoritarianism or rigidity or whatever, to systematised lifelong education, then schools, colleges and universities must change. The value-system upon which existing systems are said to be predicated, liberal humanism and individual growth, remain the basis for a lifelong system, but value-systems are not at the heart of this concept. An extension of opportunity for individuals or of equality for groups, may be expected to be an eventual outcome of lifelong education, but this is not what it is primarily about. The main element in this concept of lifelong education is that of functional responses to social, economic and cultural change. In short, meeting society's new needs is the most important argument, - any society, that is, whether it be industrialised or not, democratic or totalitarian. It is, of course, unexceptionable to argue that an education system which meets society's needs is preferable to one that does not, or that one that is more integrated will achieve its purposes better than one that is not. At least this is true when such needs and purposes meet with our approval. Therefore, what the functional-integration model of lifelong education entails seems to be a re-organisation of the existing institutions of provision in order to serve the needs of society and of individuals over the whole of their lifetime.

Such developments have always been implicit in education systems, but the need of societies to adapt to rapid technological, social and economic change has now made it imperative to put a lifelong system in place. It is also suggested that the

sheer speed of change is so great today as to
constitute a potentially destabilising factor in
individuals and societies, and there can be no
doubt that this view of lifelong education is
related to one of social tensions and social
crisis, and in particular, to the need for workers
to be able to adapt to the application of new
knowledge and technology to the processes of production. Even more important in times of crisis
and dislocation is the need for a re-assertion of
universal social values: the normative consensus
upon which the social order rests and which lies at
the heart of all functionalist theories of society.
The integration of individuals and groups alienated
or marginalised in their economic, social and cultural roles is also seen as an important element of
this model of lifelong education.

The functional-integration model of lifelong
education just sketched is not based upon any comparative social and political analysis, but upon
humanistic and developmental psychology and is
addressed, apparently, to universal needs of individuals and societies. An alternative, which we
may for convenience call a cultural-liberation
model, has been outlined by Ettore Gelpi using a
concept of the international division of labour as
its analytic basis. As Head of the Lifelong Education Unit at UNESCO, Gelpi has addressed lifelong
education in relation to its capacity for the cultural liberation and social emancipation of individuals and groups marginalised in the processes of
production and the worldwide distribution of
wealth. He has concerned himself therefore with
issues of the Third World and the North-South division of wealth and poverty, with migrant workers
and people culturally marginalised and economically
exploited by the operations of international corporations. He has concerned himself particularly
with workers' education and with struggles to gain
some control over the productive processes which
divide individuals, groups and societies.

Gelpi's cultural-liberation model of lifelong
education is obviously more politically oriented
than that described as the functional-integration
one. This is not to say they are necessarily
incompatible, for to subscribe to one does not mean
the other is thereby invalidated. But they certainly focus upon different aspects of lifelong
education: Gelpi's humanistic utopianism is concerned much more with conflict and struggle than

with integration and consensus. His is an openly
political conception of lifelong education, and he
sees it as both potentially reproducing and transforming existing social structures of inequality.
Gelpi too focuses particularly upon education and
the labour market, and the capacity of lifelong
education for transforming the international division of labour. But in his model the educational
institutions themselves are transformed rather than
merely functionally integrated, so that a whole
range of cultural institutions become the setting
for lifelong education processes. Whilst Gelpi's
is certainly not a 'de-schooling' vision, it does
involve a far more radical view of educational
institutions than that taken by the functional-
integrationists, and it throws open for debate the
whole issue of where learning is located if not in
traditional institutions.

Gelpi takes lifelong education to be, amongst
other things, an instrument of social policy. And
whereas one model of it stresses those elements of
a lifelong system which are already in place, his
tends to focus much more upon the obstacles which
must be overcome before it could be achieved. For
Gelpi, lifelong education is an object of social
and political struggle against, at best, the
inertia of the bureaucratic apparatus. At worst,
lifelong education must coexist in dialectical
relations with 'apartheid, colonialism, racism,
lack of intellectual freedom, physical violence ...
the violence inflicted by man upon man in order to
tame his fellows.' Whether lifelong education
reduces or connives at these evils will depend upon
who controls it: Gelpi has little faith that
bureaucrats or traditional educationists could be
capable of constructing it as an instrument of
social policy on such global scale.

Given such contrasting views about the idea of
lifelong education, what point could there be in
defining recurrent education as a strategy to
achieve it? Would it be a strategy to achieve the
functional integration of educational systems or
through cultural liberation to transform the international division of labour? Following Gelpi,
there is no reason to suppose that functional integration would contribute to such a transformation.
On the contrary, there is plenty of evidence to
suggest that what is essentially a bureaucratic
model of lifelong education would tend to reproduce
the existing division of labour and the distribu-

tion of wealth in the world, to the disadvantage of all those people who suffer marginalisation as a result of it.

The example of lifelong education suggests the futility of defining recurrent education in terms of other education concepts: the same result would be achieved if the terms 'adult', 'continuing', 'permanent' or whatever were substituted. Either the definition becomes tautologous or else it simply begs all the questions of meaning that inevitably arise.

Why bother to 'define' recurrent education at all when the effort could be better put into constructing it as a form of social welfare policy? What this would require is very different from the academic theorising or the bureaucratic de-politicising of traditional adult education on the one hand or the visionary utopianism of radical educators on the other. Neither of these approaches begin to conceptualise education as a form of social policy in which the struggles of opposed interests and the play of ideologies, rather than the market-place of ideas, determine outcomes.

Traditional adult education theory has become rather self-consciously academic in pursuit of the status of a discipline: the refinement of techniques of adult teaching and learning, for the moment at least, seems to occupy centre-stage alongside philosophical, psychological, sociological and historical conceptualisations of provision. Radical educators offer powerful critiques of the forms of oppression and exploitation, but in describing these forces paradoxically point up their strengths. Scrupulously avoiding hopelessness, they nevertheless have little to offer by way of social policy analysis. Change there certainly is, but it tends to be on a parochial scale rather than the global one of the political critique itself. The days when exaggerated claims for the political effectiveness of education were routinely made are over, for the time being at least, and the truth is probably as Gelpi suggests, that education systems are a potential for both liberation and oppression. Official reports scrupulously avoid a political view of education in any case, and construct priorities in a social policy vacuum: social policies are not inherent in education as such, however, being constructed from professional ideologies and imposed by the political system out of the struggles of contending interests. As a result, lifelong education tends to be thought of as an object of 'political will', whatever that is, or else it is conceptualised in such a loose way that it is impossible to grasp as an object of social policy at all.

To construct recurrent education as a form of social welfare policy, instead of trying to define it in terms of adult or lifelong education, offers us access to a well-established tradition in this country of social welfare policy research and analysis. Instead of a sterile and de-politicised functionalism on the one hand and romantic utopianism on the other, it would enable us to consider in a practical way the possibilities of education in relation to the redistribution of wealth and opportunity in society. In society as it actually exists, that is, rather than in a society we believe ought to exist. The issue of publicly provided access to education cannot really be separated from that of access to work, housing, leisure, health and social security, and to perpetuate recurrent education as an exclusively 'education' idea would be quite impractical in people's lives. Recurrent education is a social welfare policy which is inextricably linked with the fate of social welfare itself, and its analysis and construction could only satisfactorily be achieved in the same terms as the analysis and construction of all social welfare policy.

We now know a good deal in Britain about how to study and analyse welfare policy, both in terms of alternative models of social welfare and of policy formulation, practice and outcomes. We can certainly learn from this discipline the opportunities and obstacles which are likely to be met in constructing recurrent education as a form of social welfare policy. This is likely to be a sobering exercise if, as is commonly supposed, it is regarded as a strategy of equality which redistributes educational opportunity in society. Most educational policy since the Second World War has addressed itself to equality in some sense or other but few attempts have been made to measure the effectiveness of such policies in relation to other variable factors which influence people's life chances. There is little evidence to suggest that public expenditure is an effective strategy of equality, and most policy analysts would concur that the structural inequalities of society have so far proved impervious to education policies aimed at a more egalitarian distribution of wealth and opportunity. It may even be the case that the promotion of greater inequality has been an unintended outcome of such policies. There is no reason to suppose that recurrent education as a strategy of lifelong learning or whatever, would be any more effective than any other egalitarian education policy. (See Nilsson, Ch. 28)

So there is no point in constructing recurrent education as simply another education policy directed towards greater equality in society, because all the evidence suggests that such policies, although they may be almost universally embraced in some sense or other, do not actually work. Social policies are constructed from conflicts of interest and value, and a policy which appears to command universal assent may well not achieve its aims in the end. The case of paid educational leave, for example, which is often regarded as a typical recurrent strategy, is as much if not more addressed to employment than to educational provision. In which case, an unintended consequence of the policy may be to expose a conflict of interest between the employed and the unemployed, between those engaged in salaried, waged and unwaged work, thus promoting greater inequality rather than equality.

To avoid defining recurrent education as an educational strategy and instead to construct it as a policy of social welfare seems in the light of experience to be more realistic. The impact in this country of education policies addressed to redistribution and equality is minimal: it would appear that redistributive policies need to be directed much more closely to the social relations of production itself. The mere expansion of provision has not prevented an actual widening of social class differences to wealth and opportunity.

Recurrent education as a form of social welfare policy should therefore be addressed as much to employment and to all those factors which determine people's life chances. This has very significant consequences for the 'policy community' of recurrent education, for there are no reasons why educationists should have a dominant role in policy formation: on the contrary, it should probably be modest. This approach would perhaps avoid the pitfalls of tautological definitions of education concepts, whereby, for example, paid educational leave is a strategy of recurrent education, which is a strategy of lifelong education, which is a strategy of an alleged 'master concept' of lifelong learning, and so on. It might also help to avoid problems raised in professional adult education discourse, focusing as it does upon the nature of adult learning in a context of humanistic philosophy rather than one of production and politics, which are themselves the proper context of humanism. The utopiansm of radical educators is always morally appealing, but in the end it is more or less remote from problems of policy formation in societies such as ours.

Recurrent education as a form of social welfare policy requires attention being paid above all to a real world of conflicts of interest and value, to a policy community which reflects a subordinate function for educationists, an awareness of the widespread failure of education policies to have a redistributive impact, to the need to evaluate the outcomes, intended and otherwise, of policies, and so on. Only if recurrent education is addressed to problems of social welfare, rather than to problems of education, will it be a strategy worthy of the name. We need to think of it as a social welfare idea then, rather than an education idea as such.

## Bibliography

Advisory Council for Adult and Continuing Education (1982), Continuing Education: from policies to practice.

Dave, R.H. (1976), Foundations of Lifelong Education (Pergamon Press/UNESCO Institute for Education).

Demaine, J. (1981), Contemporary Theories in the Sociology of Education (Macmillan).

Duke, C. ed. (1985), Combating Poverty Through Adult Education (Croom Helm).

Freire, P. (1985), The Politics of Education (Macmillan).

Gelpi, E. (1985), Lifelong Education and International Relations (Croom Helm).

George, V. and Wilding, P. (1984), The Impact of Social Policy (Routledge and Kegan Paul).

Himmelstrup, P. et al eds. (1981), Strategies for Lifelong Learning 1 (University Centre of South Jutland and Association for Recurrent Education).

Illich, I. (1971), Deschooling Society (Calder and Boyars).

Knapper, C.K. and Cropley, A.J. (1985), Lifelong Learning and Higher Education (Croom Helm).

Knowles, M.S. et al (1984), Andragogy in Action (Jossey-Bass).

Le Grand, J. (1982), The Strategy of Equality: redistribution and the social services (Allen and Unwin).

Lovett, T. et al (1983), Adult Education and Community Action (Croom Helm).

Thomas, J.E. (1985), Learning Democracy in Japan: the social education of Japanese adults (Sage Publications).

Thompson, J.L. (1983), Learning Liberation: women's response to men's education (Croom Helm).

# SECTION 2: THE POLITICIANS AND RECURRENT EDUCATION

# 9.  CONTINUING EDUCATION - CONSERVATIVE ACHIEVEMENT

Dr Keith Hampson, MP

Once, education was thought of as the key to
creating a fair and more just society in Britain.
Disillusion set in some time ago. Public disen-
chantment, moulded in the main by school developments, in the 1970s infected attitudes to education
as a whole. Higher education ceased rapidly to be
the sexy political subject it was in the mid-1960s.
Those who criticised lack of interest and a fall in
priority for higher education were castigated for
special pleading.
During Sir Keith Joseph's tenure at the
Department of Education and Science, the mood was
one of reform but overlain by a strong disenchant-
ment. For the quality and nature of education was
in the eyes of Mrs. Thatcher one of the 'supply-
side' constraints which she felt needed radical
reform. Change in education, however, could only
be within restrained resources. 'What can we
afford?' was the constant refrain.
Adult and continuing education only emerged as
significant in the Government's second term of
office. The awakening came from a combination of
'supply-side' concern at our prospects as an
advanced industrial nation and the mounting tide of
unemployment.
Through the pressure of economic events, the
Government has translated the concept of continuing
education into reality over the last three years or
so, but some of the repercussions dawned slowly.
Course development and more flexible teaching
methods, in-service training for further education
teachers and staff development workshops have come
belatedly on the scene. One obvious reason must be
that programmes have evolved on an ad hoc basis.
Conservative interest in continuing education

has stemmed directly from its vocational significance. Ministers became acutely aware of Britain's chronic shortage of skilled manpower in critical areas and increasingly worried. Moreover, since unemployment amongst the unskilled is some five times that amongst the skilled, the obvious lesson is that one should do everything possible to turn the unemployable unskilled into a more employable skilled workforce, a policy which in turn would help to ease wage pressures caused by skill shortages.

To Sir Keith Joseph and his colleagues in the DES, this meant that reform of the school curriculum and examinations was the first priority, followed by pressure on higher education to switch the arts/science balance more towards the applied sciences and technology. But in 1983, Sir Keith said: 'Regular updating has long been a requirement of such life and death professions as midwifery and airline pilots, and it is equally important that those professions most closely associated with jobs and wealth should also move quickly in this direction'. In his last two years Sir Keith became a very enthusiastic supporter of initiatives in continuing education and actually took the lead in asking Cabinet colleagues for more resources for PICKUP. Peter Brooke, of all ministers, was probably the most receptive to such ideas and deserves recognition for maintaining the PICKUP momentum.

Dissatisfaction with the style, tone and nature of school education led naturally to a greater degree of interest in retraining. A drift heightened by the stark traditional opposition of much of the school world, that has always resented what it sees as education subservient to the whims of employers. But as always, the politics of education lie in the schools. Parents can vote, and with parental concern at standards in the schools mounting and the two year long teachers' dispute, the schools inevitably attracted ministers' attention.

In 1979 I wrote that: 'Traditional attitudes are deeply entrenched and there is no money for a global approach. The way forward can only be by developing a series of complementary activities on a number of fronts... Only incremental changes, not sweeping transformations, have a chance of getting Tory support. There has indeed been no "big bang" reform. No great announcement or open conversion'. (Roderick, G. and Stephens, M. (1979)).

A consensus of view between the Departments of Education, Industry and Employment emerged in 1981 when they jointly published the White Paper A New Training Initiative. But in the October of the previous year, the DES produced its own Green Paper Continuing Education. It ably, if rather boringly, highlighted four central issues where it proposed immediate practical help: the need to make higher and further education more entrepreneurial, their closer collaboration with industry and business, the need for an information network of appropriate courses to be made available to employers, and changes in students' entry qualifications. From it sprang the PICKUP initiative launched by the DES in 1982. The same lessons were not lost on the MSC which rather more dramatically launched in December 1983 its Adult Training Strategy.

There was a Department of Employment White Paper, Training for Jobs, published in 1984 and one in 1985, Employment: the challenge for the nation. In the DES Green Paper, The Development of Higher Education into the 1990s, published in May 1985, there was a valuable chapter on 'Education throughout Life', which opened in ringing terms: 'Opportunities for education should be available throughout life - for career purposes and for greater personal fulfilment - and the need increases with the pace of technological change'.

1985 might in fact be seen by future generations as a seminal year - the year of 'lift-off'. A Standing Committee on Continuing Education was established to try to promote greater collaboration between the UGC, NAB, the Open University and the Scottish Education Department. The University Grants Committee and the National Advisory Body for Local Authority Higher Education issued a joint statement, 'Open Education and the Needs of Society', which included consideration of whether continuing education required a reinterpretation of Robbins's first two objectives or should be established as a new objective. They determined that there should be a new objective: 'The provision of continuing education in order to facilitate adjustment to technological, economic and social change and to meet individual needs for personal development'. An interdepartmental committee of civil servants was established. Within the DES, PICKUP was launched in 1982 as a pilot project costing less than £1 million a year, but in 1985 its funds tripled to £5 million. In November 1985 the

Department of Employment and the MSC launched the Adult Training Campaign to increase awareness of the importance of adult training and updating by bringing together and coordinating all Government departments and making a massive publicity effort to stimulate interest in the public.

Bit by bit, the initiatives have mounted and produced a quiet revolution - like so much Government policy, largely unsung and unnoticed, even by the mass of the Conservative Party. It would be nice to think that on at least one occasion, the educational debate at the Tory Party Conference was about more than just the return of grammar schools.

Overall, however, continuing education and re-training have seen a greater expansion of resources than any other area in the educational field. With mounting unemployment, retraining assumed new importance. The number of adults in various training and retraining projects will reach a quarter of a million by the end of 1986; that is more than double the 1983 figure, despite the closure of some lesser used Skill Centres. A wide range of agencies have been tapped.

As with so many developments in further education, progress owes most to the Manpower Services Commission, a body which is seldom given enough credit in the educational world but has been a most creative body and has been particularly important in making the educational world wake up to the fact that its customary lead times - 5 to 15 years - are absurdly long. Between 1985/86 and 1986/87, MSC expenditure on non-advanced further education rose by 60%. Its spending on the Open Tech rose from £8 million to £11 million and there was a 14% real increase (to £260 million) in the remainder of the MSC's adult training budget. Not all of this 'action' has of course been good value for money!

Faced with this competition, the DES started to get its act together, despite the risk of some duplication of effort. The traditional providers of adult learning, such as the WEA, university extra-mural departments, and above all the Open University, have however, received less attention than they merit. They have tended to suffer from the prevailing prejudice in favour of industry-geared programmes. Though one vice-chancellor, who has been keen on PICKUP, has reportedly said that continuing education is too important to leave to an extra-mural department.

There has been a small but steady decline in

real terms in the Open University's grant since its peak year of 1980/81, though numbers of undergraduates have risen from 60,000 to 67,400.

Though we may be short on a proper long term strategy, at least there have been the odd shafts of light to cheer up believers in adult and continuing education, whereas after labouring mightily for years the Russell Committee produced a thorough report with a soundly based strategy that was promptly pigeon-holed and perceived by both Conservative and Labour Governments as impracticable. The fact that initiatives are piecemeal does not devalue their worth in themselves, and the more seeds scattered the more chance they have of germinating into a comprehensive programme.

Though piecemeal and uncoordinated, the trends are clear. There are powerful pressures pushing Government in the direction of continuing education. First is the general economic picture. Recession can work miracles - even without anyone noticing. There has been a steady and mounting concern over the poor quality of training and growing recognition of the importance of retraining. Britain has a long way to go to match anything like the range of training presented in other countries, as Mr. Bryan Nicholson, chairman of the Manpower Services Commission, himself stressed in March 1986 in a ferocious attack on the poor record of British managers in investing in education and training.

The education world has come a long way when its Secretary of State can argue - as Sir Keith Joseph did in The Times of 16 January 1986 - that 'in times of great technological and economic change there is a direct relationship between the practice of continuing professional education and the competitiveness of industry and commerce'. The evidence is clear and growing.

Take, for example, the findings of Competence and Competition, the report published by the National Economic Development Council and the Manpower Services Commission, which looked at the three overseas economies we find most difficulty competing against - the United States, Japan and West Germany. It showed that we are investing in adult training, retraining and updating only a fraction of what these countries have done for some years. These competitors clearly believe that updating people in their skills and knowledge is good for business, and they invest in this crucial linkage. This is not the case with us.

The point is reinforced by findings in a recent research study entitled <u>Adult Training in Britain</u>, conducted by IFF Research. This reported that the UK workforce as a whole receives about 14 hours off-the-job training a year compared with the 30 to 40 hours considered to be good practice in West Germanuy. The research found that high-performing businesses are twice as likely to train employees as are low-performing companies and that the high performers train at least twice as many of their staff as low performers.

There seems to have been a long-standing belief on the part of many British workers - and indeed amongst the unemployed - that participation in adult education does not provide any significant advantage in the labour market. Yet there is clearly a great number of 18 to 30 year olds who never achieved their potential at school or college and are stuck in jobs beneath their potential capacity. They must be encouraged to improve their prospects, particularly when parts of industry are experiencing shortages of appropriately skilled people. There are obviously strong attitudinal barriers to overcome. It might not readily occur to someone who has worked in a shipyard all his life - and his father and grandfather before him - that he might have done, or might now do, something else. And the self-confidence to take the plunge may not be there.

There is already an acute national shortage of computer scientists and to some extent the UGC did not help by cutting back in the early 1980s on the technological universities, such as Bradford, Brunel and Salford. The National Computing Centre recently showed that despite a predicted massive increase in demand for computer staff, fewer than a third of the companies they surveyed actually did any training in the area. Its survey indicated that in a great many IT areas there would be a 50% shortfall over the next five years. In April 1984, the Secretary of State for Industry, Normal Tebbit, established a special IT Skills Shortage committee under a Department of Trade and Industry junior minister, John Butcher. It identified a chronic shortage of information technology manpower. To redress the problem the number of people trained in computer skills would need to double each year. Retraining is the only way this can be achieved.

Ministers whose concern stems in large part from their 'supply-side' economic beliefs tend not

to see solutions in terms of direct government
intervention. In preparing measures to alleviate
the problem, the Government sees its role as primarily that of a catalyst, encouraging industry
itself to become more involved. There has been a
reluctance to pump Government funding into the
universities or other institutions of higher education to provide the extra places. The DES has not
the funds and the DTI has a different, more hands-
off ideology, which says that employers themselves
must take the major share of the responsibility and
cost of training.

Nevertheless, it is paradoxical, given the
rhetoric of both the present and last Labour
government, that the proportion of part-time degree
level students has grown so slowly. From 1974 to
1978 the proportion of part-timers in universities
grew from 8.7 to 8.9 per cent. Between 1979 and
1984 the proportion has grown to 11%. But in the
public sector institutions from a peak in 1980 of
45.9%, it had fallen by 1984 to 42%. Part-time
work in the non-advanced FE sector dropped from 85%
in 1974 to 80% of a smaller total of students in
1984.

The Lords Select Committee on Science and
Technology (1985) argued that a hands-off approach
would not suffice. 'If they think that the
nation's problems can be solved without spending
any money they are deluding themselves', the report
said. It is obviously in the national interest
that more adults should be motivated to re-enter
education and training. And no Government can duck
its responsibilities if employers continue to pre-
fer to poach experienced staff rather than engage
in the expensive process of training and developing
talent themselves. Too little is currently spent
by companies and there are huge financial disincen-
tives to individuals to take on the responsibility
themselves.

The Government (Cmnd. 9653, 1985) agreed with
the Lords Select Committee that Britain 'lags
behind its competitors in investment by employers
in the updating and retraining of their work-
forces'. And it argued forcefully that 'initial
education and training can no longer be - even if
it ever was - an adequate basis for continuing
professional competence'. Yet in the same response, the Government stressed that the primary
role of government is 'to reinforce the workings of
the training market by ensuring that adequate

information systems about training needs and training courses are available'. This is, in fact, the
area on which they have most successfully concentrated.

The little NEDDY for the computer industry has
stressed the need for a 'national training focus'
rather than the Butcher ad hoc committee into skill
shortages. But the very existence of that committee indicates an awareness which did not exist a
decade ago. And one development with enormous
potential is the National Priority Skills scheme
through which MSC grants are available to help
employers meet their key skill needs by retraining
existing employees or training newly recruited
staff.

There are two basic problems. How to ensure
that all potential adult students have easy access
to up-to-date and accurate information, in sufficient detail to help them match their needs and
circumstances against course content and conditions. Secondly, how to ensure that the recurrent
opportunities on offer are relevant. Without that
perception they will not trigger the necessary
interest on the part either of the company or the
student who is looking for a course germane to the
demands of his or her job.

A key element has been the Further Education
Unit. It has done valuable service in assessing
curricula. It has also commissioned and sells a
computer database with which FE colleges can keep
track of all company contacts to assist them in
curricular design and marketing. It is symptomatic
that it had to urge colleges and validating bodies
to give immediate and top priority to a review of
engineering courses 'to make sure that they are
relevant to the needs of students in or about to
enter jobs involving new technology'. Also note-
worthy is the FEU's Flexible Learning Opportunities
pamphlet, issued in 1983.

The difficulties of maintaining relevance were
highlighted by the Training Opportunities Scheme
(TOPS). It came under increasing criticism for
training redundant skills. In line with the
Government's philosophy, the MSC replaced it by the
Job Training Scheme, the intention of which is to
relate training more to the needs of the local
labour market. It has special provision for disabled people.

The reorganisation of the MSC's adult programmes reflects the growing belief that training

and retraining resources have to be sharply targeted at specific employment needs. The MSC's adult training provision is now essentially grouped into two programmes - the Job Training Programme and the Wider Opportunities Training Programme. Within the former, about 54,000 adults will be engaged in the Job Training Scheme in the current financial year, at a cost of about £159 million. Also within the Job Training Programme is the 'Training for Enterprise Scheme', providing basic management training opportunities for some 16,000 people aiming to start new businesses, and embracing a Management Extension Programme which trains unemployed managers for allocation to small firms short of resources. A third scheme 'Access to Information Technology' promotes computer based skills. The Wider Opportunities Training Programme offers basic skill training and general support in areas like literacy and numeracy through a range of modular full and part-time courses. Around 40,000 adults on this programme are unemployed.

The MSC has addressed a number of specific problems related to the disadvantageous position of women in the labour market. Facilities have been improved to help women to return to work after a long absence. But the structure and timing of retraining programmes seriously inhibits their use of women. This is where distance learning comes into its own. The Open University has an MSC sponsored 'Women in Technology' to prepare women for re-entry into further education or employment. Open Tech programmes try to take account of the difficulties of domestic commitments as well.

Distance learning has tremendous potential, both because of its relatively low unit costs, the flexibility it provides for students who can study at home with tapes and videos, and in using to best advantage scarce expertise. The Government has particularly favoured distance learning for management training, and the Open Business School has been developed by the Open University and the British Institute of Management. Tutored distance learning is under discussion between the MSC and the Alvey Directorate to develop and offer a series of course modules in modern electronic and IT skills for companies who find it difficult to release scarce staff.

Though the Open Tech is expanding at the technician level, it has not enjoyed the impact which Jim Prior hoped for when he developed the idea in

Opposition and pushed it through as Secretary of State for Employment. There are currently some 120 pump-priming projects. There is now also a comprehensive guide to Open Tech courses, the Open Tech Directory. During 1985/6 some 50,000 people benefited from training supported by the Open Tech. One particularly valuable Open Tech initiative is 'Southtek', which links Brighton Polytechnic, FE colleges and local companies in the development and sale of distance learning packages. The MSC has put in £1.7 million to extend the operation nationwide, and has since put up £6 million to get the Open College of the Air off the ground.

Unemployment has thrown into sharp relief the lack of education and training amongst the ethnic communities. Many first generation immigrants made redundant in middle-age find that their standard of English must improve if they are going to stand a chance of getting any job. Provision for basic courses in literacy and numeracy has increased markedly with the establishment - in the first year of the new government - of the Adult Literacy and Basic Skills Units as a fully fledged and permanent resource, advisory and development unit. Despite the overall severe restraints of public expenditure that year, £500,000 was found for it. Well over 100,000 students attend basic courses in England and Wales. And there seems to be sustained demand for provision of all sorts. Local authorities, often using individual volunteers and voluntary organisations, have created an efficient service, generally speaking. But the provision can vary enormously in quality and quantity.

Going one stage further, there are now a considerable number of 'Second Chance' courses set up by the WEA. Again, since they are run during the day they are primarily for the unemployed: to widen horizons and boost confidence, and lead them, it is hoped, into other types of educational work which can give them qualifications of some sort.

Many sections of industry are quite unaware of the range of educational services which could be made available. But there has in fact been a real breakthrough in appreciating the need for better information, both to excite interest and to help people to find the right opportunity to develop their particular talents. One of the most striking differences over the past five or six years has been the sheer weight of information available on adult education of all kinds. There are now pamphlets and books and leaflets of all sizes and types, from a plethora of sources. A range of information booklets, explaining in simple terms what is available both to employers and to individuals, is now available in Job Centres. Libraries are also increasingly used. Some local authorities are producing free newspapers on adult education provision.

Promotional material can of course be misleading. So there is still a great need for accurate, comprehensive and efficiently coordinated information. Individuals must be able to find the right opportunity to develop their particular talents. Currently, the provision is difficult to understand and gain access to. A person might not even know whether it is 'education' or 'training' they need, 'adult' or 'further' education, what might suit them best or where an appropriate course is available.

They need guidance. Since so many potential adult students are concerned about their time and other constraints, there is an important missing link if there is no-one to whom they can talk, to help them sort out what they should do and where it will lead.

The system must be made more attractive if people are to be more willing to enter. Counselling services are therefore essential if we are going to accept a society in which the majority of people change their career several times in a working life. The need is of course more acute when they are also unemployed.

Ideally, we should be looking for arrangements to help workers prior to redundancy. The White Paper, 'Training For Jobs' (January 1984) stressed the importance of training packages to help employees facing redundancy. But the coordination effort is immense, particularly trying to identify and inform firms facing redundancies. One success story is in Sheffield, where five colleges have formed a consortium to undertake joint publicity and provide courses for the redundant.

Job Change programmes, MSC funded but run by adult education centres one day a week for six months, are geared to attracting older people from management, boosting morale and helping to identify their aptitudes. The Birmingham Polytechnic based Job Change Project is a successful out-reach programme for the over-forties.

We are in sight of real progress in a number

of other directions related to helping the unemployed, though each scheme in itself tends to be rather small beer. This would be a criticism of the excellent initiative of the Department of Education and Science called REPLAN. This was launched in March 1984, initially for three years, but was renewed in 1986 for a further two years. Its aim is to encourage the development of better educational opportunities for unemployed adults. New kinds of course, new approaches to teaching adults and new ways of publicising the openings are supported by pump-priming grants. In its first two years REPLAN established eight field officers covering England and Wales, coordinated by the National Institute of Adult Continuing Education. The overall budget was set at only £2.5 million over three years, though the MSC helps out on some of the development projects. The money is also channelled to approved Local Authority schemes through the Education Support Grant mechanism.

At another level entirely is the critical question of access and that long-neglected area of British post-school education, credit transfer. It is disgraceful that the conservatism of British higher education should have delayed this essential step for so long. I remember making speeches on the subject in 1977! It took a painfully long time for the Open University to breach the universities' resistance, and only in 1983 did the Government throw its weight behind the OU by funding a three year development programme for a computer data base called ECCTIS (The Educational Counselling and Credit Transfer Information Service).

A pilot scheme was established, initially only in the South West. Information on all degree courses in the universities, advanced further education courses in the polytechnics and the colleges with 70% or more advanced work is being gathered. With details on the qualifications needed for entry to or transfer between courses in mid-course, including alternatives to 'A' levels, and opportunities for mature students. In August 1985 the then Secretary of State for Education, Sir Keith Joseph, announced the Government's commitment to extend the scheme into a fully operational national service.

Typically, the long term arrangements for the financing, administration and continuing support of a national ECCTIS are a bone of contention. Without sufficient funding, there will not be the necessary publicity for its services. The key is to make it available to the widest audience at the cheapest cost. For libraries and school careers officers the system is available on microfiche. But by linking into PRESTEL, knowledge of the opportunities will be available in the home. Adult learning could take a gigantic leap forward as PRESTEL spreads. ECCTIS has also entered into experimental local collaborative agreements with LEAs. They will collect and collate local information on a regularly up-dated basis in return for access to the national data base for its schools.

In March 1986 the Council for National Academic Awards (CNAA) launched a 'Credit Accumulation and Transfer Scheme' (CATS) covering institutions of higher education eligible for CNAA degrees. Basically, what is involved is a 'clearing house' type of arrangement, through which students can 'build' their own degrees. Periods in different institutions, which in the past would not have been taken into account, can now be treated as 'credit blocks' which together lead to a degree. It must make sense to associate this with ECCTIS.

Following encouragement by George Walden, then Minister for Higher Education, a total of 15 universities decided to contract in. The volume of inquiries has also been larger than expected. The scheme has received good support from industry. More than 50 companies declared an interest in the project in the first few weeks.

Printed directories can fall easily out of date. Computer data bases are therefore essential and must be promoted across the entire field, not just at degree level. There are a wide variety of guidance systems, often funded by the MSC and related to the careers service, which should be drawn on. Birmingham, for example, has an ambitious computerised record scheme incorporating city-wide information to help individuals to find jobs and discover what they need to prepare for them.

Ad hoc developments are no bad thing in terms of spontaneity and innovation, but there has to be more work done on inter-agency liaison and the development of more concerted national advice. And if better guidance leads to a more effective use of resources and instruction more appropriately suited to an individual's requirements, then it will be money well spent.

The DES recognised this in 1984 when it asked

the Unit for the Development of Adult Continuing Education to examine the entire field. Their report, The Challenge of Change, was published in May 1986 (UDACE 1986). It proposes that a permanent, nationally coherent framework should be established by a 'National Unit for Education Guidance for Adults'. Local Education Authorities should receive Education Support Grants from the DES to develop detailed local guidance schemes which could then be co-ordinated. The latter should certainly be done, after which consideration could be given to a national unit. Let us sort out and improve local information first, then link it into the Education Conselling and Credit Transfer Information Service.

There is a very welcome variety of initiatives currently receiving government backing. But there must come a point where greater coordination is achieved, or the duplication will be ridiculous and a waste of scarce resources. Some schemes involve the private sector, others a more adventurous use of existing public sector provision. Bridging the gulf between the commercial and academic worlds has been a slow process. There are faults on both sides. The slowness of British industry to draw on higher education reflects a poor perception of the ability of academics to be relevant and able to cope with industry's specific technical problems. But it has also to be said that the universities have proved highly resistant to change. Some have hardly thrown themselves into links with industry with any great gusto. How good are their industrial liaison officers, for example. Are they too often simply second-raters?

Both sides would be well advised to remember that courses planned in conjunction with industry need not lose sight of the values of liberal education, if they are to develop personal responsibility and open-mindedness. However both workers and employers are attracted to short practical courses. Reflecting this, BTEC and City and Guilds courses are being restructured to provide a wider choice of modules which can be built into nationally-recognised qualifications.

At the end of the day what bedevils progress most of all is the lack of incentive to the individual learner. Actual or suspected financial barriers are identified by the reports of the Advisory Council for Adult and Continuing Education as major factors dissuading adults from taking up opportunities. Equally, employers, bothered at the investment they might lose to a competitor, hesitate before releasing and paying for staff to enrol on up-dating or refresher courses.

For the latter there should be tax relief. For the students, the Government White Paper, Training for Jobs (1984) proposed a loan scheme. Typically, only a pilot scheme has been launched. Barclays and the Cooperative Bank share the cost of the loans with MSC, which has £5 million available to lend in 1985/6. A course has to be vocational and last no more than a year. A loan covers 80% of the course fees and is interest-free during the length of the course and for three months afterwards. In its first year about 10,000 trainees received loans ranging from £500 to £5,000.

There is amazingly instinctive caution about so many initiatives, which is remarkable when one considers how central to the government's prospects is its uncaring image on the jobs front, but is all the more remarkable in this area of student finance where there is such a strong radical wing of the party passionately committed to student loans. Since the MPs of this disposition tend to be involved with the Education Committee and not the Employment Committee, they seem to have totally overlooked this loan initiative. Any stimulus to adults to return to course work is better than none, and the educational world should therefore resist its usual knee-jerk reaction against student loans, and the Government should get cracking with a proper nationwide scheme.

But the real revolution in attitudes must begin in the Treasury. At least there must be greater freedom for the unemployed to be able to take appropriate courses while retaining their supplementarty benefits. Even in the present febrile climate of politics, the Treasury is hardly likely to loosen the purse strings enough to facilitate anything as dramatic as tax relief or adult education vouchers.

The inability to spend its budget other than through local authorities or other agencies has always hamstrung the Department of Education and Science. But even when it has had direct funding opportunities, as in the case of university extramural departments, it has timidly failed to exploit them. Years ago, DES could have used its grants to develop extra-mural departments into units which could in large part operate as internal brokers for

continuing education.

The DES now has some direct spending capability. And its chosen instrument for advancing its approach to continuing education is PICKUP, (which stands for Professional, Industrial and Commercial Updating). It is essentially the funding satellite of the DES that matches the MSC. Only there is a funadmental difference in the size of it and the scale of its resources. It is mini-satellite.

It is important to keep the scale of the programme in proportion. It had only three staff when it was launched in 1982, with a budget of less than £1 million. The following year there were five staff, then England and Wales was divided up into ten regions, each with its own full-time development agent. Since then there have been other developments such as PICKUP development officers in 17 universities to help lecturers negotiate and develop courses. PICKUP had its funds increased to £6 million in 1986.

From the beginning, the Government emphasised that PICKUP projects were to be self-financing. As William Shelton, the then Minister, in launching the programme said: 'Employers will pay an economic charge for a good product tailored to their requirements'.

Marketing is one of PICKUP's most important tasks. College staff are encouraged to analyse systematically what the college has to offer and where there might be opportunities in the locality for selling their activities. Just what can be achieved with a real marketing drive, as against merely advertising, is demonstrated by Wigan New Enterprise Ltd., a bold co-operative venture set up by Wigan College using £500,000 from the EEC's Social Fund and £500,000 raised from PICKUP, local business and the council. Its four project managers travel around local firms and design responsive programmes. They claim in three years to have created 1,300 new jobs.

Assuming the first step is taken and programmes are well tailored to the needs of the client, they are still relatively useless unless people know about them. By and large advertising for further education pogrammes is a jumble of announcements in Job Centres, course guides and a smattering of local authority posters. Both marketing theory and common sense dictate a more coordinated approach.

Basic to adult learning is the fact that there

is no common need. There has to be a variety of providers and as wide a range of openings as possible. In areas such as distance learning it is impossible to forecast just what developments are likely to emerge. It is therefore unwise to try to plan and direct too much from the centre. Such a pluralist approach fits well with a Conservative government's predilections. It has favoured pump-priming and matched funding in a wide range of activities. This promotes local ingenuity but schemes can then often lack permanence. There has to be further consideration of long-term funding. And though the variety is there, the scale of the opportunities in total is by no means adequate. There is undoubtedly money to be made from tailoring continuing education to industry and commerce: Salford University has more than doubled its non-UGC funding. So growth will develop its own momentum.

On the other hand, the Government must have regard to the policies of our competitors and inject more resources into proven areas. Educational institutions are not noted for swift change. Tighter purse strings have been quite salutary some ways, but money talks - particularly so after a period of restraint. Not all continuing education should of course be employer directed. The educational world is already somewhat resentful of what - in its eyes - is the philistine approach of the Government.

What I believe we still need is a fully-fledged 'national development unit' for adult and continuing education, which will span the binary divide. Should the educational bureaucracy be cut and the UGC and NAB merge, such a development unit could be an arm of the new body. It should have a Government-determined budget, could assess the resources throughout higher education which could be drawn on; determine where growth might be concentrated and where research should be focused.

If ministers are numbed by the thought that after more than 30 years of egalitarian educational policy, a staggering building programme, the training of thousands of teachers and the emission of millions of words about education, standards in our schools are so depressingly low, what untried solutions are there? Put it another way. Why not accept that there will always be underlying inadequacies, that thousands of pupils will never learn as much as they could, or have the motive or

stimulus to do so? And make the priority the
availability of new opportunities after school and
throughout life? It is a prospect exciting and
positive, but the corridors of Whitehall are filled
more with caution than a sense of urgency.

References

Cmnd. 9653, The Government Response to the Second Report of
the House of Lords Select Committee on Science and Tech-
nology, 1984/85 Session: Education and Training for New
Technologies, HMSO, 1985, pp.34-6.
House of Lords Select Committee on Science and Technology,
Session 1984/85 2nd Report, Education and Training for
New Technologies.
Roderick, G. and Stephens, M. (eds), Higher Education for
All?, the Falmer Press, 1979, pp.144-5.
UDACE, The Challenge of Change, National Institute of Adult
Continuing Education, 1986, p.8.

124

# 10. CONTINUING EDUCATION AND THE LABOUR PARTY

Andrew Bennett, MP

Recurrent education, continuing education, second-chance education, whatever we choose to call the extension of education into adult life, is essential for our prosperity, democracy, enhancement of our leisure time and the development of a co-operative, understanding and peaceful society. Education ought to be a basic requirement in life, like food, water or shelter, something that is essential for all our lives, not some rare malt whiskey to be savoured only by the few.

The education system we have at present - learning between the ages of 5 and 16 for all and for a minority between 16 and 21 - is becoming increasingly irrelevant to our present day needs, where technology and society are rapidly changing.

The concept of adult education has always been central to the traditions of the Labour Movement with the National Extension College, the Workers' Educational Association and Ruskin College, but it gained wider popularity at the end of the 1960s and beginning of the 1970s. Following the ILO Convention in 1974 several countries adopted legislation giving workers the right to educational leave. Unfortunately, just when the need for recurrent education was becoming recognised, confidence in the whole education system in Britain began to erode.

Until the mid-1970s there had been a general political consensus: education was seen as a 'good thing' and the agreed aim was to expand the system. Even the Conservative government, with Margaret Thatcher as Education Minister, produced a White Paper in 1972 entitled, 'Education: A Framework for Expansion'. The paper argued for the expansion of nursery education and said of higher education,

'The government considers higher education valuable for its contribution to the personal development of those who pursue it; at the same time they value its continued expansion as an <u>investment in the nation's human talent</u>' (my emphasis).

The education world of the 1950s and 60s had to cope with large classes and educationalists were looking forward to the day when school rolls would fall and more attention could be given to developing the curriculum and raising the standards for all pupils. Before this, however, the consensus on education had evaporated. Sadly for the Labour Party Jim Callaghan started the 'Great Debate' on education without the correct terms of reference. He, and particularly Shirley Williams, ought to have refuted the Black Papers and the likes of Baroness Cox, and proclaimed that state schools in the 1970s were doing a good job, especially in the way they coped with the school population 'bulge'. Only with success in the minds of everyone ought we to have questioned how to do even better. Unfortunately, the debate became about educational standards with the strong implication that public money was being wasted and that teachers were ineffectual, even though, in reality, standards were rising.

Since then education has become a legitimate target for cuts in government expenditure. Why did the consensus disappear? The primary cause was a sense of disillusionment, not with education itself, but with the education system. The system put forward the wrong values. Parents and teachers saw education as 'getting a good job'. What should have been an enlightening and enjoyable experience was, for far too many, made into a production line of unpleasantness. If you succeeded the reward was to be financial security and status. Success was measured merely by examinations. And not just examinations, but examination grades. Those who succeeded were able to exploit their scarcity value and demand high salaries.

By the mid-1970s the goal posts had been moved. The oil price rises of 1973 produced a recession in the western world which, we now realise, was to have long-term effects. Unemployment began to increase steadily and young people leaving school or higher education found they were denied the opportunity of 'choosing' the career most suited to them. They had to take what they could get. Not suprisingly the <u>raison d'etre</u> of the education system was brought into question. Furthermore, it began to be implied that the education system was, perhaps, the cause of our economic ills.

At the same time it began to dawn on government that the world was entering a new technological era and that Britain was falling behind her competitors. The cry went out that we needed more science and technology training in schools and colleges, and less of the 'wishy-washy' arts and social sciences. Very little was said then about out-dated management techniques, the lack of training of the workforce and lack of investment in our industries.

The debate about extending education ceased when the Conservatives came to power in 1979. The monetarists were determined to reduce public expenditure and the public services were thrown into disarray coping with cuts and threats of cuts. Rational planning was not the order of the day but cash columns were. Education was an easy target due to the falling school population and disillusionment with the system generally.

In this climate, it is not surprising that the idea of recurrent education has not had the prominence it deserves. It is, however, recurrent education that has an important part to play in any economic renewal. With the decline in the number of 18 year olds in the population it is a very appropriate time to put recurrent education into practice. Spare places in higher and further education should be offered to mature students and post-experience courses should be developed to meet the needs of the economy.

Before these changes can come about however, there needs to be some radical rethinking in education. We are prone to see education as something that comes in boxes. We are all supposed to learn the same thing at the same age and if we happen to miss a box then it is lost for good. Little account is taken of when individuals are ready to learn. But learning naturally takes place in mixed age groups; at university summer schools, for example, you can find whole families studying archeology together, or the enthusiastic child dragging its parents along to the museum. Computers, of course, are the most dramatic example of mixed age group teaching. How many parents must there be who have learnt about computers from their own children?

Education in reality is something which takes place during a whole life-time, and we are not all ready, or motivated, to learn the same things at the same time. The education system must be adapted to coincide with natural learning patterns of individuals. We must not close the doors of our schools at the age of 16 and say 'You will never enter here again'. Nor must we leave youngsters so fed up with school that they have no thirst for learning, or any wish to return to education in whatever form. We must work towards a situation where it will be commonplace to see mum and dad studying in the same class as their son or daughter.

Returning to education at the moment is seen as a freak activity and takes a great deal of courage on behalf of the person concerned. Given the acknowledged shortage of skilled personnel in our industries today, however, it should be an easy task to persuade the public at large that adults should at least consider retraining in new skills. This would I hope encourage the habit of recurrent education.

Employers could do much in this sphere by regularly retraining their workforce either on site or in further education colleges. It was tragic that one of the first acts of the Thatcher government was to abolish the 16 Industrial Training Boards and establish voluntary bodies in their place. In France, Belgium, Sweden and the Netherlands employers are obliged to pay a small percentage of their wage bill into a training fund for their workers. It is mostly used for work-related training but courses of general education can be provided. If employers in Britain paid just 1% of their payroll into a training fund this would provide £1,500 million per year.

The present government's solution to the problem is to introduce training loans, but this is grossly unfair to those who cannot afford to take on the burden of a loan. It also does not solve the great problem of the lack of investment in training by British employers.

Whilst more emphasis on science and technology in education is undoubtedly needed this must not be at the expense of the arts and social sciences. Human society still has many complex problems which cannot be solved by technology. The mining industry, for example, may have the engineers and technology to produce coal efficiently but it did not have the management skills necessary to avoid the conflict at 1984/85.

The needs of communities, whether local, national or international change constantly and in order to cope with these changes society needs individuals who are capable of analysing problems, coming up with solutions and, more importantly, having the skills to implement them. As society becomes more complex we will need more skilled administrators, teachers, managers, psychologists and social workers. The skills to avoid conflict are not found on an integrated circuit or in a test tube.

Just as recurrent education has a major role to play in the regeneration of the economy, it is also vitally important to the continuation of democracy. In Britain we proudly claim to be a democracy and free education is the minimum requirement for this. A fully democratic society, however, depends upon everyone having a high degree of knowledge and self-confidence to participate. Otherwise, elections are little more than a sham and an excuse to retain power in the hands of the elite.

In a highly complex society such as ours the democratic process depends upon the ability of the population to make decisions based on informed opinions. If we do not educate our people to keep in touch with developments in science, technology, economics, then we are allowing them to lose touch with reality.

There is then a growing tendency to defer to self-appointed experts or the newspapers. If we allow this we have taken away the ability of people to think and make judgements for themselves. We cannot, of course, expect people to become experts on everything but we can, at least, teach them how to question, how to find out the truth of certain issues and to recognise when they are not being told the truth. Access to recurrent education can be seen as a democratic safeguard.

Education is essential for democracy, it is essential for economic development and in these days of the shorter working week and increased unemployment, it is an important factor in our leisure time. Work-free time, whether enforced or achieved, is not now simply an opportunity to do nothing. Leisure time, because it is becoming a greater proportion of our lives, needs to be more constructive, and this requires a certain degree of education. (Not that the idea of armchair relaxation should be abandoned). Hobbies become all the more interesting with the addition of a little extra knowledge on the subject, whether it is keeping salamanders, pigeon fancying, motorbike scrambling or attempting cordon bleu cookery.

Education is needed for democracy, economic prosperity and an enjoyable leisure time. Through these we might hope to create a more peaceful society, a society where people can express adequately and rationally their feelings about the world in which they live. Education gives people the knowledge and the confidence to have some impact on their environment whether at local, national or even international level. The riots of 1981 in Manchester and Liverpool illustrated the alternative methods of making an impact. On these four grounds the case for recurrent education becomes overwhelming.

To make recurrent education a reality serious consideration has to be given to the financing of students. Dependants of students cannot be expected suddenly to drop their standard of living and adapt to the impoverishment of present day student life. We need to give consideration to a scheme of education insurance, perhaps similar to the present National Insurance scheme, so that mature students can be guaranteed a reasonable income during their studies. This would also enable people who find themselves unemployed to undertake training or study. The present social security system which actively discourages study during periods of unemployment is a major hindrance to the development of recurrent education.

A system of recurrent education could also go some way to solving the problem of the lack of students in higher education from working class backgrounds. Too often these young people are deterred from pursuing their studies either because of their own bad experience of the system or because they come from families with no tradition of further and higher education. At a later stage in their lives, when they perceive the benefits of education, it often seems too late to return to studying. The financial responsibilities of a mortgage and a young family plus simple lack of knowledge of the system militate against a second chance in education for these people. It is essential in developing a policy for recurrent education that it does not become a prerogative of the middle classes. It should redress the balance of the

130

present education system, so that the talents of this group can be exploited to the benefit of themselves and society.

An advisory service is a small but important part of a recurrent education system. There is such a plethora of courses now at a variety of institutions that an individual cannot be expected to oversee all developments in the education field. This service would be particularly important for those who come from families with no experience of post-school education and who find it intimidating to approach institutions directly.

It is often assumed that, because the Labour Party argues for an expansion of the post-school education system, they are somehow arguing for a dilution of academic excellence. This is, to say the least, an illogical argument and one designed to serve the educational elite who happen to be good at examination techniques. Any developments in the education system must be accompanied by high educational standards. Resources are an important factor in achieving high standards. They allow flexibility and developments in new directions and keep morale high among staff.

Motivation of the student, however, is equally important and this is one of the most important challenges to the whole education system today. Our school system is very good at teaching people that they are failures. Failure or low grades at 'O' level geography or chemistry implies an 'unsuccessful' person. But maybe the education system is measuring the wrong things.

Maybe people fail geography and chemistry because they cannot see any reason to succeed in those subjects. The key to successful learning is motivation. Take for example, driving a car. Most people manage to acquire this complex skill after they have left school and success is not limited to those with good academic qualifications. Or take learning a language. Children in Wales, or in immigrant communities, are often conversing quite happily in two languages by the time they are five years old. How is it then that our education system cannot produce fluent French speakers after 5 or 7 years secondary schooling?

How is it that we can class a young lad as an educational failure when he is capable of maintaining his own motorbike. Perhaps an 'O' level in motorbike maintenance would have measured his abilities better.

Of course, we cannot expect every pupil to be self-motivated in every subject. That is the challenge to educationalists, how to tap into that stream of motivation within us all that makes education a joy rather than a task. Motivation is the key to high standards and a recurrent education system is much more likely to tap this valuable resource than the all-or-nothing approach we have at the moment.

The principle of recurrent education is particularly important in the field of teacher training. As a former teacher myself I know the teaching profession would be enriched if we could encourage more mature students to enter the profession. Allowing individuals to pass through the education system and then simply end up on the other side of the desk makes little sense. Perhaps we should also allow practising tradesmen and professionals to teach part-time in our schools as they used to do in our colleges of further education.

The Labour Party proposes to develop a whole framework to make recurrent education a reality. The first priority would be to introduce a system of paid educational leave. This is defined as leave within normal working hours, with no loss of income, promotion or pension rights. At the moment this is available to only 7% of employees. It must be extended to cover far more employees at every level of employment.

A system of assisted educational leave would also be established which would give employees the right to unpaid leave and to return to their job without loss of wage increments, pension rights or promotion opportunities. Entitlement to this type of leave would be based on length of service with a statutory minimum entitlement of 4 weeks per year of service.

Eventually, it is hoped to give every adult an entitlement to at least 1 year's further education, to be used for any course of study they wish. These schemes of entitlement would also be matched by an increase in the present number of courses available and the development of new courses to meet the requirements of the new consumers in education. Education for the unemployed, for example, or access courses for adults proposing to enter higher education, or special classes to encourage women into science and technology. Greater emphasis would be given to part-time courses and to distance learning techniques along the lines of the Open Tech and the Open University.

Such radical changes in the education system will require a significant increase in resources. The money can be made available; it is a question of political will how government money is used. It is plainly absurd that we can find vast amounts of money to perfect our weapons of destruction but not, it seems, for revolutionising our education system.

Recurrent education seems a little like Third World Aid. Everyone agrees that it is a good idea, but very little actually happens. And, like Third World Aid, if we do not treat recurrent education seriously and find the money now, the long term consequences will be disastrous.

11. THE PRIORITY OF RECURRENT EDUCATION:
A SOCIAL DEMOCRATIC PARTY (SDP) VIEW

Anne Sofer

All education policy must be about recurrent
education. Unless any single stage in education
leaves the recipient with a desire to go on learning at the end of it, it has failed. We should
really, when we talk about recurrent education, be
talking primarily not about administrative processes of allocations of resources, but about this
crucial issue of motivation. The Hargreaves
Report, 'Improving Secondary Schools', submitted to
the Inner London Education Authority, talks about
the most fundamental sort of achievement being the
achievement of the desire to achieve.
Another recent report of great significance
was 'Competence and Competition' the comparative
study of four different countries' systems of
vocational education prepared by the Institute of
Manpower Studies for the National Economic Development Council (NEDC) and the Manpower Services Commission (MSC). It was clear from this comparison
that Britain, unlike West Germany, Japan, and the
United States, is lacking in commitment to, and
high expectations of, its education and training
systems. It is not only a question of government
investment: it is industry, trades unions, and
individuals themselves in other countries who seem
more prepared to invest in education.
The SDP Education and Training Policy Document, written three years ago, anticipated this
approach. We saw that the basic problem in this
country was a raising of sights; a changing of the
cultural assumptions. There is, of course, also a
problem of resources from which we did not shy
away. But even more important is the need to
convince people that a better education system is
important and can be achieved. To some extent, the

record of the Conservative Government has, ironically, done part of the job for us. In 1984 a
Gallup Poll found that 64% of people thought that
we did not give enough attention to education: this
represents a huge increase from the figure of 34%
of 1959. So the climate is probably more favourable for a great leap forward than it has been for
years.

The opening paragraphs of our document propose
the twin justifications for our approach:

> Education is the key to the fairer and more
> prosperous and self-confident society Social
> Democrats are working for. We believe that
> the skills and intelligence of our people
> can be increased and that we can and must
> transform ourselves into a technologically
> sophisticated, internationally competitive,
> highly skilled economy.
> We also believe that people, both at work
> and in their own communites, are far more
> capable than has been generally assumed of
> running their own affairs and taking respon-
> sibility for decisions. We believe that the
> future of democracy in a pluralist society
> will depend on a far higher level of par-
> ticipation and a deeper and more concerned
> understanding of each other.
> (Education and Training, Policy Document No.
> 6. SDP, 4 Cowley Street, London SW1).

In proposing to bring the education system and the
needs of the economy closer together we are aware
of the traditional liberal educationalists' reservations about such a statement, but think they are
exaggerated.

> Educationalists have traditionally resisted
> the notion that education should 'serve the
> needs of industry' and have insisted instead
> on education's prime function of 'developing
> the individual'. We believe the dichotomy
> is now becoming increasingly irrelevant and
> that the barriers that have been erected
> between 'Education' and 'Training' are prov-
> ing harmful to both. 'Serving the needs of
> industry' is no longer a matter of turning
> out docile wage-slaves content to spend
> their lives on one repetitive and meaning-
> less occupation. Such a way of life is fast

disappearing. Rather industry now needs far more people who can think independently and apply a range of skills in a versatile way. These are qualities also needed for personal autonomy, and for life in the sort of devolved democracy we strive to achieve: they are qualities which both the Education and Training establishments in this country must now bend their efforts to enhancing. (ibid p.1)

This approach has a major implication for the administration. That is the urgent need to bring together the Department of Education and Science and the training functions of the Manpower Services Commission. We propose to make one department of them - a 'marriage of equals' rather than a take-over - and, by a phased plan, unite area boards and local education authorities and devolve decision making to them. This administrative change would be backed by legislation spelling out the entitle-ment of all individuals to further education and/or training. (The extent and nature of this entitle-ment is dealt with later in this chapter.)

The second major implication of our approach is that the whole community will have to involved.

If we are to achieve the great stride for-ward in educational standards which we are seeking it cannot be done by teachers and trainers alone. There will have to be a raising of expectations at all levels. This would not be a wholly new experience for our nation. After the great Education Acts of 1870 and 1944 there were similar great shifts in popular expectation, and history indicates that when we do upgrade our expec-tation of levels of achievement, people respond by doing better. One of the sever-est problems at the moment is that so many people feel that education is not for them: an early experience of rejection or failure has killed their confidence in themselves as learners.

We must bring this confidence back to life, and foster a new attitude, one which takes for granted that education is 'for life' and that recurrent periods of learning - whether of a new skill, or more theoretical know-ledge or new leisure interests - become part of the fabric of normal life for everyone. This will involve far more of the community than at present, both as teachers and learners, and a breaking down of professional and institutional barriers. Places of learning and means of learning will become more varied and groups of learners more heterogeneous. (ibid p.2.)

This constant insistence on 'education in the context of society' means that throughout our discussions the implications for recurrent education are borne in mind: the connections between education now and education at some future stage in an individual's life; the connection between the person being educated and the rest of the family; the transfer of skills and qualifications; the importance of part-time education.

Thus, though our policy document follows the conventional chronological approach - from under 5s through schools, colleges and universities to what is traditionally known as 'adult education' at the end - in writing this article I have had to select the relevant passages from throughout the text. For instance, in our policy for the under 5s, our proposals, based on the 'two guarantees' of one year's pre-school education and a 'Young Family Centre' in every neighbourhood, are developed in the context of the needs of the whole family, not just the individual child.

Another important benefit of pre-schooling at its best is the improved quality of family life. Not only does it give the parent (usually the mother) a measure of freedom, but it should also seek to increase parents' knowledge and above all, enjoyment of their child. Long term, children given a good start in life are better able to pass on those benefits when they themselves become parents.

In simple societies, with traditional family structures, parents were more sure of their role. In today's society, with its weaker family ties and more fragmented communities, a child's first years can be a time of anxiety rather than pleasure for its parents. Many feel isolated and lacking in self-confidence. Preparation for parenthood, in schools, adult education and

137

attached to ante-natal classes is important. Even more valuable is the mutual support system a good play group or nursery class can offer.
(Education Matters No. 4. Policies for the Under Fives. SDP, 4 Cowley Street, London SW1).

Similarly, in our consideration of secondary education we are concerned to promote the link to later educational experience for all pupils, not just (as at present) the academic elite.

In the two years before the statutory school leaving age two bridges must be firmly built. One is the bridge to the working world and the world of adult responsibilities: this means more time spent at work and in the community understanding the processes of our very complex society. The other is the bridge to continuing education: introduction to the range of opportunities for learning outside and after school is essential if a new attitude to lifelong learning is to develop. For many under 16s spending time in a more adult education institution (Further Education or Adult Education) may be a key motivating factor in their educational progress.
(Education and Training, Policy Document No. 6. SDP, 4 Cowley Street, London SW1).

However, it is what happens in the years after the statutory school leaving age that must be of most interest to those who espouse the cause of recurrent education. Our philosophy is clear.

The phase of education starting when compulsory education stops should be seen as a continuum, lasting throughout the rest of life. Particular age-groups and vocational groups will share common interests and problems but the education and training that is available to be voluntarily pursued should be flexible, responsive to need and of use to all sectors and age-groups in the community.
(ibid p.22).

We place great emphasis on establishing the

habit and expectation of recurrent education early,
and making sure that young people get the guidance
they need.

> Because the need for recurrent education and
> training will grow, and because the range of
> courses will inevitably become more complex
> (though we hope better co-ordinated), we
> recommend a strengthening of the duties,
> training and staffing of local education
> authority careers services. In future they
> should have the duty to keep track of all
> school leavers in their area for at least
> two years, making sure they are getting the
> careers advice and counselling they need.
> In addition the service should expand to
> take over an Adult Advisory Service role,
> giving advice on education and training
> opportunities to all adults who need it,
> whether to enable them to change jobs, to
> improve their basic skills, or to make more
> creative use of their leisure.
> (ibid p.22).

Our proposals for the 16-19 age-group include
the introduction of the 'Education Benefit' (linked
to our new 'Basic Benefit' system) to give financial support to young people in full-time education, the establishment of a credit transfer system
between the various courses (including - very
importantly - the Youth Training Scheme (YTS)) and
an upgrading and quality control of all vocational
courses.
In higher education we see the present drop in
the 18-22 year old age-group as a golden opportunity to widen the somewhat narrow scope of the
present provision. As we put it in our response to
the University Grants Committee's consultative
exercise last year:

> More must be done to encourage people who
> did not proceed into higher education at 18
> plus but would like the opportunity to do so
> later in life. This will necessarily in-
> volve the provision of access and prepara-
> tory courses geared to their needs for many
> such students. Attention should also be
> paid to ways of accrediting students with
> learning they have gained through their life
> experience as a means of satisfying entrance

requirements. Mature applicants without 'A'
level qualifications must no longer be seen
as exceptional, but as a major source of
recruitment to higher education. Last but
not least, many more courses should be provided on a part-time basis: ideally, all
full-time qualifications should be available
through part time study as well.
(Education Matters No. 1. The Future of
Higher Education, p.4. SPD, 4 Cowley
Street, London SW1).

The need for the universities and polytechnics
to diversify to meet demand is likely to accel-
erate.

Within all the professions there is a growing need for re-training and up-dating
courses in mid-career. Demand for non-
vocational courses is also likely to increase. The SDP believes that continuing
education must become an increasingly important part of universities' provision.
(ibid p.5.).

But this pressure should not be borne only by
the state-funded educational institutions. We
believe that industry should assume a far greater
responsibility for training and re-training and in
our policy paper on industrial strategy we have
proposed a system of fiscal incentives to encourage
this.
We believe that among the most misguided and
parsimonious actions of the present Governemnt must
be the cuts in support to the Open University - the
most innovative as well as the cheapest of post-war
experiments in the field of higher education.
Distance learning techniques should, we believe, be
more fully exploited, not less.
To conclude this summary of SDP policy, it is
worth quoting in full the end of the section on
adult education. It encapsulates our optimism
about education, our belief in the pooling of
experience and our conception of the partnerhship
between local and central government.

The final aim is that unmet and unarticu-
lated needs must be assessed and planned for
by a positive national campaign. Here we
are thinking about what is generally thought

of as 'adult education', not only qualifica-
tion-bearing courses, but the vast field of
education for basic needs (numeracy, literacy, English as a Second Language), education for leisure and interest, education for
democratic participation.

We would establish a <u>national development
council</u> and local development councils. The
latter would consist of all the bodies which
have an interest in adult education in a
local area, and they would be charged with
drawing up a plan for their area in consultation with their local education authority.
This would imply some additional local
expenditure, but it should also be a way of
drawing out the ideas which would need only
'pump-priming' money or could be self-financing.

A central sum of money would be made available to be administered by the national
development council on the same basis as
Urban Programme funding (75% DES, 25% LEA)
against which bids could be made. The criteria for funding would be that schemes
should be either:

(a)   catering for needs not previously met -
      either of particular sectors (e.g. the
      handicapped) or geographical areas, <u>or</u>
(b)   extending work of this sort which <u>has</u>
      not yet reached its full potential
      (e.g. literacy), <u>or</u>
(c)   establishing innovative cost-effective
      schemes where a relatively small 'set-
      ting-up' grant could establish a ser-
      vice to large numbers. For example,
      such schemes could include the use of
      local radio and/or voluntary groups, or
      the development of 'out-reach' tech-
      niques.

At present only half of 1% of total current
expenditure on education, science and the
arts goes on 'adult education'. The pace of
change in society, the increase in leisure
time and the need to raise educational
expectations at every level demand that this
percentage should be raised.

(Education and Training, Policy Document No.
6. SDP, 4 Cowley Street, London SW1).

Discussions within the SDP on recurrent education have not stopped with the production of these policy papers. They do, we feel, to some extent represent a consensus among progressive educationalists - consensus that is easier to arrive at than to put into action. The reason for this is partly money, and partly the innate conservatism of institutions. In our further thinking about how to develop policy we have been trying to think of ways to overcome this conservatism and to force institutions into a more responsive habit of mind.

We are interested in pursuing the idea of an entitlement of - say - two years' education or training for all adult citizens. This could be taken at any time, full or part time, all in one go or by stages, and on any one of a complete range of courses. The entitlement would be held as a sort of voucher (if one dare in educational circles use the term!) cashable by the individual. The effect of this on institutions could be extremely radical. They would be forced, if they wanted to stay in business, to provide what people wanted.

It would be possible to phase in this scheme by giving vouchers first to the long-term unemployed, or to those who had had no education or training since they were sixteen. This again would have the effect of giving birth to some very different types of course. None of these ideas has been worked out in detail, but we see no reason in principle why there should be any limitation on course-providers under the scheme - though there would have to be a validating body akin to the Council for National Academic Awards (CNAA), for the individual courses.

There are knotty problems in reconciling this scheme with the existing student grant system - and even knottier problems in trying to divert money from the latter into the former. We hope of course for more resources for education as a whole - our Education and Training Policy Document, produced before the last election, proposed an increase of one billion pounds on the current government expenditure projections. Half of this was to be directed to the post-16 sector. But it is naive to expect that any government in the near future will produce as much money for education and training as we would want. A measure of redistribution will be the only way of unlocking what is needed for recurrent education.

Our proposals for higher education generally propose a shift in the direction of a two year general (or more general) degree for all - followed, either at the time or later, by a further period of academic study or vocational preparation. This, we feel, would be a more appropriate provision for the great majority than the highly specialised three year single subject honours degree course which is the current norm. It would also make possible a more equitable distribution of our educational resources between the present well-provided academic elite and the very poorly provided rest of the population. However, whether this is practicable or politically feasible is an issue we have not yet resolved. The discussions continue.

For a new party we feel we have covered a fair amount of ground. We have the advantage of starting afresh and having fewer previous commitments to square with new thinking. Politics apart, it is an area in which new thought is more important now than ever before, and we are more eager to discuss any new ideas.

## References

'Competence and Competition:' Training and Education in the Federal Republic of Germany, the United States and Japan. MSC and NEDC, 1984.
'Improving Secondary Schools.' Report of the Committee on the Curriculum and Organisation of Secondary Schools. ILEA, March 1984 (The Hargreaves Report).

## 12.  ON THE NATURE OF POLITICAL PROGRESS

Gerry Fowler


Many of the contributors to this volume are
sanguine about what has been achieved in the development of recurrent education in Britain since
1974. That is unsurprising; they are dedicated
practitioners, or theoreticians who are delighted
to find evidence that their theories are in course
of being instantiated in practice. My own thesis
is that much of the undoubted progress made is
rooted in historical near-inevitability, or in
political pragmatism, and does not rest upon a
fundamentally changed perception of what is educationally necessary or desirable. Even Dr Hampson,
although a practising politician of the party
ruling at the time he was writing, is a theoreti-
cian and an enthusiast who wishes to see an evolving pattern in the policy changes he describes. It
is apposite to point out that he has (unjustly)
never secured preferment in the Government he sup-
ports.

The central difficulty with the implementation
of a system of recurrent education is that it
postulates a wholly new way of looking at the
educational needs of each person throughout his or
her life, including early life (Lawson 1977). It
denies the domination of childhood education, or
the 'apprenticeship model' of education, as for
most the complete preparation for life, work and
retirement. It turns its back upon the mediaeval
notion, apposite to the time and still dominant in
the professions as well as the crafts, that there
is an immutable progress from apprenticeship,
through practice as a journeyman, to mastership, in
which state one knows, perhaps with occasional
refreshment of knowledge, all that one needs or is
likely to need to know (cf Fowler 1974). Yet the

Minister of whatever party, along with the majority of those who advise him and who provide the information upon which that advice is based, is primarily concerned with the management and improvement of what exists. Concern lies with what is, and with what it might with effort become, rather than with an alternative, better suited to the needs of a new century and new millennium.

Despite some increase in the number of political advisers to Ministers over the past twelve years, Britain still has a governmental system radically unlike the American, in a way perhaps even more significant than the 'separation of powers' of which the textbooks make much. In the United States, the top echelons of the 'civil service' change totally when a new administration takes office. In Britain they go on for ever, pupil replacing master, their expertise supplemented only by that of one or two imported advisers in each Department, few of whom initially understand the machine of which they have become cogs - and many of whom are young and inexperienced, because they are also paid but a middling salary. This is not even like the French system, where each new Minister brings with him his own 'cabinet' of undoubted experts in his departmental sphere of activity.

To make matters worse, the dichotomy between the amateur Minister and the professional civil servant is itself false. For the civil servant is of necessity no more than a professional adminis- trator, who may know little of the theory of the area subject to his administration. In the Department of Education and Science he is unlikely to be a professional educator or educationalist. The Minister may of course not be a professional at all, except a professional politician. But at least he is more likely than not to be an amateur (in the proper sense of the word) of the policies he propounds; the civil servant recently trans- ferred from Industry or the Treasury may find them boring, if not odious.

In theory, educational expertise is provided by Her Majesty's Inspectorate (HMI). And so it is. Inspectors are recruited by virtue of their excel- lence at doing what is done, and sometimes because they have ideas about how it might be done better. Their numerical composition reflects a childhood- education philosophy, and their paucity of exper- tise in post-18 education of any kind is exacerbated by the exclusion of the universities from their remit. Architectural education is judged by those trained in building and the constructional skills; there is but one qualified architect in the Inspectorate. It is believed that the crucial problem of teacher supply, the lack of candidates for the 'shortage subjects' - Mathematics, Physics, and Craft, Design and Technology - will disappear if higher education institutions are given more money for recruiting them rather than other students, while even to the least tutored eye it is obvious that the problem lies in salary relativities for those qualified in these disciplines, and in the election of subjects made by thirteen and fouteen year olds at school. (These examples come from 1984-85). What hope is there then that these excellent people will renege upon their training and experience, and propound a fundamental change in educational objectives and organisation?

Ministers bear their own sacks of experience and prejudice upon their backs, as do all Members of Parliament, and for that matter Peers of the Realm. Often it is vicarious experience - that of constituents, or of employees, or perhaps even of tenants. Their vision is thereby narrowed. They look to an amelioration of early schooling, or to an easier progression of youthful talent as the chief if not sole objective of educational policy. There is of course nothing wrong with these objectives, save that they exclude others, by constraining options within a traditional framework. The constraint has become the more acute as the availability of funds has become less, by virtue of the poor performance of the national economy as well as in consequence of deliberate restriction of public spending. As Robert Lowe said of the system of payment-by-results, 'If it shall not be cheap, it shall be effective; and if it shall not be effective, it shall be cheap'. Effectiveness is measured by short-term perceived gain, and cheapness by the Treasury.

It is then pointless to look to the British political structure to produce a revolutionary change in the bias and weight of educational policy. What has been said of central Government applies equally to the Local Education Authorities (LEAs), where officers are what they are because of their success in doing what is expected in the traditional system, and elected members bear the concern of worried parents, and of employers looking at the failure of the school system to assuage their unjustified guilt at not being able to employ more young people. What we want is more of the same, but better - higher - standards, and more immediate applicability of knowledge and skills. This may be a recipe for educational ossification, and for the replacement of the aim of widening the intellectual capability of the individual by that of maximising his or her immediate economic utility, but it is undoubtedly what the majority seek.

The decade of the 1960s was, in respect of the schools, preoccupied with questions of structure (Kogan 1971). It began with the legalising of 'middle schools' (8-12 or 9-13) by the simple act of allowing them to be declared either 'primary' or 'secondary'. By Circular 10/65 (1965) the focus was on the comprehensivisation of the secondary system, but that very Circular was to admit that there were no less than six possible and acceptable structures of secondary education, some of which effected mutations in primary structures too. At the same time, the Plowden Committee was preparing its report recommending preferred methods of primary education, and the value of pre-school or nursery education (Plowden Report 1967). In essence, the whole of this political process was concerned with structure, with the extension of the period of childhood schooling (cf the raising of the school-leaving age, deferred but finally fixed in 1968, as well as nursery schools), and with the assumed improvement in average educational attainment and hence in social equality (vid. esp. on RoSLA: Crossman 1976, and Wilson 1971). It is true that many believed that comprehensive schools would produce less social separation than the old tripartite system, and hence greater social understanding and stability, but it was always the argument that talent was being wasted and that the nation could ill afford this which was most widely persuasive, and which blunted right-wing attacks on the reform.

If talent had been wasted, it followed logically that there must be more than previously suspected who could profit from higher education endon to school education. There were. Qualified demand for higher education places from schoolleavers had been rising, was continuing to rise, and was confidently expected to rise yet more rapidly. By 1970 the Secretary of State for Education, Edward Short (now Lord Glenamara) could say in a private conversation that the then projection of 727,000 places required by 1981 was clearly an underestimate, and that planning should proceed on the basis of a requirement of one million (cf Education Planning Paper No. 2, 1970). The Kingsley Amis school of thought, that 'more means worse' (always more precisely expressed as 'the same number drawn from a larger qualified pool may result in a higher average level of final attainment' - a totally uninteresting proposition), was routed. At the same time, the growing number of students, allied to the student unrest in Britain which was a mild off-shoot of more violent manifestations of discontent in Europe and America, produced a political demand, immediately conceded, for some further democratisation of higher education institutions, with increased staff and student representation in their governance (Education No. 2 Act 1968; DES Circular 7/70).

What is significant about all of these developments is that they were essentially the extension and improvement of what already existed. The school and higher education strands of the process came together in the expansion of teacher education; C.A.R. Crosland's greatest triumph as Secretary of State for Education (1965-67) was to ensure that the supply of new teachers doubled in only seven years (Kogan 1971). Oddly, it was the first reform to be reversed, as Government wrestled with the decline in the school population anticipated for the late 1970s. At the same time, decreasing class sizes by increased teacher supply was replaced as a political concern by increasing them through school closures (Hencke 1978; Fowler 1979).

The 'management of what is' is further exemplified by the emphasis of the mid-1960s on study of the applied or applicable disciplines. By 1967 the University Grants Commiteee (UGC) was aiming at a 50:50 division of university places between technology and natural science on the one hand, and arts and social science on the other. By 1972, the target had slipped to 47:53. By 1976, the Prime Minister (James Callaghan) could publicly complain that there were '30,000 unfilled higher education places in science and technology' - and whose silly fault was that? (Callaghan 1976; Fowler 1979).

One branch of this same theme was the foundation of the thirty polytechnics in England and Wales, which denied the tradition of expanding higher education by promoting through merit to university status worthy institutions, but had its roots in the alternative tradition of local encouragement of the applied arts, often through part-time study, with wider opportunities for 'mature' students rather than school-leavers, and with as much emphasis on professional qualification as upon academic degrees (Robinson 1968; Burgess and Pratt 1971). Nevertheless, this was of itself but an alternative tradition, and its development was a major act of evolution, but not one of revolution.

An element of continuity between the 1960s and the 1970s was the growth of the Open University, first presaged in 1963 and founded in 1969 (see Nick Small's contribution to this volume, and Perry 1976). Today it caters for the higher education and continuing education needs of over 70,000 adults. Even here however an attempt was made, through a research study, to divert it to the education of eighteen-year-old school leavers; this was when the present Prime Minister was Secretary of State, and unsurprisingly (school modes of study being radically different from those of the Open University) the experiment did not justify further use of this mode of solving a traditional problem by unconventional but cheaper methods. It does however serve to demonstrate the preoccupation of politicians with new means of expanding and improving what is already done, preferably less expensively, rather than with effecting a radical change of direction.

The Russell Report on adult education (1973) also bridges the gap between the decades, since it took four years to produce. Unfortunately, it also recommended 'more of the same', and more meant more expensive. It revealed little acquaintance with the work of OECD on recurrent education or of UNESCO on lifelong education (OECD 1971, 1975a and 1975b; UNESCO 1976), and it preceded the publication in Britain of Houghton and Richardson's symposium on Recurrent Education (1974). Happily, the Report did suggest that adult education should concentrate more than in the past upon the needs of the hitherto educationally deprived (whether deprived in basic skills, or in political and social knowledge); and it did look to the future in recommending the establishemnt of a Development Council.

This was the thin foundation upon which the few achievements of the Department of Education and Science hitherto have béen built. The Conservative

administration in power when Russell reported
ignored his recommendations. The successor Labour
administration was in 1974 able to do a little to
remedy the weakness of provision for the adult
educationally deprived. It might not have happened
had not Illich written of a community of teachers
and learners, suggesting that voluntary effort
might be mobilised, outside the paid teaching profession (Illich 1971 and 1974). It might not have
happened had not the British Association of Settlements (BAS) mounted a campaign to mobilise political opinion in favour of funding their own minimal
adult literacy scheme (Fowler 1979). It would
never have happened had the civil service had their
way. It would never have happened had BAS not
lobbied Crosland's former Parliamentary Private
Secretary, and he in turn approached a minister and
a political adviser who were doctrinally committed
to recurrent education.

It could not have happened but for the pure
chance that the Treasury had under the previous
administration miscalculated the future rate of
inflation as it would affect the universities. DES
was entitled to spend a further £6.5m, in origin
because of underfunding of the universities. In
the end, the universities received £4m, the polytechnic building programme benefited by £1.5m, and
a new adult literacy programme began with the
princely funding of £1m in the first year. Even
that was achieved, after a fortnight's wrangling,
only by appeal to the Chief Secretary to the
Treasury, who raised no objection provided that the
total demand on public funding was not increased.

Such accounts are sometimes disregarded as
'anecdotal' by political analysts. They should not
be, for there is no other way to understand the
workings of the political machine, save by being
part of it. Old Cabinet records are as much anecdotal, the story-teller being in this case the then
Secretary to the Cabinet, who always records decisions accurately, but much less the flavour of
discussion.

Recurrent education thus had its birth as an
element of public policy in a decision taken by
Ministers in 1974, against strong civil service
opposition, with no role played by the Inspectorate, and with no funds available save those stemming from a re-ordering of political priorities.
Opposition continued. In 1976 Ministers were told
that the release of voluntary effort organised by

150

the new Adult Literacy Unit was being supported by some LEAs through the secondment of their own staff, in return for commensurate funding. This was indubitably illegal, since central Government funds were flowing to LEAs by a route which no law sanctioned. Ministerial action solved the problem, and thence stemmed the Adult Literacy Resources Agency and the subsequent Adult Literacy and Basic Skills Unit (Fowler 1979).

But opposition was not restricted to the civil service. It was as strong among traditional practitioners of adult education. In that same year District organisers of the Workers' Educational Association expressed reluctance to give preference in their activities to the Russell priorities (because, be it said, of the democratically expressed wishes of their existing members), although the power of the purse largely solved the problem. From top to bottom, the system is geared to what is, rather than to what should be.

None of this should surprise. In 1973, at an inter-governmental conference of the Organisation for Economic Cooperation and Development concerned primarily with recurrent education, a British representative claimed that we had long practised recurrent education, save that we called it 'adult education'. The following year officials in DES smirked when the term was first mentioned by incoming Ministers in the new Government. Yet in the end views changed before the Labour Government left office; why?

We cannot find the explanation in any change in the central educational concerns of most politicians between the 1960s and the 1970s, beyond those occasioned by the declining birth-rate (decline of the demand for teachers, and the need for school closures), and by a lack of the old faith in the socially· equalising effects of educational investment. Otherwise, the 1970s witnessed a renewal of the battle for comprehensivisation of secondary education culminating in the 1976 Act, subsequently repealed by the 1979 Conservative Government. They saw an almost evangelistic concern with the standards of school education, which reached its zenith with Prime Minister Callaghan's 'Ruskin speech' of September 1976, and the 'Great Debate' (as vacuous of result as of content) which followed it. They were the decade of a renewed concern about the nation's supply of engineers and applied scientists (vide Callaghan's speech), sparked off by the new

technologies and the 'horizon industries'. All of
this was old hat, with new trimmings, reflecting
concern about the structure and improvement of what
existed (Fowler 1979). But it was in the last of
these traditional but regarbed themes, the need for
servants for a changed technology, that one of the
keys to an apparent encouragement to recurrent
education lay.

The Manpower Services Commission (MSC) was
established in 1973, as an arm of the Department of
Employment, primarily to coordinate the work of the
Industrial Training Boards and to plan the satisfaction of perceived manpower needs. Almost at
once its purpose was perverted, because of the
spectre of rising unemployment, and especially
youth unemployment. It was part of the mythology
of British democracy that nothing brought about the
demise of a Government so surely as high unemployment; how else could one explain the Labour land-
slide of 1945 than by the intolerable number of
jobless nevertheless tolerated by the National
Government in the 1930s? Pragmatism dictated that
funds should be channelled through the MSC, and new
programmes entrusted to it. The alternative was to
build up education through the LEAs. But even in
the mid-1970s it was commonly asserted in Government circles that the LEAs could not be trusted,
since once money was transferred to them, it became
theirs rather than the Government's. Who knew to
what inappropriate function they might divert it?

The MSC thus became the Topsy of the 1970s and
1980s, and just growed. Leaving aside Training
Opportunities Progammmes (TOPS), Skillcentres, and
Open Tech, all aimed at adults, we have proceeded
through Job Creation (non-job creation) and Work
Experience on Employers' Premises (WEEP - many did,
at the paucity of training provided), the Youth
Opportunities Progamme (YOPS) and much else, to the
Youth Training Scheme (YTS) and the Technical and
Vocational Education Initiative (TVEI). If one
leaves aside all other criticism of these programmes, such as their failure to provide permanent
employment for some half of those engaged on them,
or their use by employers as an extended selection
process heavily subsidised by the taxpayer, the
fact is that they are short-term training programmes not designed as a foundation for further
study, and of themselves leading nowhere save to
unemployment as the skills inculcated become obsolete.

No-one would wish to disparage the achievements of the MSC and its programmes. For the first time since the collapse of the old apprenticeship system Britain has a youth training scheme comparable with that of our Continental competitors. But it does not link with the structure of education, and its examinations and qualifications. (Contrast the intention of DES' Certificate of Pre-Vocational Education, the rival offering: FEU 1985 and 1986). Nor is it a building block in a wider structure of learning; it has no relevance to the theses of continuing or recurrent education at all. Even Open Tech, still patchy and often specialised, cannot be seen as a general facility for re-education or for the renewal of the participant. It is an attempt to deal simultaneously with the problems of unemployment and of the need for trained manpower in the 'horizon industries'. At least it spurred DES, still otherwise obsessed by the improvement of what is, to the inception of the 'PICKUP' programme; but that too has been done partly at the cost of subordinating broader educational objectives to those of narrow vocational retraining.

There lies the rub. What is demanded by a period of very rapid technological changes, which inevitably results not only in the loss of traditional jobs but also in a diminution in the total number of hours worked for pay, while at the same time making possible an improvement in the average quality of life and an increase in longevity, is not simply retraining programmes designed to meet the demands of the latest scientific advance. It is a much broader system, permitting repeated re-entry for both vocational and non-vocational reasons, subsuming job and career changes, but also leisure, 'productive' retirement, and the more general satisfaction of the needs of the mind and the body (cf ACACE 1982). This too may seem a traditional goal: 'mens sana in corpore sano'. But it is one hitherto reserved for the leisured classes, while the childhood education of the masses has been geared to success in the processes of production, distribution and exchange, with subsequent education reserved mainly to those triumphant in the rat race. Politicians and civil servants alike find it hard to break the mould. It is easier to devise training programmes for a changed industrial age, than to recognise that the post-industrial age makes quite different demands.

DES has at least grasped the nettle of credit transfer in higher education, with the creation of the Educational Counselling and Credit Transfer Information Service (ECCTIS). That too was the result of the partial assimilation of new ideas in the late 1970s. But policy towards school examinations, and achievement in childhood, remains essentially unregenerate. The new General Certificate of Secondary Education (GCSE) will of course in time be a great improvement on its precursors, since it is designed to measure the achievement of 80% of the age-group, and the measurement is to be by continuous assessment as well as formal examination. But it is still measurement of the past rather than assessment of the future, and there are at present no plans to relate it either to public training programmes or to adult re-entry to the education system. The proposed 'AS Level' (half a General Certicate of Education Advanced Level pass) is merely a desperate last effort to broaden the English school curriculum, in recognition that its traditional narrowness is inapposite to an age of rapid vocational change. It too is not yet perceived as the foundation of future adult learning, and it is not even clear what weight, if any, the universities will attach to it in granting entry at eighteen. These are improvements - but improvements to a modernised mediaeval and Renaissance system of education.

Over the past twelve years the stakeholders in the education system have backed away from a thoroughgoing examination of one of the keys to any move from an apprenticeship to a recurrent model of education, the system of grants, awards and entitlements to financial support. Even the Advisory Committee for Adult and Continuing Education (ACACE) did not grasp this hot potato. The reason was simple enough: such an examination entails the scrutiny of the desirable level of public expenditure, and its purpose. That is reserved to the Treasury, and to the Cabinet. The creation of ACACE itself bore witness to their power in this area. It was a triumph of the political will of DES Ministers in 1976-77, but of a will which recognised that any attempt to proceed to Russell's recommended Development Council was foredoomed (Fowler 1979). The word 'Development' carried the clear implication of increased public expenditure. DES officials were chary about setting up even an advisory body; as with the Central Advisory Council for Education, buried in 1967 but pronounced dead only in the 1986 Education Act, its advice might be costly of implementation. After six years of valuable life, ACACE was killed. Admittedly, it was replaced by the Unit for the Development of Adult Continuing Education (UDACE), but units reporting only via intermediary and essentially powerless bodies to Government are not as dangerous as committees of the eminent of all shades of political opinion.

The award and entitlement system has thus been neglected. There was a research study on Paid Educational Leave, but little practical came of it, largely because the Trades Unions Congress, despite the occasional genuflection in this direction, has been preoccupied with more immediate concerns in the spheres of industrial relations and of pay levels and relativities. The system of means-tested Educational Maintenance Awards (EMAs) for 16-18s proposed by Mrs Shirley Williams when Secretary of State was first whittled down by her Labour Cabinet colleagues, and then scrapped by the incoming Conservative administration in 1979.

The Leverhulme Study's proposal for two-year degrees, which whatever its weaknesses would at least have entailed scrutiny of the period for which maintenance awards were mandatory for school-leavers entering higher education, and hence of the possibility of releasing resources for other categories of student, seems to have died from neglect (Leverhulme Report 1983; cf Evans 1980). The brave if sometimes misguided Sir Keith Joseph at least got the issue onto the political agenda in 1984, but made no progress because of the perceived intention of substituting loans for grants, and the almost unanimous hostility of the existing stakeholders to such a notion. His successor as Secretary of State, Kenneth Baker, has in 1986 revived Joseph's enquiry into the awards system. It is doubtful if he will make much headway either, not least because of Treasury fear of the initially higher cost of a loan system, as well as of the divorce of this issue from that of the desirable long-term structure of education.

So long as schooling remains compulsory to 16, it is the 16-18 gap which is crucial. It is at 16 that the greatest drop-out from education occurs in Britain, not 18. While MSC training programmes fail to link with the continuing education system, and while they but not 16-18 education attract public financial support for the trainee or student, the total pattern of provision must remain disjointed, designed to 'cool out' and to produce caste stereotypes at 16, but not to encourage re-entry or the acquisition of qualification by accretion. Yet the divorce between education and training is perpetuated by the existence of the rival empires of DES and of the Department of Employment/MSC.

A similar phenomenon may be observed with the slow development of credit transfer in Britain. ECCTIS and other more limited schemes mark substantial progress. But they are not geared to the assessment of training programmes for credit purposes, and still less to that of experiential learning. Quite apart from the reluctance of many (not all) British universities to give adequate credit to studies undertaken elsewhere, the complexity of the educational and professional qualification systems add to the difficulty of instituting effective credit transfer. Complex modern industrial societies have compartmentalised all activites; to break down the barriers in order to restructure to meet changed need is then a task of great political and organisational difficulty.

The persistence of traditional systems may be seen equally in DES projections of higher education student numbers for the 1980s and 1990s. Without entering into the controversies whether Report on Education 99 (1983) or Report on Education 100 (1984), or whether Variant Y or Variant X is to be preferred (the ancient Mysteries were less obscure), one can assert with conviction that inadequate allowance is made for recurrent re-entry to the system for updating, career change or a satisfying life in an age of increased non-remunerative activity.

The failure of the case for recurrent education to make any impact on the University Grants Commiteee (UGC) was revealed starkly in 1986 when, in calculating the grant to London University they cut the weighting of part-time students at Birkbeck College from 0.8 to 0.5 of a full-timer, at the same time proposing a reduction in its student intake. The process of a century of 'academic drift', and the disregard of the needs of the less advantaged, was to grind inexorably forward. Yet Birkbeck seemed fortunate to those in the polytechnics who had tried to keep the flag of part-time higher education flying, not least on the ground that its utility is great for the mature returner. There the National Advisory Body of Public Sector Higher Education (NAB) has decreed that part-time day students shall count as 0.4, and part-time evening as 0.2 of a full-timer. Because such work can thus only exist by 'riding on the back' of full-time, for which adequate financial provision is made, it is increasingly seen by staff as peripheral, although NAB has often said that it wishes to see it develop. Money is the key to the system, and financial allocation rarely accords with rhetoric.

Despite such discouragement, the polytechnics have in general maintained their efforts to provide for the recurrent needs of mature learners. Often, as with much management education, this has to be by offering courses at a full cost fee, which advantages those in employment whose firms are willing to second them and pay for them. Yet the City Polytechnic still runs courses for members of ethnic minority communities in business, law, accountancy and language. Some eight thousand part-time and short course students pass through the Polytechnic of Central London's doors each year. Brighton Polytechnic pioneeered, albeit with MSC money, the most successful Open Tech scheme to date, Southtek. Lancashire Polytechnic, with Lancaster University, sponsors the Open College of the North-West scheme, designed to ease the re-entry to education and progression into higher education of those who left school at the statutory leaving age. Most polytechnics offer advice and short courses with a hidden subsidy to those seeking to establish small businesses, or nursery groups, or local advice centres - or to contribute in a host of other ways to the life of the community.

Perhaps the most radical scheme, and certainly the one which most neatly fits the recurrent education thesis, remains North East London Polytechnic's system of Independent Study, leading to a Diploma of Higher Education or subsequently to a degree, or even a postgraduate qualification. Nearly all the students are of mature years. The great majority lack the normal 'school-leaver' qualification for entry to higher education and left education after the completion of the period of compulsory school attendance. There are more women than men, and a high proportion come from ethnic minorities. The student devises, with guidance, and with tuition in study skills, his or her own programme of study, drawing upon elements of more conventional programmes offered by the polytechnic, but focusing upon a practical problem or cluster of problems, or upon the design or creation of an artefact of practical utility or aesthetic value. The standard of achievement, scrutinised by external examiners, an Advisory Committee, and the Council for National Academic Awards, is that of conventional discipline-oriented programmes of study.

The significant feature of many of these developments in the polytechnics is that they have received little or no political encouragement. The political process has become in large measure disjoined from the innovations of practitioners. The centre, inevitably concerned with the maintenance and improvement of what is, has lost touch with the periphery, where innovation happens. Of course, this is not wholly true; for example, the Royal Society of Arts has its 'education for capability' scheme which has recognised such innovations as Independent Study. But this seems to be one of those periods in educational history when the inward-looking cast of mind of those who should lead means that those who do lead, fighting in the trenches, are sometimes hindered but rarely helped. Educational history has much in common with military.

Conservatism at the centre is paralleled locally and in some institutions. The universities could have been brought into the general system of education in Scotland and Wales had the last Labour Government's proposals for devolution been accepted; they resisted them. The LEAs in England favour neither a regional tier of government, which would again permit the unification of tertiary education and for that matter the training system, nor the grant of corporate status to institutions over which they have historically exercised direct if often very theoretical control. Change is thus inhibited. It is indeed mere resistance to change - the desire to preserve existing jobs and present power structures - which here overwhelms party political differences.

Guidance and counselling systems, also central to recurrent education, have received very patchy local support. Although some fifty have been established, many have quickly died, from lack of minimal local funding. They have relied too heavily on the zeal of a few. That is to say, they have been accepted into the social structure as worthy charitable ventures, but scarcely yet as part of necessary public provision. Recurrent education has achieved that stage of development which schooling had in early Victorian England. The best example of all is that of the longest established system, the Educational Guidance Service for Adults in Northern Ireland. It was threatened by, of all unlikely agents, a Labour Government, although it was one of the few recognisably non-sectarian Socialist ventures in that province (see Eagleson and McGowan's chapter). It was saved, but after great waste of time and effort, and at a cost to the public purse which, were it possible to compute it with precision, would have accounted for its funding for two or three years.

In short, the battle is not won, but scarcely joined. That so much progress has been made in the last twelve years is the result of a collocation of social factors, allied to the proselytising of the dedicated. High unemployment, rapid technological change, and a perhaps unjustifiable but deeply entrenched credo about what determines electoral success have led to measures originally designed as palliatives, but broadly consistent with the philosophy of recurrent education, and increasingly difficult to reverse. Preaching has led to an inchoate grappling with the problem among policy-makers. If the preaching continues, the politicians may yet find the conviction, and the means.

## References

ACACE 1982, Continuing Education: From Policies to Practice, Leicester Advisory Council for Adult and Continuing Education.

Burgess, T. and Pratt, J. 1971, Technical Education in the United Kingdom, Paris, OECD.

Callaghan L.J. 1976, Speech of the Prime Minister at Ruskin College Oxford, London, HMSO.

Crossman, R.H.S. 1976, The Diaries of a Cabinet Minister Vol. II, London, Hamish Hamilton.

DES Circular 10/65 (1965), London, Department of Education and Science.

DES Circular 7/70 (1970), London Department of Education and Science.

Education No. 2 Act 1968, London, HMSO.

Education Planning Paper No. 2 1970, Student Numbers in
Higher Education, London, DES/HMSO.
Evans, N. (ed) 1980, Education Beyond School, London, Grant
McIntyre Ltd.
FEU (1985), CPVE in Action, London, Further Education
Unit/DES.
FEU (1986), Supporting IT in CPVE, London, Further Education
Unit/DES.
Fowler G.T. 1974, in Houghton, V. and Richardson, K. (eds)
1974, Recurrent Education, London, Ward Lock Educational
(in association with ARE).
Fowler, G.T. 1979, in Bernbaum, G. (ed) 1979, Schooling in
Decline, London and Basingstoke.
Fowler, G.T. 1984, in Alexander, R.J., Craft, M. and
Lynch J. (eds) 1984, Change in Teacher Education,
Eastbourne, Holt Rinehart and Winston Ltd.
Hencke, D. 1978, Colleges in Crisis, Penguin, Harmondsworth.
Illich, I.D. 1971, Deschooling Society, London, Calder and
Boyars.
Illich, I.D. 1974, After Deschooling, What? London, Writers
and Readers Publishing Corporation.
Kogan, M. 1971, The Politics of Education, Harmondsworth,
Penguin.
Lawson, K.H. 1977, A Critique of Recurrent Education, ARE
Discussion Paper No. 1, Nottingham Association for
Recurrent Education.
Leverhulme Report 1983, Excellence in Diversity, Guildford,
Society for Research into Higher Education.
OECD 1971, Equal Educational Opportunity: A Statement of the
Problem with Special Reference to Recurrent Education,
Paris, Organisation for Economic Cooperation and Develop-
ment.
OECD/CERI 1975a, Recurrent Education: A Strategy for Life-
long Learning, Paris, OECD.
OECD/CERI 1975b, Recurrent Education: Trends and Issues,
Paris, OECD.
Perry, W. 1976, Open University, Milton Keynes, Open Univer-
sity Press.
Plowden Report 1967, Children and Their Primary Schools,
Report of the Central Advisory Council for Education
(England), London, DES/HMSO.
Report on Education 99, 1983, London, DES.
Report on Education 100, 1984, London, DES.
Russell Report 1973, Adult Education: A Plan for Develop-
ment, London, HMSO.
UNESCO 1976, Lifelong Education; the Curriculum and Basic
Education Needs, Bangkok, United Nations Economic and
Social Cooperative Organisation.
Wilson, J.H. 1971, The Labour Government 1964-1970, London,
Weidenfeld and Nicolson, and Michael Joseph.

# SECTION 3: RECURRENT EDUCATION IN PRACTICE

SECTION 3: MANAGEMENT EDUCATION IN PRACTICE

## 13. IMPROVING SECONDARY SCHOOLING: STARTING FROM WHERE WE ARE

Roger Mercer

This paper has two aims. First, to set secondary schooling within a broader strategy of extending educational opportunity throughout the life span of the individual. (I take secondary schooling to be the schooling between the primary stage and leaving school. For many it will be 11-16; for some it will be 11-18). The main focus in this paper is on the last two years of compulsory schooling since that, in my view, exerts a crucial pressure on the rest of secondary schooling. Second, to identify 'budding points' for possible change, development and improvement, within, say, the next decade, but starting from where we are.

Bolam (1985) describes the initiatives of the present government as being the most radically interventionist of any post-war government. Various white papers (HMSO 1983, 1984, 1985, etc.) spell out very clearly government aims. This interventionist strategy is significant and important because it changes the context and the ground rules within which schooling operates and, paradoxically, provides both more direction to what is happening in schools and also increases teacher responsibility and autonomy. It also provides precedent and mechanisms for governments of different political views to implement their policies.

The messages of research on bringing about effective change in schools indicate that the context is more important than the specific innovation, that the implementation - getting change to happen in practice - is the most difficult part, and that 'fidelity' - implementing the change as designed - is well nigh impossible (Berman, 1981; Dalin, 1978; Fullan, 1982; Fullan and Pomfret, 1977).

I would argue, along with Tim Brighouse, that in some ways present provision of secondary schooling is fundamentally flawed, that the answer is not more of the same but rather 'different things'; this I try to do by raising questions about structure, how learning takes place, teacher stress, pupil alienation and relevance.

The present structure of secondary schooling (i.e. school subjects, pupils in classroom batches of 30, held together by a complex timetable arranged in 40 minute slots, with subject department rigidities) perpetuates the structure of Grammar Schools early in this century. Subjects such as Classics have all but disappeared, and new subjects have appeared: others have been transformed (Drill into Physical Education, Movement and Outdoor Pursuits). However, these changes have taken place within the same structure. This structure acts like a deadweight on secondary schooling (see Ball, 1985; Benn, 1984 and Moon, 1984). In secondary schools teachers see themselves essentially as teachers of one or more subjects. Raffe (1984) reports that young people who have recently left secondary school recall that experience as a collection of disjointed subjects.

Possibly the key to good primary practice is that it is about 'development' and 'development' is part of the 'hidden curriculum' and as such remains hidden. A further comment made by Raffe (1984) is that while secondary teachers are knowledgeable and skilled in the transmission of content and see the need to update themselves in this field, they are relatively ignorant of the context within which they work, and lack the knowledge base and skills associated with organisational analysis, effectiveness, development, etc.

Question: What structures in secondary schools are consonant with, and supportive of, an extension of the notions of 'development' and of 'lifelong learning'?

Sir Cyril Burt clearly must answer for much of this. Many teachers still work on the psychometric assumptions of the normal distribution of 'intelligence'; and even if individual teachers do not do so, schools are organised on that basis ('lower ability band'), as are GCE examinations with their built-in failure rate. What happens if people accept the school teachers' assessment of them?

Current government initiatives to move from

norm-referenced testing (how well people do in relation to certain 'norms') to criterion-referenced testing (how well people do a range of things - hence the notion of 'pupil profile') is probably a move in the right direction.

Question   What policies, structures and practices are consonant with and supportive of evaluation and. accreditation procedures which are appropriate in a democratic society?

Many teachers see themselves as being committed people who are doing a worthwhile and demanding job which is not adequately valued. It is a job which is becoming more difficult as more demands are placed on them and as resources are seen to decrease. Gifted teachers have always existed and will continue to make their impact. What I am suggesting is that increasingly teachers who ply their craft and their subject exclusively within the confines of a classroom are not likely to be the most effective. Effectiveness is likely to imply a notion of a 'wide-angle' and reflexive perspective of a variety of contexts - including that of lifelong learning.

Question   How can teacher stress be kept to manageable proportions and be used productively to promote new structures and new patterns or learning which are consonant with lifelong learning?

For a significant minority (say 20%) of pupils, mainly boys and mainly from a working class background, the experience of the latter years of compulsory schooling has been a wounding experience and the antipathy to 'education' appears to persist for up to 10 years after leaving school. (See ACACE, 1982, p.7).

Question   Stated in a traditional and possibly inappropriate way the question might be: 'how is the love of learning to be engendered?' More pragmatically the question might become 'how can young people come to form a view that learning, training, education and development are possible, necessary and do in fact take place over the whole lifespan?'

In the last decade apprenticeships for boys have disappeared, as has the 'carrot' of paid employment at 16. (This first pay packet used to be symbolic for many young people of the transition from the dependent status of child to that of adult wage-earner). In the absence of 'work hard at school and get a good job', much of what happens at school (see Tolley, 1983) has become irrelevant to both pupils and teachers. Another external factor is the changing nature of the job market. In the last decade 1.5 million unskilled and semi-skilled jobs have disappeared in extractive and manufacturing industries. The growth areas are financial and administrative services, design engineering and high technology, all of which require professional and vocational qualifications, multi-skills, new skills, some higher level skills and some de-skilling etc. The Institute of Manpower Studies Report (NEDC/MSC 1984) highlights our lack of educated, trained and qualified manpower compared with Japan, Germany and the USA.

Question Given this analysis, what are the implications for the curriculum and for the ways in which secondary schooling is arranged?

Improvements will probably cause disruption in the short term, and therefore some loss of efficiency, all the more so because any one school may well be involved in a dozen or so different change initiatives at any one time.

The triggering mechanisms and sequences of responses, individual initiatives and developments at all levels are so complex that they need to be monitored and controlled by knowledgeable, well informed and committed people at all levels. These processes and outcomes must be sensible, sensitive, humane, robust and workable in the light of individual and national needs in the last decades of this century. I list those I think necessary.

## 1. Changing the context

### (i) Radical intervention

Government interventions are intended to provoke changes. The Technical and Vocational Education Initiative (TVEI), the introduction of the General Certificate of Secondary Education (GCSE) and the Certificate of Prevocational Education (CPVE), the Microelectronics Education Programme (MEP) and DES Circulars 8/83 (on the monitoring of the school curriculum) and 3/85 (on priorities and targeted funding for the in-service education and training of teachers) are examples of such initiatives, initiatives whose impact is now being felt in secondary schools.

(ii) <u>Reorganisation</u>

Rogers (1985) suggests that in the next fifteen years, as school rolls fall, traditional Sixth Forms may disappear to be replaced by Tertiary Colleges. Such changes may sufficiently destabilise the situation so that change can take place, and new and more appropriate practices and traditions may be institutionalised. These new post-compulsory education arrangements may look more like the North American Community College, and even the 11-16 schools may be rendered more open to outside influences.

2. <u>Examinations</u>

(i) <u>What is examined</u>?

It is suggested in the Hargreaves Report (ILEA, 1984, pp.1-2) that what is currently examined at 16+ is restrictive and, for many young people off-putting and counter-productive. Achievement as measured by the present examinations involves most of all a capacity to express oneself in written form, a capacity to memorise propositional knowledge and to organise material within strict time limits. The Report (ILEA 1984 pp.1-2) suggests that there are three other currently undervalued aspects of achievement which those in secondary schools need to address, and which should form touchstones to judgement on their effectiveness or otherwise.

a.  This aspect of achievement is concerned with the capacity to apply knowledge rather than with knowledge itself, with the practical rather than the theoretical, with the oral rather than the written. Problem solving and investigational skills are more important than retention of knowledge...

b.  This aspect is concerned with personal and social skills; the capacity to communicate with others in face-to-face relationships; the ability to co-oper-ate with others in the interests of the group as well as of the individual; initiative, self-reliance and the abil-ity to work alone without close super-vision; and the skill of leadership. This aspect of achievement remains virtually untapped by the 16 plus examination...

c. This aspect of achievement involves motivation and commitment; the willing-ness to accept failure without destruc-tive consequences; the readiness to persevere; the self-confidence to learn in spite of the difficulty of the task. Such motivation is often regarded as a prerequisite to achievement, rather than as an achievement in itself. We do not deny that motivation is a pre-requisite to the other three aspects of achievement, but we also believe that it can be regarded as an achievement in its own right. For some pupils come to their school without such motivation, yet the school succeeds in generating it in them and, in such circumstances, both the school and the pupils have made an important achievement. By contrast, the schools actively reduce the motivation and commitment of pupils, thereby causing further under-achievement...

If a school does not attend to this aspect as a central feature of its work, then achieve-ment in the other aspects becomes improbable.

## (ii) Breaking the 16+ age-related lockstep

Many teachers in secondary schools would see themselves (and their pupils) as trapped in the present examination system, and relatively powerless to do anything about it. One par-tial answer, and a move in the right direc-tion, would be to shift from the present sys-tem of examining towards a system of accredi-tation which would systematically take account of the four aspects of achievement noted above. One such initiative is recorded earlier in this book (see Brighouse's chapter). In four LEAs attempts are being made by individual schools, backed by other schools and working cooperatives with the support of local education authority, local industries and the Examination Board to produce and validate school-based certification of achievement. The Hargreaves Report (ILEA 1984) suggests that 14-16 year old pupils should work for much of the week on modules of half a term in length, which could be then accumulated towards accreditation. Handy (1984) suggests monthly reports by the clients on how well the school is doing in meeting their learning needs.

3.  ## Management Development

Management activity includes managing innovation and change. Those in school tend to concentrate on maintenance management rather than on change management. There are many reasons for this, but increased awareness of the need for change management and an emphasis on increasing the knowledge base and skill training is one possible starting point. Insofar as managers - at all levels - create the context in which learning and teaching take place in schools - and this context is very important in bringing about change - managers and the choices they make do make a difference. Cameron (1980) argues that strategic choices made by managers in a wide range of American enterprises, including educational ones, are of greater importance than even environmental factors. Stewart (1982) makes the same kind of point in a British context while Styan (1984), speaking about English Secondary Schools highlights the importance of forced choices - and these are the kind of choices that are now to be faced because of falling rolls, and because of government intervention.

4.  ## Where the action is

Teachers, pupils, parents and others can and do initiate change which is then carried through by confident, well informed and well qualified teachers. The broader policy ini-

tiatives and strategies for introducing lifelong education all imply that the teachers are
confident, well informed and well qualified.
Also implied are changed emphasis in initial
professional training and increased (and different) kinds of professional updating, staff
development, in-service training and retraining. But that is another story.

## References

ACACE (1982) Adults: their educational experience and needs,
Advisory Council for Adult and Continuing Education.
Ball, S.J. (1985) English for the English since 1906 in
Goodson, I.F. (ed) Social histories of the secondary
curriculum: subjects for study, Falmer.
Benn, C. (1984) Secondary reform: time to move on, Forum
26(2), 32-34.
Berman, P. (1981) Educational change: an implementation
paradigm in Lehming, K. and Kane, M. (eds) Improving
schools using what we know, Sage, 253-286.
Bolam, R. (1985) Lecture given at Sheffield City
Polytechnic, 13 June 1985.
Cameron, K. (1980) Critical questions in assessing organi-
sational effectiveness Organisational Dynamics, Autumn,
66-80.
Dalin, P. (1978) Limits to educational change, Macmillan
Fullan, M. (1982) Meaning of educational change, Ontario
Institute for Studies in Education.
Fullan, M. and Pomfret, A. (1977) Research in curriculum
and instruction implementation Review of Educational
Research, 47(1), 335-397.
HMSO (1983) Teaching quality, Cmnd. 8836.
HMSO (1984) Training for jobs, Cmnd. 9135.
HMSO (1985) Better schools, Cmnd. 9469
ILEA (1984) Improving secondary schools (The Hargreaves
Report).
Moon, B. (1984) Challenging the deference curriculum, Forum
26(2), 35-37.
NEDC/MSC (1984) Competence and competition, National Econo-
mic Development Council/Manpower Services Commission.
Raffe, D. (ed) (1984) Fourteen to eighteen, Aberdeen
University Press.
Rogers, R. (1985) Sixth sense of savings, The Guardian,
9 April 1984, p.13.
Stewart, R. (1982) Choices for the manager, McGraw Hill.
Styan, D. (1984) Notes of a meeting on 5 November 1984.
Tolley, G. (1983) 16-19: the changing scene Secondary
Educational Journal 13(1), 3-4.

# 14. 16-19: THE CRITICAL STAGE FOR RECURRENT EDUCATION

Ray Morgan and Frank Molyneux

After a major comparative survey of European approaches to provision at 16+, it was concluded that:

> all questions of higher education and all questions of further professional training depend for their answers on decisions taken about the immediately post-compulsory period of education.
>
> (King 1978)

This finding is of particular importance to the development of recurrent education whose advocates regard it as axiomatic that the present 'front end' model of education with compulsory school serving for most as 'a terminal apprenticeship for life' (Houghton & Richardson 1974) is now totally inadequate. Further they argue that if recurrent education is to be regarded as a practical alternative

> its acceptance will require a reconsideration of every facet of existing education provision.
>
> (Flude and Parrott 1979)

It follows that such a review will have to be rooted in the compulsory sector, more especially in its assumptions, purposes and values, its methods and most urgently in its attitudes towards older pupils. The 14-19 age group is of particular concern at this time as its numbers are declining significantly thus forcing a review of provision in financial terms. In addition school leavers can no longer 'escape to work', a marked feature in this country until the late 1970s with under a half remaining in education compared with more than double that proportion in the United States, Japan and Sweden. Of those entering employment between 40 and 50 percent received no further training compared with 14 percent in France and 9 percent in West Germany (Richmond 1981).

Therefore even before the full political impact of massive youth unemployment had been felt, the official view was that more and better education and training for the 16-19 age group was urgently needed. Some of the purposes which this improved provision was expected to fulfil were described in the late 1970s as

a.  encouragement to continue learning beyond 16 and indeed 18, whether for personal satisfaction or otherwise;
b.  encouragement to develop maturity, and especially: independence of thought and action; self reliance; an appreciation of social and moral values, of rights and duties; acceptance of adult responsibilities; the ability to play a constructive part in family and in the community;
c.  help with acquiring the social and other skills needed in adult life ... and the knowledge and self-confidence needed to cope with the practical business of day to day living;
d.  opportunity to acquire job-specific knowledge and skills and qualifications and to become equipped to meet employer requirements;
e.  an understanding of the demands which working life makes on the individual, a grasp of the place of industry and commerce in the life of the community, and of the rights and responsibilities attached to employment;
f.  access to advice and guidance on personal problems and to effective vocational guidance and counselling.

(DES 1979)

These officially perceived needs certainly do not conflict with the tenets of recurrent education but the manner of their fulfilment will be the cause of dispute unless, as argued elsewhere in this book, there is an accompanying perception of recurrency as an aspect of social welfare policy. Also, as other contributors properly insist, it will be the fostering of positive attitudes to post-school opportunities for education and training within compulsory schools which will ensure the secure rooting of any system of recurrent education. The question now arises in practical terms whether young people will have any real choice about 'escaping the system' at 16+. The 'front end' is extending whether we or they like it or not. Any change in the fundamentals of schooling prior to 16 is unlikely to occur overnight as all the lessons of comparative education show. Thus the immediate focus of change comes back to the 16-19 stage.

However, as implied above, the sheer uncoordinated variety and waste of the present largely fortuitous provision at this stage seems likely to force organisational changes in the near future. For those increasing numbers remaining in full time education provision is made in school sixth forms (where staffing problems are acute), in sixth form centres and colleges - largely a response to staffing and other problems - in Colleges of Further Education and less commonly but with more radical implications in the so-called Tertiary Colleges.

In addition, the political conseqences of the dramatic increase in unemployment among 16-19 year olds and the acknowledged fact that the country's educational system 'produces one of the least trained forces in the industrial world' (MSC 1982) has stimulated an equally dramatic response from a Conservative government. This has taken the form of an unprecedented intrusion into the 16-19 sector by the Department of Employment through the training programmes of its agent the Manpower Services Commission.

Since the late 1970s these programmes have received much financial investment and their impact on increasing numbers of young people are considered elsewhere in this book. In effect, they are rapidly raising the age of first leaving the system to 18 for many who have succeeded least within it. They thus deserve particular attention from those advocating recurrent education whether or not they approve or question the circumstances of their introduction.

Within these same circumstances the Department of Education and Science, conscious of the challenge to its influence and power, has felt obliged to explore the vocationalisation of upper school curricula via its 17+ Certificate of Pre-Vocational Education. Again there is much of interest in CPVE

173

for the supporters of the principles of recurrency.
These are exemplified in a later chapter but clearly include the search for personally relevant educational experiences in a course leading to a
national qualification. In short, an attempt to
provide a motivating experience for the individual
learner as opposed to the often debilitating cram-
ming process which teachers and students experience
as GCE at the Advanced level is used as a multi-
purpose filtering instrument prior to higher education or middle level employment.

Even more radical and contentious is the MSC's
incursion into the heart of the upper secondary
school with its Technical and Vocational Education
Initiative for the 14-18 age group. This cannot be
the place to detail and comment upon the TVEI's
early history but it cannot be ignored that despite
initial resistance in some areas, money has proved
a great stimulus to LEAs fallen on very hard times
(whatever their reservations about its source) and
those interested in recurrent education will note
that TVEI again seeks to address the apparently
intractable problem of motivating those who have
traditionally achieved least at 16+. Thus they
will need to look closely at the results of TVEI's
cross modular approach to the curriculum, the use
of profiles and behavioural objectives in assessment, the working out of the idea of negotiated
units and the stress on careers and personal
guidance (Powell 1985).

Clearly there are many aspects of the mid-
1980s which contain the seeds of radical changes in
the provision available to the age group in question. We must note the proliferation of courses in
schools and colleges, the novelty and power of the
MSC policies, the blurring of the schools-colleges
divide and the questioning of traditional forms of
assessment against a background of rapidly changing
employment structures and the competing claims of
political strategies. These include, unusually for
Britain, a particularly strident and radical form
of conservatism enjoying successive electoral terms
with a large majority which has ensured the continuation of, for instance, the innovative tendencies of MSC.

Thus it is our contention that any objective
view of the situation confronting the advocates of
recurrent education suggests that it is an appropriate time to urge the need for a principled
approach to the problem of reform at the 16-19

level. The present confusion of provision is widely criticised and a more cost-effective approach is politically unexceptionable but the strength of vested interests should not be under-estimated and appears to many to have influenced the slow and often mysterious decisions of minis-ters concerning post-16 reorganisation plans put forward by hard pressed LEAs in recent years. A rationalisation of the present arrangements and a drawing together of provision for the age group is beginning to appear as party policy at least among the opposition. Should this be articulated with sufficient vision and belief in the principles of recurrency, it might, as in Sweden, play a signifi-cant part in the shift towards a wider system or recurrent education.

The Swedish experience also indicates that effective change will not be achieved by tinkering with administrative arrangements. There will have to be a guiding philosophy to facilitate changes in curricula, teaching methods, assessment and guid-ance as well as changed relationships between traditionally separate and autonomous institutions. The necessary changes in attitude by many practi-tioners will take time and need much genuine dia-logue and ultimately compromise as well as the sort of financial input at present apparently available only through the MSC.

Educational change following such a rational-empirical model has not thus far been a notable feature in this country in the 1980s and conse-quently it still seems unrealistic to predict any rapid progress towards a recurrent based pattern of provision at the 16-19 level (Molyneux 1979). In organisational terms the logical first step would be to establish a post-secondary or tertiary sector at 16+ to overcome the present lack of articulation between activities for young and older adults and a resource system better able to respond to the rapidly changing requirements of an evolving post-industrial economy (Stonier 1979).

In practice, as suggested above, only a series of politically suspect decisions by ministers, who under the present law are not required to offer explanation or even act within a stipulated period, have prevented the more rapid spread of Tertiary Colleges. Thirty-five were listed as operational in 1984, and many more such colleges are planned - that is, institutions providing all maintained provision at the 16-19 level in a given administrative area. Defined thus they are comparable to the post-1970 Swedish Gymnasieskola with its vocationally grouped lines of study in two, three and four year courses and acting also as a threshold stage to degree level higher education. In recent years about 90 pecent of those leaving the compulsory nine year school at 16 have entered the Gymnasieskola with significant numbers entering as mature students at 18+. It is worth noting that this embryonic recurrency has perhaps proved too popular and from 1984-85 those applying directly from the Grundskolan were given priority in applying for favoured lines of study. Thus in April 1986 the Swedish National Board of Education announced that no less than 97 percent of those leaving the compulsory school had applied for admission. We should also remember that socialistic Sweden does not pay unemployment benefit to those young adults who cannot find work but refuse the opportunity to enter a Gymnasieskola with a study grant or an approved course of training.

However, to avoid facile comparison, we should remember that (as detailed by our Swedish contributor) Sweden adopted recurrent education as the basis of all post-school provision a decade ago. This followed a generation of political debate and structural reform of first the compulsory school system, the 16-19 sector and finally higher education. In no sense has structural reform and the adoption of the recurrent principle achieved all of Sweden's educational goals but despite the political blasphemy which its Social Democratic policies represent to the new Conservatism it is difficult to deny the country's long record of economic success and industrial harmony. The writers' observations at first hand over the last six years in the Gymnasieskola cannot but leave us reflecting sadly on the contrasts between our two countries so far as the prospects for those leaving compulsory school are concerned. There are no panaceas in the hard world of educational change but surely the time has come for a principled attempt to create some constructive order within the daunting jungle of education, training and unemployment which currently faces the 16-19 group. We believe that the principles are available now. The need is for a little vision and much more political will.

# References

Department of Education and Science (1979), 16-18. Education and Training for 16-18 year olds. A Consultative Paper (Annex).

Flude, R. and Parrott, A. (1979), Education and the Challenge of Change. A Recurrent Education Strategy for Britain, Open University Press.

Houghton, V. and Richardson, K. (eds) (1974), Recurrent Education: A Plea for Lifelong Learning, Ward Lock Educational.

King, E. (1978), The Education of the 16-20 Age Group - A Comparative Approach, Coombe Lodge Report, Vol. 8, No. 15, Blagdon F.E. College, Bristol.

Manpower Services Commission (1982) Youth Task Report, London.

Molyneux F.H. (1979), 'Perception, Problems and Priorities' in Recurrent Education and Lifelong Learning, World Year Book of Education 1979, Kogan Page.

Powell, B.L. (1985), The Changing Face of Education (Unpublished Lecture), WAB, Cardiff.

Stonier, T. (1979), 'Changes in Western Society - Educational Implications' in Recurrent Education and Lifelong Learning, World Year Book of Education 1979, Kogan Page.

## 15. THE CHANGING CURRICULUM AT 16+ - A WORKING VIEW OF CPVE

Phil Hodkinson

It is clear to many of us actually working with young people that our traditional school curricula dominated by public examinations can be damaging to the longer term learning prospects of many of them. Despite the best efforts of a lot of teachers the apparent irrelevance and authoritarianism of the later years of secondary school seem to stifle the intellectual vitality of many (including some very able) and destroys any willingness of the lower achievers to get involved in further or continuing education. From the point of view of recurrent education this is unacceptable. It has also become a highly charged political issue and government's concern over Britain's well documented inability to retain its young adults in formal education and training programmes has produced various attempts to 'vocationalise' curricula at 14 or 16+. These are referred to in general terms elsewhere in this book and the notions examined that the pupil will be motivated by the new and greater curricular relevance to prospects of employment and that the economy will benefit in the longer term from young adults better prepared to respond to whatever employment may be available. Whatever reservations teachers may have about such initiatives they are obliged to work with whatever tools are to hand and in a period of great professional uncertainty. Moreover, many like myself have taught through the period of comprehensivisation, become accustomed to 'mixed ability' as a normal fact of professional life but remain very frustrated by the durability of traditional curricula and assessment. What follows is one such teacher's experience with one opportunity for curriculum change at 16+. As indicated elsewhere in

178

this book the 16-19 stage can be viewed as potentially vital to those seeking to shift towards
recurrent education. My implied question is - does
CPVE conribute to or have potential for making the
post-16 stage into a better basis for recurrent and
continuing education?
What is CPVE?
The Certificate of Pre-Vocational Education
(CPVE) is a new one year course for young adults
initiated by the DES at 16+. The course, which at
present must be full-time, consists of three parts:
Core, Vocational Studies and Additional Studies.
Students must also complete a minimum of 15 days
work experience.

## The Core

The syllabus for the Core consists of a large
number of objectives, grouped under aims in ten
overlapping areas (Appendix-Table 1). The vast
majority of these objectives refer to skills, and
very few specify content. They are mainly open-
ended and wide ranging. CPVE also specifies appropriate styles of work and teaching, new types of
assessment and the development of real student
responsibility. In an attempt to escape the load-
ing of several traditionally used labels, the Joint
Board for Prevocational Education (the examination
board controlling CPVE) are creating their own
language.
Work in CPVE should be <u>integrated</u>. Within the
core the ten areas are covered in a linked and
interlocking way. In addition, work in the Core
and Vocational areas should be integrated as far as
possible. <u>Experiential Learning</u> is another 'buzz'
phrase. Students should learn by doing and experiencing things for themselves. The idea of <u>negotia-
tion</u> is perhaps more radical. Each student should
agree, through negotiation with his or her tutor,
an individually tailored programme of activities
within CPVE. This recognises individual needs,
interests, ability and achievements. It requires a
very open-ended structure to most parts of the
course.
The implications of these principles leads to
the use of the word <u>delivery</u> instead of teaching.
There are not CPVE teachers, only tutors. We
guide, advise, provide resources, but seldom
instruct or give information in a didactic manner.
According to the jargon, we are <u>facilitators</u>. The

implications for staff/student relations are profound. If teachers make all the rules and take all
the decisions there is no student responsibility or
genuine negotiation. We become more like a solici-
tor or accountant advising a client, and must learn
to accept that sometimes our advice, no matter how
sound, will be ignored.

CPVE assessment is also radical. It is based
on the use of Profiling. Each student keeps a
running record of her/his achievements throughout
the course. This Formative Profile is compiled by
the student negotiating with his/her tutor(s). It
helps guide student choices throughout the course,
pinpointing and recording both achievements and
needs. When the course ends, a final statement or
Summative Profile is drawn up, having been moder-
ated by the Joint Board. This Summative Profile is
based on a computerised bank of statements, which
are in turn related to the original core objectives.

## Vocational Studies

In order to organise the Vocational aspects of
CPVE, all occupations are classified into five
Categories, each sub-divided into clusters (Appen-
dix-Table 2). This is a departure from the previously universal Occupational Training Families
(OTFs) used by the Manpower Services Commission.
Vocational studies in CPVE are also modular, and
the modules are of three types. The Introductory
Modules are broad and generalised, covering a whole
Category. Exploratory Modules cover a single cluster. They are paired: one is theoretical, the
other a practical project. Finally, Preparatory
Modules are specific to a particular aspect of
vocational work. All students must complete a
minimum of four modules, but not necessarily at all
levels. However, Preparatory Modules must be
accompanied by appropriate Exploratory Modules, and
these in turn must be linked with the relevant
Introductory Module.

## Additional Studies

Each CPVE centre must offer a programme of
Additional Studies, although not every student need
choose them. No student can spend more than 25% of
her/his time on Additional Studies. This part of
CPVE is deliberately not specified, but could

include, for example, O level subjects or leisure activities.

## CPVE at Houghton Regis School

We decided to pilot CPVE because it seemed the best available one-year sixth-form course. Like many other schools we had grown dissatisfied with existing courses, although we mourned (perhaps prematurely) the imminent demise of CEE. We made a deliberate choice to run CPVE for all our one-year sixth formers. This was partly expediency, for the sixth form is small; and partly to avoid CPVE becoming a course for the less able. We began, in September 1984, with 30 students, with a very wide ability range indeed.

The timetable was blocked. Core CPVE was labelled as such for 16 35-minute periods per week. The existing sixth form General Studies and Social Education programmes, which were for all sixth formers, were also counted as Core. Vocational Studies had 8 periods, and within this block students could choose one of three parallel Vocational courses. Individual tutorials were timetabled against a range of Additional Studies. Many students also signed up for evening classes run by the Community College.

Our central tool for teaching CPVE was the integrated assignment (Appendix-Table 3). Each one would cover a wide range of core areas, and they were designed to be open-ended and to allow varieties of individual experience. Most were group activities. Adult life is often a matter of working with others. In our view, too much of traditional education is concerned with students working in isolation.

The 'Study of the Local Community' involved firstly, the students deciding which aspects they wished to explore. They then organised themselves into groups of four or five, each focusing on one aspect. Each group then decided what to find out, and how. Obviously the library was consulted, but most of the methods were fieldwork - questionnaire surveys, visits, interviews with local people, etc. The group then had to decide how to report back. One girl made an excellent video programme about environmental problems, especially a local derelict chalk quarry. Another group produced a database on micro-computer. Others produced more conventional written reports or poster displays.

The 'Mini-Co' exercise is a simulated business, using a published kit (Bray 1983). We had two companies, each with its own elected Board of Directors and each raising its own capital. One ran discos for local 14 to 16 year olds, the other washed cars and ran a tuck shop.

One assignment was a one week residential trip to the Yorkshire Dales National Park. Students self-catered in holiday cottages, and had to live together in groups, plan and cost menus, buy food, cook and balance the books, as well as completing an assignment on Planning in National Parks.

The key elements in all these assignments are that students were involved in deciding how to make the assignment work, by negotiating with peers and staff. Staff, who were timetabled in teams of two or three, acted as advisers. Ideally, like good sports coaches, we modified the students' own practice to make it better, and suggested possible approaches or avenues they had not thought of. We very seldom told them what to do.

## Problems

Piloting any new course is never an unqualified success. Here are just a few of the problems we encountered.

## Transition from year 5

We underestimated the problems of a sudden, radical change in methods of working. For the first two weeks many students were totally disorientated. They had been trained for ten years to follow a teacher's every instruction like reluctant sheep. To have to make decisions and to take responsibility are much harder. We were plaintively asked to sit them behind desks and tell them what to do - by students who had patently failed when just that had been done in the past.

## Student Attitudes

Some of our students could see little point in what they did. They dodged work and truanted. Anyone who believes the rhetoric about 'relevant curricula' or 'purposeful study' should come and speak to Amanda! There are three reasons for these problems. Firstly, this particular group were difficult because of a few leading negative personalities; secondly, too many of them had drifted back into the sixth form because mother wanted them off the streets, but they didn't really want to be with us; thirdly, they were conditioned by previous educational experiences to judge a course by content and qualifications rather than by process. Buying a second-hand car was boring for girls, regardless of the actual tasks involved, and discussion is not 'work'. Some also felt that if CPVE did not give General Certificate of Education Ordinary levels, then it was valueless. What a sad indictment of traditional education!

## Tutoring and Guidance

Each student met his/her CPVE course tutor for an individual tutorial about once a month. This was to clear up problems, assess progress, decide on future action and to complete the Formative Profile. Neither tutors nor students proved up to it. Staff were inexperienced in building relationships one to one in a private interview. The students perceived the sessions as 'checking up' on errors and omissions. They gave evasive and inventive answers, avoiding the necessary trusting relationship. This tutorial process was made worse because our profiling was too long-winded, and students did not understand many of the objectives we were trying to assess. The problem arose because of the difficulty of measuring individual student attainment on well over 100 core objectives, when within each assignment each student has a different experience, and much of what happens is (rightly) beyond the direct supervision of staff anyway. Furthermore, the student needs to be in control of this process, and the language used by the Joint Board hinders this.

## Working as as Team

Staff found team integration difficult. We all came from different departments, with different ideas and approaches. Most of us had previously only taught 'in splendid isolation'. The team-teaching generally worked well, but never involved more than three staff at any one time. The problem was one of communication between teams so that one team knew what the others were doing.

## Conclusion

Despite all this, the result was highly worthwhile. Much excellent work was achieved, and the
growth in maturity and confidence of most of the
students must be seen to be believed. Out of our
original cohort of 30, almost half got jobs before
the course had ended - three were employed as a
direct result of work experience. Many of these
same students were unemployable when the course
began. CPVE is a course where both students and
staff got out what they put in. The shirkers
achieved very little. Those with energy and
commitment achieved a great deal, regardless of
ability. That is not a bad educational philosophy.

## Future Plans

At Estover, where I now teach, we are trying
to learn the lessons of the CPVE pilot schemes. We
are part of a consortium involving several other
schools, and the Plymouth College of Further Education. This means that we can offer students a vast
range of Vocational courses.
Within our Core programme, we aim to be more
flexible than at Houghton Regis. Students will be
able to negotiate which assignments they do, and
there will be scope for individualised work to
complement group assignments. There will be a
carefully structured introduction to the course,
with a series of short assignments designed to help
students learn the new ways of working and learning. The Profile is being redesigned and simpli-
fied, although Profiling remains the most intransi-
gent of our problems with CPVE.
Already, CPVE is acting as a link between
compulsory education and the adult world, in a way
that many traditional 'academic' courses did not.
However, its value to many students is undermined
by the competition with YTS. YTS is only open to
16 and 17 year olds, and a student completing CPVE
is at present denied a full two year YTS afterwards. Also, YTS trainees are paid, but CPVE students are not. These circumstances mean that true
flexibility, designed to meet the needs of an individual is unattainable. At present, the 16 year
old faces a confusing choice of alternative routes,
and once the choice is made, future options become
irreversibly constrained. If it were possible to
complete a full two year YTS after CPVE, and vice

versa, and if both attracted the same levels of remuneration, students would have a real chance to plan their own programme of continuing education and training, modifying choices as experience and interests develop. Surely that would be to everyone's advantage.

## Reference

Bray, Elizabeth (1983) The MiniCo Kit Longman: York.

## Table 1: CPVE Core Areas

Personal and Career Development
Industrial, Social and Environmental Studies
Communication
Social Skills
Numeracy
Science and Technology
Information Technology
Creative Development
Practical Skills
Problem Solving

# Table 2: Vocational Modules

| Categories | Clusters | |
| --- | --- | --- |
| Introductory Modules | Double Exploratory Modules (examples only) | Preparatory Modules (examples only) |
| Business and Administrative Services | Control of Organisations<br><br>Services to Business | Typewriting<br>Book-keeping<br>Reception Skills |
| Technical Services | Information Technology and micro-electronic systems<br>Service Engineering | Product Design<br>Electronics<br>Computing<br>Motor Vehicle Engineering |
| Production | Manufacturing<br><br>Craft based Activities | Materials technology<br>Fabrication and Welding<br>Finishes and Decoration |
| Distribution | Retail and Wholesale | Customer Service<br>Stock Control<br>Display |
| Services to People | Health and Community Care<br><br>Recreation Services<br><br>Hospitality including Food and Accommodation | Childcare<br>Nutrition<br>First Aid<br>Geography of Tourism<br>Beauty Therapy<br>Care of Elderly<br>Accommodation Services |

Table 3: Some Integrated Assignments used at
         Houghton Regis

Mini companies
A Study of the Local Community
Image and the Media
Planning a Foreign Holiday
Buying a Second-hand Car
A Simulated Planning Enquiry
Planning in National Parks
Housing and Recreation in Houghton Regis
Study of a local Industry
Role of women in Science and Engineering
Planning a CPVE Core Assignment

# 16.  FEU SUPPORT FOR RECURRENT EDUCATION

Philip Barnard

The Further Education Unit was established in 1977, and is an independent body funded by the DES with a remit to promote, encourage, and develop the efficient provision of further education in the UK. The sector of educational provision to which the FEU primarily relates is constituted by the 600 or so colleges of further education officially described as 'major establishments'. The number and size of these colleges has expanded greatly in the last forty years. Their main role has been to provide vocational education and training for school-leavers, but they also make substantial provision in other curriculum areas and for other client groups, including adults. In 1984, out of a total of about 1.6 million students enrolled for non-advanced courses in colleges of further education in England, just over 800,000 were over 21.

At the time when the FEU was established, colleges of further education were receiving increasing numbers of young students whose records of achievement at school were modest and who did not have specific vocational aspirations. With very limited resources, the FEU made it a priority to offer curriculum guidance to colleges on work with this new pre-vocational clientele.

In 1979 the FEU published 'A Basis for Choice', which was the report of a study group on post-16 pre-employment courses. This report laid down principles of curriculum design to which the FEU has consistently adhered. Among the most important of these were that educational provision should be learner-centred, based on an analysis of the learners' needs and aspirations, implemented with the active involvement of the learner, and drawing on and relevant to the learner's experience

189

outside the classroom. The report identified aims which were considered to be basic and contributory to the whole range of possible successful outcomes; the objectives associated with these aims constituted a common core for teaching and learning, and were in this sense to be offered as an entitlement which guaranteed breadth, balance, and opportunities for personal development.

With the support of the FEU, many staff working in colleges have adopted this approach to curriculum design and development in their work with adults. The same principles have been found to be valid in work with new client groups, including long-term unemployed adults, adults on work preparation courses, and adults following professional, industrial or commercial updating (PICKUP) courses.

The FEU is ready to extend its definition of 'vocational' to cover learning needs arising from changes taking place at any stage in an individual's life, affecting occupation in a broader sense rather than narrowly in the context of employment. A feature of recurrent education in these terms would be that on the basis of previous successful experience of educational support for life changes, adults would readily turn to educational agencies to help them cope with new challenges. The continuity of successive learning experiences would be maintained by the continuity of curricular principles.

From the early 1980s, the FEU was able to offer support specifically targeted on the education of adults. Funds became available to commission a small number of curriculum development projects in this area. One of the first of these was a study of curriculum design, undertaken by the University of Surrey, covering a wide range of provision, including that made through Local Education Authority adult education centres, which have annual student enrolments totalling some 1.6 million. The FEU was also invited by the DES to manage a programme of curriculum development support for PICKUP provision, and, in 1984, a similar programme in support of REPLAN provision for unemployed adults (discussed by Charnley and Stock in chapter 4).

In 1984, the FEU set up an Advisory Committee on Education/Training for Adults and issued a Statement on the Provision of Education and Training for Adults (FEU 1984a). Activities in progress which related to an adult clientele included not only the programmes mentioned above, but also developments in areas where the further and adult education curricula form a continuum: education for those with special needs, for a multicultural society, business studies, engineering, and management education, as well as projects within the FEU Experimental Colleges programme. In all, about one third of FEU research projects now relate to an adult clientele.

Most FEU research projects are undertaken by practitioners working in educational establishments, and involve the design, piloting, and evaluation of learning programmes and activities. A curriculum development model comprising the following elements, namely, needs analysis - design - implementation - evaluation - staff development and support, is adopted for most projects, and this constitutes a framework which facilitates the development of learner-centred curricula. Reports on projects contain descriptions of the development of provision, and frequently also examples of learning schemes and learning materials, which have been evolved by colleagues working in the field and can be readily adapted. This is the most widely available form of support offered by the FEU.

The FEU Statement on the Provision of Education and Training for Adults drew attention to an expanding clientele whose education/training needs arise in a wide variety of situations such as employment, unemployment, community service, family life, recreation, and disability. The development of guidance on curricular issues and themes has been undertaken by the FEU largely in the context of provision made to meet such needs.

For example, effective PICKUP provision requires some form of marketing. PICKUP research projects piloted methods of marketing research and the creation of databases designed to support education/training provision. Marketing consultants were then commissioned to undertake research and report on ways in which commercial marketing methods could be adapted and practised in further education and adult education. It is hoped that the guidance which emerges will draw colleagues' attention in a more focused way to the practical relationship between responsiveness to needs, publicity, and curriculum development.

PICKUP and adult training have also provided contexts for the development of guidance on flexible learning opportunities, since the access of adults to learning is notably restricted by their other commitments. Among FEU publications on this theme are: Flexible Learning Opportunities, (FEU, 1983), which provides a conceptual framework; a number of reports on flexible learning in action; a guide, published jointly with the Open Tech on Implementing Open Learning in Local Authority Institutions (FEU/Open Tech Unit, 1986). Open learning is sometimes presented as a cheap way of enabling employers to update their skills; it is less often seen as the only way in which a wider range of learning opportunities may in practice be offered to a wider clientele, including unemployed adults.

The emphasis placed on qualifications gained in initial education and training has had a highly restrictive effect on the access of adults to qualifications and training. Two approaches have been adopted by the FEU to overcome this barrier to recurrent education. The first is to seek to ensure that the issues of accreditation and credit transfer/progression are explored when new curricula are developed. Recent REPLAN projects in the area of training for work in leisure and tourism offer specific examples of this, as in The C.C.P.R. (Central Council for Physical Recreation)/ Community Sports Leaders Award (FEU, 1986). The other approach is to promote alternative routes of access to further education and training which take account of adult experience and adult habits of learning. Support for the piloting and evaluation of access courses is an obvious example of this, and there have been several FEU projects in this area. Special attention has also been given to the assessment of prior experiential learning. Exploiting Experience (FEU, 1984b) illustrated the need for the development of techniques and methods, and more recent projects have followed this up with the aim of offering guidance, providing examples, and identifying issues.

The FEU approach is based on the assumption that the knowledge and skills available within the education/training system can be offered more effectively and shared more widely to benefit more individuals and society as a whole. It offers a prescription which seeks to take into account learners' aspirations in respect of personal development, educational progression, and employment or occupation. The student-centred approach has been effective with youngsters who have not taken advantage of educational opportunities offered at school and with adults who lack confidence in their ability to learn (though its effectiveness is not, of course, restricted to under-achievers). It is an approach which aims to involve and develop the whole person. The present adult education/training scene includes pressures on the one hand to restrict training to the satisfaction of immediate and narrowly defined work-based requirements, and on the other hand to treat adult education as part of the leisure industry, the development of which should be determined by market forces. Under such pressures it becomes difficult to maintain a clear perception of how to implement educational aims and values. In attempting to uphold this perception, the FEU offers curriculum prescriptions which apply across a broad range of education and training and to learning experience from childhood to retirement. Curricular consistency and continuity of this kind is a prerequisite for the advancement of recurrent education.

## References

FEU 1979, A Basis for Choice, London, FEU.
FEU 1983, Flexible Learning Opportunities, London, FEU.
FEU 1984a, Statement on the Provision of Education and Training for Adults, London, FEU.
FEU 1984b, Exploiting Experience, London, FEU.
FEU 1986, The C.C.P.R. Community Sports Leaders Awards, London, FEU.
FEU/Open Tech Unit 1986, Implementing Open Learning in Local Authority Institutions, London and Sheffield, FEU and MSC.

N.B.  FEU publications are available from: Publications Despatch Centre, Department of Education and Science, Honeypot Lane, Canons Park, Stanmore, Middlesex, HA7 1AZ.

# 17. THE INTERFACE BETWEEN EDUCATION AND TRAINING

Carol Dalglish

Ten years from 1975 have seen some dramatic changes in post school education and training. The need to use both the words 'education' and 'training' indicates one of the major issues that has come out of these changes. The established meanings of these two terms have been challenged. Education is generally accepted as providing a foundation of knowledge; it is about the development of the mind and powers of thought. The education system as a whole has tended to emphasise the academic. Training on the other hand is generally seen to be rather mechanistic, to be about skills acquisition and to be almost exclusively to do with employment. The division between these two terms and the systems which are involved with their implementation are not nearly as simple and clear cut as these descriptions might imply.

Post school education has largely been the responsibility of the local authorities through their further and higher education institutions and through universities. Training has largely been the responsibility of industry and the former training boards which serviced industry. This too is simplistic. Both further and higher education establishments have long provided vocational education for industry and commerce. They have worked with employers and training boards to provide education and training which is appropriate to the needs of young people in employment. The distinction between education and training is extremely difficult to draw in practice. Is a doctor educated or trained; or an engineer or an architect or a writer? All are 'trained' within the education service.

Despite this the two traditions of education

194

and training have grown up very separately. There is suspicion between the two, there is a different vocabulary, a difference of emphasis and a very strong sense that they are not understood or appreciated by those of the other tradition. Events in the 1970s and 80s have called these attitudes and distinctions into question. The rise in unemployment, the decline of British manufacturing industry, the fall of employment opportunities particularly at the bottom end of the market and the very rapid increase in new technology have all brought about an environment in which change is essential. The agent of this change has been the Manpower Services Commission.

The Manpower Services Commission came into being following the Employment and Training Act of 1973. The Commission is separate from Government but accountable through the Secretary of State for Employment to Parliament. It has ten members representing the Confederation of British Industry (CBI), Trades Union Congress (TUC), Local Authority Associations and professional educational interests. The aims and objectives of the Commission formulated in 1977 are:

a)  to contribute to efforts to raise employment and reduce unemployment;
b)  to assist manpower resources to be developed and contribute to economic well-being;
c)  to help secure for each worker the opportunities and services he or she needs in order to lead a satisfying working life;
d)  to improve the quality of decisions affecting manpower;
e)  to improve the effectiveness and efficiency of the Commission.

The structures within the organisation have altered over the years of its existence but there are two main concerns following on from the aims and objectives; services related to employment and services related to training. Over the ten years or so of its existence the Manpower Services Commission has produced many papers relating to employment and training opportunities. The most significant of these relating to training is a consultative document on the New Training Initiative published in May 1981. It proposed three objectives for training for the rest of the decade.

Objective 1 - to develop occupational training, including apprenticeship, in such a way as to enable people entering at different ages and with different educational attainments to acquire agreed standards of skill appropriate to the jobs available, and to provide them with a basis for progression through further learning.

Objective 2 - to move towards a position where all young people under the age of 18 have the opportunity either to continue in full-time education or to enter training or a period of planned work experience combining work related training and education.

Objective 3 - to open up widespread opportunities for adults - whether employed, unemployed or returning to work - to acquire, increase or update their skills and knowledge during the course of their working lives.

All three of these objectives call into question existing patterns of provision provided by both the training and education traditions. It is objective three that will be discussed here.

In October 1980, the Department of Education and Science produced a discussion paper entitled 'Continuing Education - Post Experience Provision for Those in Employment'. Within this document education is described as follows:

> Education should be construed broadly as embracing areas of activities which might be regarded as training.
> (DES Continuing Education October 1980)

It is a narrowly conceived document which relates only to the role which established educational institutions should play in providing education and training for employers. The definition which it presents of education, that of an all-pervading, all embracing term, represents one of the fears that many training institutions have, that co-operation with education is not possible, that education will 'take-over' whatever activity it sees as being within its brief. The paper does however indicate an increasing awareness of the post initial needs of adults. This theme was also contained in publications from the Advisory Council for Adult Continuing Education (ACACE) and particularly in Continuing Education: from policies to practice (ACACE, 1982).

In April 1983, the Manpower Services Commission produced a discussion paper 'Towards an Adult Training Strategy' (MSC, 1983). This document identified areas that would need to be developed to provide better adult training. These areas included:

a) Information and advice services.
b) The need for local response.
c) New systems for delivering learning.
d) Recognition of the special needs of certain groups such as women and ethnic minorities.
e) Co-operation between providers.
f) The need to influence opinions and attitudes about recurrent education and training.

The Manpower Services Commission did not see this as its task alone but the responsibility of all those involved in education and training. Although emanating from a very different tradition, the Manpower Services Commission document 'Towards an Adult Training Strategy' comes close to seeking answers to questions that have long been asked by those in continuing and recurrent education.

The Manpower Services Commission's methods of operation have been met with some hostility. This hostility has not been lessened by the fact that substantial sums of money have been made available to the Commission to bring about the changes considered desirable, at a time when education is experiencing serious financial cutbacks.

Economic pressure is no doubt the driving force behind the change. This in itself does not invalidate the need for change. Education is of great significance in a world of change. Economics may be the reason for the speed, but this does not imply that mechanistic, narrow, skill-orientated provision is what is required, nor would it be fair to represent the Manpower Services Commission as seeing the solutions to the problems in such narrow terms. It is increasingly important that adults have learning opportunities which provide them with an understanding, an adaptability and an appreciation of life other than the economic as well as the necessary vocational skills. This requires education and educationalists, who provide both vocational and non-vocational education to join in a network of provision with trainers and training providers so that adults can benefit from a wide range of opportunities.

It will become increasingly important for the

benefits of learning, both vocational and non-vocational, to be promoted. The proposals in the 'Adult Training Strategy' would benefit the whole of the post-school sector and should not just involve the strictly vocational. Perhaps the most significant and the most difficult to achieve of the objectives, is the co-operation between pro-viders to offer a local response to answer the needs of the community. This requires the two traditions to come together, to respond in the ways that they are best able to provide a coherent service.

Many Authorities are moving towards the concept of recurrent education. One model which is attempting to bring together all providers in a coherent network is the State Mill Centre in Rochdale. This is a local authority initiative, using a renovated mill to bring together a range of providers in offering a coherent training and education network for adults in the community. The Centre has as its aims:

* To develop a coherent education and training strategy for the Authority.
* To develop a network of training and education provision including a variety of providers.
* To develop a network of information on train-ing and education for employers and individ-uals.
* To encourage maximum participation and re-source sharing.
* To assist in the revitalisation of local industry.
* To identify training and education needs of industry and individuals and facilitate provi-sion to meet these needs.
* To develop services and support for the self employed.
* To provide information and guidance services.
* To ensure access to training and education opportunities for all regardless of gender, disability or ethnic origin.
* To promote the development of new delivery methods and appropriate curriculum.
* To encourage and undertake staff development.

The providers involved in this initiative include further education colleges, the local Skill Centre, the Adult Education College, private train-ing organisations and voluntary and community organisations. A significant feature of each of the developments is the co-operation and involvement of a range of agencies, including the customer, to ensure that the service matches the community's needs. Real efforts are being made to open access to the widest range of people irrespective of their gender, handicap or ethnic origin. It is an attempt by the Local Education Authority to provide a service which is understandable and coherent, which will offer a range of recurrent opportunities for education and training using existing facilities.

This attempt to bring the two traditions together in a local setting is not without its difficulties. Bringing all sides together within a partnership will promote a better understanding of the nature of learning and the constraints under which each of the systems has to operate. It will demonstrate that most training involves wider knowledge and the development of attitudes and personal qualities, and that self-confidence can be acquired through skill acquisition; and that education is not without its skill components whether these are skills of thinking, surgery or car-mechanics. Training and education are two sides of the same coin; without education training cannot be achieved to match the skill requirements of the economy; training is increasingly necessary for economic independence and economic independence is essential if people are to feel that they have some control over their own lives.

Just as training and education are two sides of the same coin, so the systems which have delivered these services must become parts in a larger system of learning opportunities from which individuals can pick, when appropriate to them and their personal or career needs, the learning opportunity they require. The system needs to be easily accessible, should not make value judgements about their choice but should offer advice, encouragement and support. Those aspects of the education and training systems that choose not to become part of such a service could find themselves without customers and be denying access to the expertise they have to offer. The time for inter-face is past. The two traditions must become part of a continuum of learning opportunities.

Despite enormous financial constraints and continuing uncertainty, the opportunity does exist to bring the two traditions into partnership to

provide a new and better education and training
service.

## References

ACACE Continuing Education: from policies to practice, 1982.
DES  Continuing Education: Post-experience vocational provision for those in employment, 1980.
MSC The new Training Initiative, 1981.
MSC Towards an Adult Training Strategy, 1983.

18.  THE MSC AND ADULT EDUCATION AND TRAINING

Geoffrey Holland

In an important speech to a national conference on educational guidance for adults, the director of the Manpower Services Commission, Mr Geoffrey Holland, outlined the manpower crisis facing the United Kingdom and the Commission's approach to the problems. The main part of the speech has been reproduced as it was delivered because it gives a clear idea of his and the commission's philosophy of vocational adult education and training.

My starting points are two in number:

a.  7 out of 10 of the people who will be working in the year 2000 are currently in the work force and it is they who will bear the brunt of the necessity for change;

b.  the world in which we - and they - are and will be living is uncertain and turbulent and likely to remain so, but there are important characteristics of that world which are quite clear.

First, those 7 out of 10 who will be at work in the year 2000 who are in the work force today. The starting point must be that it is inconceivable that what they will be doing in the year 2000 will be identical with what they are doing today. It is much more likely that, by 14 years from now, they will be working in quite different environments, on quite different products and services, using technologies of which we may still be unaware or applications of existing technologies still undreamed of.

It is this generation which will undoubtedly bear the brunt of the necessity for change. By the

201

early 1990s, as a result of the 2 year YTS and all the significant current developments in schools, it will be the norm for every young person to be entering the world of work later than now and with a recognised qualification or a significant credit towards one, following a period of systematic foundation education and training.

Those who are already at work are not so lucky. Consider the following:

a.    6 out of 10 of those at work left full time education at the earliest possible leaving age: for some of them 16, for some of them 15;
b.    those who left education as soon as they could did so because education had failed them - quite literally, through a process of examination designed to secure that 6 out of 10 of any cohort did drop out of full time education by age 16 (or whatever was the minimum school leaving age at the time);
c.    so the majority of those at work (the majority of the adults with whom this conference is concerned) have no happy memories of education, got little from the experience, associate educational institutions and services with failure rather than achievement and have very little interest in, and even poorer expectations of, the world of education and all its works;
d.    that would be bad enough, but when these men and women left full time education they entered a world of work in which 4 out of 5 of them secured no systematic vocational education and training as a foundation for working life subsequently. The minority were lucky enough to secure apprenticeships or traineeships of some kind. But they were the exceptions that prove the rule: most people at work have had but the narrowest training, the minimum required to do the immediate job. And that has been their experience in the world of work ever since.

These facts have the most important consequences for those who are concerned with guidance for adults. They mean:

a.    that adults are not queuing up waiting for guidance, nor are they queuing up looking for education;

b.   on the contrary, so far as many young people
     are concerned education is for 'them' and
     'they' are different and inhabit a world dif-
     ferent from that of the ordinary working man
     or woman;
c.   if education and training are on offer, the
     immediate reaction of many adults is suspi-
     cion: what have I done wrong? Am I going to
     be redundant? Why am I considered expendable?

Consider now the management for whom these 7
out of 10 of our work force of the year 2000 now
work. Let us not mince words: that management
itself is, by any international standards, under-
educated, under-trained, under-qualified and unpro-
fessional.

It is a management which, as a generality, has
the shortest of time horizons for its concerns:
this afternoon's problem, this month's or this
year's bottom line. In consequence, it is a
management which has neglected research and development, has failed to invest in and capitalise on
or sometimes even appreciate the need for innovation, and has certainly under-valued people as a
key resource.

Of course, there are exceptions - and shining
exceptions. But all the work the MSC has done
shows that what I have said is close to the truth.
Management says it values its workforce and says it
is concerned about and does a good deal of education and training of that work force. But the same
management often does not know what education and
training it is doing; and certainly has little idea
how that education and training compares with what
its competitors overseas are doing.

Not exactly an encouraging setting for any
adult who is interested in personal development, in
updating his or her skills, or in extending his
skills. Yet the requirement for all those kinds of
opportunities has never been more urgent.

And here I turn to my second starting point:
that we live in an uncertain and turbulent world
and one which is likely to remain so.

Some very important things can, however, be
said about that world. They include:

a.   that no firm and no country is an island. All
     exist in a world market place which is
     increasingly competitive. The requirement
     therefore is for people at all levels who are

aware of this and who think and look beyond their immediate environment;

b. it is a world in which innovation, quality, closeness to the customer and value for money will increasingly determine success. None of those requirements just happens. None will happen without systematic investment, by firms and individuals alike, in the development of their potential, their skills, knowledge and competence;

c. paradoxically, however, the world in which people are living and will be living is a world of local labour markets. We are competing in a world market place but most of us are born, educated, live, work and die in the same locality. The boundaries of that locality may be shifting with modern transport and modern telecommunications. But the point is that the opportunity for personal development, education and training must be brought to bear in a specific locality.

We can also say some important things about structures of employment:

a. only 1 in 5 of those at work is in manufacturing industry. That proportion is unlikely to increase;

b. people are likely to work in smaller establishments (not necessarily small firms, please note) rather than larger establishments. This is partly because small employers have always been very numerous, partly because of the trend towards decentralisation and partly because of the new technologies themselves;

c. we are now feeling the first impact of information technology. Before long it will be all-pervasive. The first impact has been on manufacturing and, in employment terms, has been negative. The next impact (already beginning to be seen) will be in the service and commercial sectors. And already we are beginning to be aware of the products and services undreamed of before which information technology is, itself, generating and making possible;

d. with the new technologies is coming a change in the structure of work: people are engaged in processes rather than the endless repetitive production of a single product. They are working in teams rather than individually. They - and establishments in which they are employed - are more and more parts of networks rather than hierarchies;

e. and these changes mean that narrow specialisms are dangerous but high grade, highly professional generalists are in demand. They mean that people are needed who are not afraid to take decisions - and are equipped to do so. They mean that inter-personal skills and information exchange are centrally important. And above all they mean that people are needed who can plan and adapt to change and the future.

A further very important set of comments can be made:

a. today people expect participation in decisions affecting their lives and involvement in the design stage of policies, programmes or opportunities;

b. more and more people are increasingly aware that they live in a world where choice is greater than it was and choices are multiple rather than simple either/or decisions;

c. and in this world, people do not want to be patronised, or have handed down solutions or offerings; rather do they look to make decisions for themselves according to their own individual circumstances and wishes. Such possibilities are increasingly put before them by the capabilities of the new technologies themselves.

All of that has profound consequences for education and training.

Late in the day as a country we have woken up to the fact that our vocational education and training system is not the envy of the world and has never been so. And rather late in the day - but better late than never - we have woken up to the fact that unless we create a thoroughly professional vocational education and training system which bears comparison with that of our competitors both in quality and in scale of effort we shall continue to be in grave difficulties in the world market place.

The vocational education and training system whose development the MSC is seeking to assist will have 7 major characteristics:

a.  opportunities and choices at all levels, for people of all ages, and in all communities will be greater and of better quality than they have been in the past;

b.  the customer, whether employer or student or trainee, will determine provision and when, where and how best he can learn;

c.  access to vocational education and training will start in schools, continue on leaving school and then continue throughout working life;

d.  competence and achievement will be encouraged, recognised and rewarded; unnecessary barriers to progression or to access to education and training will also be removed;

e.  we will have a structure of recognised qualifications based on competence, not simply knowledge, and match up the needs of modern society, modern industry and commerce;

f.  vocational education and training services will be of good quality, reliable and highly professional and will be recognised as such;

g.  there will be value for money for everyone, no matter where the money comes from (the Exchequer, the employer or the individual).

Those are the objectives we in the MSC are pursuing and we are pursuing them through programmes and developments of which you are well aware:

a.  the Technical Vocational and Education Initiative in the schools;

b.  the 2 year YTS;

c.  the Review of Vocational Qualifications;

d.  the very important Adult Training Strategy.

There is much that could be said about all of these but, for the purposes of this conference, I merely wish to focus on 3 new developments.

The first is the Training Access Point (TAP) project. Its aims are threefold:

a.  to help open up access to vocational education and training to the man and woman in the street and to every employer, large and small;

b.  to help the vocational education and training market work more effectively by improving the flow of information and by enabling the customer better to articulate his or her needs;

c.   to improve the return on investment in the development of the vocational education and training provision by making that provision much more widely available and by reducing time, effort and resource that can easily be wasted in duplication or fruitless search.

The project has 3 components:

a.   a network of Training Access Points through which enquirers will have access to updated information about vocational education and training opportunities and materials;
b.   a network of Approved Training Agents to provide support to individuals or employers by helping to assess and identify their training needs and helping them to assemble a package of provision to meet those needs;
c.   a foundation of computerised data bases underpinning these two networks.

This is clearly an ambitious project but its time has come. This year (1986/87) is a feasibility year. The task is to satisfy ourselves and everyone that the objectives I have stated are achievable and to establish how best to achieve them.

I would like to make 4 comments about the TAP project:

a.   the project is not driven by technology: it is driven by people and their needs;
b.   the project will rest upon existing data bases, notably ECCTIS, MARIS and PICKUP and we are not trying to re-invent the wheel or duplicate existing work;
c.   the project is every bit as much about personal development as it is about economic needs of employers;
d.   the project complements everything that is going on and in particular the work of the Unit for the Development of Adult Continuing Education (UDACE) and aims to work with those developments in a real and effective partnership.

Our second project is a major study of the vocational needs of 18-24 year olds and in particular the current provision and effectiveness of advice and guidance available to that age group.

The contract for the external part of the study has been awarded to UDACE and the Scottish Institute of Adult and Continuing Education (SIACE) and will run from now until October this year. This study will be in four parts:

a. an examination of the agencies offering information, advice and guidance in 7 areas in England, Wales and Scotland;

b. an examination of the experience of those who are the clients of those agencies;

c. an examination of a cross-section of employers in those areas and how they view the services;

d. a general survey of the usage of information, advice and guidance.

This will be an important study and the outcome will be the subject of a report to the Manpower Services Commission at the end of this year.

And thirdly there is the very important Restart development. In all parts of England, Wales and Scotland, the Jobcentres will be reaching out to every person who has been unemployed for 12 months or more or who becomes so in that time. In all, the outreach will be to 1½ million adults. Many have been out of work for several years.

The aim is to offer each and every one of them a positive opportunity: a job, a place in the community programme, a place on a training programme, a place in a Job Club (very successful self-help groups who meet daily in Job Centres and seek out jobs for themselves).

This is, I venture to suggest, a whole new market for adult and continuing education and one we have not yet seriously addressed. The experience of our pilot Restart schemes in 9 very different areas makes clear not only that the majority of those who have been out of work for some time are very keen to work and very keen to make a new future for themselves, but also that, once contacted, once offered an opportunity, once joined in self-help groups, they want to continue. Already in the pilot areas the Adult Education Service and the Further Education Service are beginning to play an important part.

I draw the opportunity to your attention. It is a new challenge. It will require new offerings, presented in new ways. It will not be easy but it will be rewarding. Those who have been without work for a long period of time may be sceptical about the world of education which may have failed them earlier in life. But that world of education has a unique opportunity to show that it will not fail those people twice.

I think it is clear from all that I have said that I and all of us in the MSC welcome the UDACE report 'The Challenge of Change'. We have no doubt at all about the importance of developing educational guidance for adults. It is a top national priority. And we have no doubt at all about the general thrust of the report with its emphasis on local networks supported by partnerships and resources backed by some kind of National Unit.

I leave you, however, with 5 issues which badly need to be addressed if we are to carry forward the recommendations. They are these:

a. who are the customers? May I suggest that employers are every bit as much potential customers as individual men and women and that is particularly true of those who are self-employed or who have their own small firms;

b. the customer will not just arrive on the doorstep. Outreach and taking education guidance to the customer will be the names of the game;

c. the customer will not arrive at all if the offerings of the education service are not right. ─Increasingly the customer will expect to determine the time, place, pace and manner of his learning. Those who are engaged in guidance will have a two-way role: they must reach out to the customer but they must also reach out to the provider and influence change in provision;

d. in developing educational guidance for adults, we must employ to the full the new technologies and their potential. In general, information is best moved around and accessed through technology. Increasingly, with expert systems, the new technology can support advice as well. Let us not have humans doing what machines and new technologies can do better and, incidentally, what the customer will expect new technology to be providing;

e. and finally, let us ensure that whatever guidance we offer fosters independence rather than dependence, choice at every point, and recognises the importance of the individual deciding for himself or herself.

Above all, let us work towards a society in which educational guidance offers a window on a world of opportunity which is relevant, accessible and fun. We are far from that at present.

# 19. RECURRENT EDUCATION AND INDUSTRY

Allan Ainsworth

It is difficult to synthesise a general view of recurrent education from the standpoint of industry as a whole. The views expressed, therefore, are those of the writer as an individual and are in no way representative of his Company, or indeed of the Confederation of British Industry (CBI) whose 'School Panel' he chairs.

A number of critical observations need to be made right at the outset. Although there is increasing recognition that education should become more consumer orientated, and that there should be greater liaison, contact and interchange between education and industry and commerce, we must not believe that all educational outputs should be capable of precise definition and be measurable. There is a school of thought that there should be greater clarity of objectives, and measurement should be provided of inputs and outputs. I would not disagree with this provided it is accepted that there are many aspects of education, the preparation for life for example, which go beyond the immediacy of preparation for the world which opens up on leaving the formal educational system, be it at 16, 18 or 21.

Educationalists tend, not unnaturally, to be subject orientated and bound by a range of curriculum requirements linked to particular examinations and to the entry requirements set by the universities. Education finds it difficult to come to terms with the concept of acquiring skills through training which is a fundamental requirement for industry and commerce. The split between education and training still exists and although the relationship between the two is better understood, it continues to affect attitudes. This is reflected

211

in education's approach toward pre-vocational education, and industry's suspicion that education pays little heed to its needs. In turn industry finds it difficult to define its needs other than by generalisations reflecting:

communication skills,
numeracy,
a broadly based curriculum,
economic awareness,
positive attitudes to self-reliance,
abilities to relate to others as members of a team.

This though is not unnatural. The banking sector would have a different set of needs for its recruits at age 16, from say the engineering industry. In trying to bring these together there is bound to be a tendency to express these needs in terms of aspects of personality, of character, of motivation rather than specifically defined subject know-how.

It is at this point that industry and recurrent or continuing education start to come together. In effect both require positive attitudes towards further education and training, and these attitudes must at least start to develop within the school system. It must also follow that there should be an appropriate infrastructure to meet these needs after the period of full-time education has been completed.

I hope to consider various aspects of this in the remainder of this paper.

Survival in a fast changing commercial and technological world is the principal objective that most companies would accept, coupled of course with providing an acceptable rate of return on the capital it employs. The need for competitiveness, the need to adapt to technical change is nothing new.

Continuous adaptation to new methods, new processes, new materials has been with us continually. It is not new. Industry has adapted, sometimes with ease, often with difficulty, and employees and managers have had to learn new skills and techniques. In the past such changes have not been anticipated by thorough preparation, training has been later rather than sooner and attitudes toward change have been a major problem on the part of both management and organised labour. In other words changes are not new; the rate of change has perceptibly increased and we now talk of an employee having to learn new skills on a number of occasions throughout a normal working life span of say 40/45 years.

Clearly industry and commerce are responsible for initiating and planning, and implementing many of these changes - they after all are responsible for investment decisions and government though its fiscal policies can positively assist, or stand on the side-lines to let so called 'market forces' operate.

Industry is, therefore, responsible for determining its needs; for responding to change and for meeting whatever new knowledge and skills are required to meet such changes. In determining how to meet such needs it can call upon a responsive system of further education (FE) through colleges of further education, polytechnics and universities. It can also expect to tap the willingness and support of its labour force to keep up to date and learn new skills that might be needed.

There is no doubt, therefore, that:

i) industry is and should continue to be responsible for the determination of the training/education needs of its employees;
ii) it should be able to build on the positive attitudes toward change of its employees, developed from their period of full-time education;
iii) at a minimum it should aim to optimise the skills and potential of all its employees recognising, however, the limitations of its own manpower requirements.

Education is fundamentally based on maximising an individual's potential. This continues into themes of recurrent education. Industry can only be expected to meet its own needs; it cannot be expected to anticipate nationally defined needs, nor to be able to meet all the aspirations and expectations of all of its employees. Industry should, therefore, recognise that many employees have potential beyond that which can be realised in their employment, that they should not place major barriers in the way of employees improving their background knowledge and skill even if they do not figure in any company manpower or succession plan. There should be a debate as to whether release facilities should be available for such employees to develop their own potential for possible use with another employer. I would argue against this, but it follows that the further education system should be able to meet this need through:

- a wider range of evening programmes (as used to be the case)
- further development of open/distance learning to give direct access to recognised qualifications.


Today we are exhorted by the Manpower Services Commission to enhance skills, to participate in and promulgate the Adult Training Initiative, and to provide training places for the two-year Youth Training Scheme (YTS). Many of these initiatives are sound; underlying the current move, however, is the aim to transfer a significant element of the cost of provision from the state to the individual employer.

There is a great deal of frenetic activity in the industrial training field from the Adult Training Initiative to methods of delivery through open learning, from the definition of competencies to the review of vocational qualifications. Industry finds it difficult to be obstructive, is sufficiently supportive to avoid the criticism that it is totally negative, but is increasingly disenchanted by the lack of coherence that is emerging.

An historical review of industrial training since the 1964 Industries Training Act would show:

- the rise and fall of industrial training boards which were committed to helping particular industries meet their defined needs;
- the extent to which they were killed by major companies and institutions who resented the bureaucracy and the imposition of levy/grant;
- the changes in attitude toward training developed in small to medium size companies and the more systematic approach that was extended in the major corporations;
- the gradual subversion of the training boards, and through the MSC, the promulgation of particular aspects of government policy;
- the commitment to continuing education and training, to the benefit of the individual, the employer, and of society;

- the resurrection of training board activities
through direct action on the part of the MSC,
bringing 'mammon' back into the training
world, and with a blurring of the edges of
industrial/company need compared to the concept of the national good.

We continue to re-invent the wheel and in
doing so probably discourage as many as we encourage. Institutions and corporations undoubtedly
benefit from pump-priming; the carrot and stick
approach has much to commend it provided we have
general agreement on where we are going. At the
moment such a consensus does not appear to exist.
We have the Manpower Services Commission (MSC) and
the Department of Education and Science (DES)
implying there is a direct relationship between
investment in training and overall national economic performance. We are compared, unfavourably,
with Germany, Japan, France and the USA in respect
of our commitment to training. Both sides see what
they want to see: there is too much looking over
the shoulder and seeing the greener grass on the
other side of the fence. Let us learn from our
competitors by all means, but for any change to be
effective it has to be developed in Britain to
achieve the balance as seen by the state, by industry and by the trades unions. Above all, it has to
be reflected to individuals. The alternatives are
stark. Either we provide a system in which the
state provides the resources and the commitment so
that all individuals are encouraged to optimise
their innate ability and skills irrespective of
needs; or we accept that industry and commerce are
best fitted to assess their manpower requirements,
that the state has a limited role in reviewing
national manpower trends, in isolating particular
shortages and surpluses and acting accordingly and
that each individual needs to be encouraged to
develop the drive and the initiative to balance his
ability and potential through marketing his own
skills. Industry can only do this on a company
basis through its own planning: the educational
system has to provide the facilities so that individuals actually seek to develop themselves.
This takes us back to the basic issues of
attitudes and values that are, or should be developed within the educational system. It is no acci-
dent that 'industry and trade', over the years have
not attracted from the universities those with the

highest abilities and potential; it has been the professions, the Civil Service, particularly during our period as a colonial power, which attracted them. Whilst not as marked today, it is a legacy like a stone round our neck.

Vocational and pre-vocational education are now coming to the fore. Initiatives such as the Technical and Vocational Educational Initiative are focusing attention on new approaches to learning and could lead, over time, to significant changes in curricula and approaches toward learning. But such changes will have little effect unless as a nation we start to come to terms with:

i) the fact that the historical conflict between capital and labour is destructive to both;

ii) the reality that profit is not a dirty word, coupled with the recognition that profit, surplus or however the difference between sales and costs is defined, is the life blood on which the overall standard of living of the country depends;

iii) we should encourage the appreciation of profit, inculcate the pride of working for a highly profitable organisation as seems to be the case in the USA, the commitment that exists to quality and peformance that epitomises Japanese industry, and the clinical approach toward efficiency that characterises German industry;

iv) the admission that industry by its lack of long term thinking on strategic issues and planning for the future, deserves censure and must accept significant responsibility for our decline as a manufacturing/industrial nation;

v) rethinking our attitudes towards greater involvement and partnership with employees as well as with consumers and suppliers. Above all there must be a positive reaction to the signals being made by the DES and the MSC for greater involvement in the development and extension of vocational education and training. Much of industry is involved with YTS; companies are experimenting with and developing new approaches to training and learning through the new techniques available - Open Tech, Distance Learning, the Open University, etc.

I have tried to argue that our industrial society has always been in a state of change, and with varying degrees of success has been able to adjust. Continuing training and education to meet the demands of new methods and technologies is not new in the industrial context. The fact that changes appear of greater degree and are more frequent and demanding requires a greater commitment to updating and re-training throughout life. I have no doubt that industry will play its part providing it is relevant to its strategic planning. The state, through its provision of education, and its ability to manipulate the climate in which industry operates, also has a major role in the initiatives taken by the DES and the MSC over recent years. It is perhaps too cynical to accept the view that the extension of the MSC into greater involvement with the educational service was to break the committee impasse of masterly talk-shops and no actions that characterised the DES for so long. There is talk of a new Department of Education and Training; I believe such a department could lead to major changes in our educational and training provision. It could give us a new start and clearly it must give a major impetus to the continuing need for all our people for education and relevant training opportunities to be available throughout life. This will need positive commitment from the state and from industry; the will is not enough, the resources to make things happen have to be provided.

## 20. A VIEW FROM THE WORKPLACE

Mike Cunningham

'What does "recurrent education" mean to NUPE members?' I was asked to consider when I was starting to prepare this chapter. Well, in my view, very little - as a term - and that is the trouble: the debate, as the phrase is, has not yet begun at that level.

However, if the 'debate' about 'recurrent' - let alone 'continuing' - education is still somewhat becalmed, and remains the preserve of practitioners and sundry enthusiasts, that is not to say that the <u>issue</u> has no reverberations amongst working-class people: it is indeed a burning issue, with traditional courses being jealously defended and some innovative ones enthusiastically embraced. The problem is that the ideas are discussed (and the decisions reached) in faraway, unenterable rooms and committees. Getting a spoonful of recurrent education is rather like receiving the occasional 'special offer' through the post.

Most ideas about why recurrent education is not 'getting through' to manual workers (and about how this problem can be solved) are premised on two serious misconceptions:

i)   course provision is more or less acceptable as it stands; more of it - and some tinkering here and there - is all that is needed;
ii)  there are no cultural (or any other kind of) barriers to participate.

These two fundamental errors go a long way, I believe, towards explaining why we seem to do a lot of running around but end up making very little progress.

Let's start off, though, on a positive note,

and look at what there is, warts and all. Firstly,
there is job-related training: some of it is
skills-training in accordance with nationally-set
standards and written into union-management agreements:

*   courses in carpentry, plumbing, electrical
    work, cooking, gardening, hairdressing, etc.

It has to be said that much of this kind of
training is in decline and running out of steam,
but courses for some newer skills are now coming on
stream:

*   computer software, word-processing.

Other job-related courses are often concerned
with promotion:

*   acquisition of supervisory skills, report-
    writing, minute-taking.

Employers will supply or facilitate the above;
they will also sometimes arrange other training,
perhaps to pre-empt a union initiative:

*   occupational health and safety.

Trade unions themselves (sometimes through the
good offices of FE institutions) put on a plethora
of training opportunities for their representatives:

*   Shop Stewards, Safety Representatives,

increasingly specialising in particular issues:

*   Law, Health and Safety, Bargaining Informa-
    tion, Anti-Racism, Anti-Sexism, Job Evalua-
    tion, Work Study, Industrial Tribunals.

While it has to be admitted that the vast
majority of trade union courses are for elected
representatives, the 1982 Tory Government's legislation on workplace ballots has spurred the entire
trade union movement to organise 'membership education', that is to say for members who are not
shopfloor representatives. Some unions have been
able to build on an existing (albeit small) base of
special courses for women and members of ethnic

minorities.

Notwithstanding the grotesque imbalance between training provision for manual workers and lower-grade clerical workers and for management/white-collar skills, we cannot say that the former are totally excluded from all forms of recurrent education. Why is it then, that the system otherwise continues to be so patently weighted in favour of that élite of articulate middle-class (usually male, almost invariably white) people?

When all is said and done, working-class people look upon the great majority of recurrent education provision as 'not for the likes of us'. And who can gainsay that? Early in 1982, the Advisory Committee on Adult and Continuing Education (ACACE) carried out a survey of attitudes to this sector of education: middle-class and/or 'educated' people thought very positively of it, while a very high percentage (33%) of working-class people had:

* virtually no education since school-leaving age;
* no regrets about it;
* no wish to benefit from any further education provision at any future point in their lives.
(ACACE, 1982)

The first two attitudes are bad enough, but the third one is even more disturbing. Why do people 'select themselves out?' My own experience, and that of colleagues, of discussing possible 'Basic Skills' courses for manual workers in the University of London shows the reasons for this profound disaffection as follows:

* poor experience of the education system;
* repeated ignoring of 'qualifications' (formal qualifications like overseas diplomas/degrees; informal qualifications such as domestic or community organising skills);
* fear of (or previous negative experience of) pre-course testing.

Even this is jumping the gun a bit: it begs the question that our targeted group is substantially aware of the courses (however irrelevant and off-putting) that are available. Time without number, our members complain that they know nothing of these courses, no matter how they are being advertised. How does this information manage to remain unseen or unread?

* It is provided top-down (fundamentally, this is probably the biggest criticism: the shop-floor, far too often, is offered no rôle <u>on its own terms</u> in the formulation of recurrent education policy - it is forced to retain a <u>passive</u> rôle).
* It reaches a very small number of people (it is common for line management to be asked to 'pass on' the information - this characteristically results in a kind of cloning, with a line manager selecting staff on the basis of his/her cultural prejudices; library notice boards, Fleet Street newspaper classified ads and the like, it goes without saying, are virtually <u>never</u> read).
* It is simply not understood (because of the 'register' of the language used, or because it is beyond the reading level of a native, a non-native, English speaker).

So much for criticisms, for the time being at least. What can be done? Even better, what has been done? The Greater London Council (GLC) in its final incarnation (1981-86) recognised that it is pointless telling everybody where Xanadu is if nobody wants to go there. Accordingly, their 'Training and Development Workshops for Manual Workers' aimed in part to assist manual workers to 'regain some of the confidence and aspirations which had been drained by traditional attitudes and assumptions about manual workers' abilities' (<u>Training for Change - The GLC's Equal Opportunities and Positive Action Training Programme</u>, GLC, 1986. Available from the ILEA Equal Opportunities Unit). I should say at this stage that I make no apology for citing the GLC so often in this chapter: the reasons are (i) that their recurrent education policy was outstanding in conception and delivery and (ii) that I am very familiar with it.

Now, restoring people's confidence is not achieved by wishing very hard. It is done by putting on special courses explicitly aimed at teaching useful skills, implicitly aimed at reconstructing confidence and optimism. These are quite often given names like:

* 'Assertiveness Training';
* 'Interviewing Techniques';
* 'Applying for Jobs'.

A proportion of such courses can advantageously be restricted to 'normally excluded' groups, such as women, blacks and the disabled.

Other kinds of course have been developed with the aim of assisting workers with yet other problems: the Trade Union Education and Skills Project (commonly known as 'Workbase') has put on scores of 'Basic Skills' courses in several London boroughs and in the University of London. These courses deal with problems with reading and writing and with English as a Second or Foreign Language.

Not only do Workbase's courses aim 'to give people confidence and independence in dealing with the varieties of written material'; they set the learning process in what is known and most familiar to the students by 'considering students' concerns as GLC employees ... clarifying workplace procedures; looking at written material at the workplace; the GLC and what it does; and the organisation of their department'. Very similar courses for manual workers in the University of London also make a feature of giving advice, information and counselling about follow-up courses in local Adult Education Institutes.

Attempts at quantifying the effectiveness of any form of education can be pretty invidious. It is nonetheless worth reporting some of the remarkable successes in certain GLC courses:

* Manual Workers' Courses: 'O' level passes and successful applications for clerical jobs;
* Women's Courses: traineeships as Customer Support Analysts;
* Courses for Deaf Staff: participation on First Steps to Management course;
* 'Second Chance' Courses: technician traineeships with day release to study for BTEC Certificates or Diplomas; staff accepted to study for Association of Accounting Technician examinations; innumerable internal promotions and acceptances on degree courses.

Some of the courses referred to above dealt with transferring to quite different work, sometimes crossing traditional frontiers of gender and race. (The rich panoply of assumptions and prejudices about exactly which people are unsuitable/ unsuited for a particular kind of job is itself enough to deter all but the most determined from applying for training). The GLC's 'Adult Trainee-ships' (particularly suitable for women) boasted spectacular success: the courses were a mix of in-house and further education college training, on-site supervision by GLC staff, and culminated in examinations set by the appropriate nationally-recognised Boards:

* Electrical Installation - 12 traineeships (of whom 11 were women);
* Painting and Decorating: 13 traineeships (all women);
* Carpentry: 4 traineeships (all women).

Equally successful were schemes to train women as firefighters and Heavy Goods Vehicle drivers. Also, similarly encouraging results emerged from career development courses designed for Asian and Afro-Caribbean staff.

A brief word is needed here about how the actual and potential students of such courses were 'discovered'. Quite simply, it could never have been achieved without extensive outreach work: this facet of recurrent education is well expressed in a report from another London organisation (the Lee Centre, Goldsmiths' College):

> not merely the printed leaflet, poster and advertisement, but staff time spent in talk-ing, listening to and encouraging individual and grouped women and men about their own potential powers to participate in, and decide, their own courses of learning.

It is worth remembering that manual workers (and most other support staff) have a poor opinion of students and of academic staff, and are gener-ally not impressed by the educational activities that they service. It is not altogether surpris-ing, therefore, if they are less than enthusiastic about participating in these activities. Any agency contemplating doing such courses would be well advised to work closely with the official! - and do so before commencing negotiations with the employer.

Finally, what about the course tutors them-selves? For one thing, they must be prepared, and able, to enable the students to develop their own potential. It is also important that as many good 'rôle models' as possible should figure among these teachers, for example women tutors on women's courses. An ex-NUPE Branch Secretary tells the illuminating story of how he would gain some immediate acceptance at the beginning of the first session when he could announce that, although he was now studying at Ruskin College, Oxford, he had previously been employed as a low-paid porter/cleaner.

Having set up courses that people actually want, and filled them with the right people, and got good tutors, it would be foolish to imagine that nothing else needs to be done.

For one thing, the students need to be made to 'feel special' - 'course lunches' have always proved very popular (they also make a nice contrast to the regular perquisites conventionally accorded to more 'senior' staff). Sometimes the support needs to be more specific: the GLC thoughtfully appointed a 'Counsellor for Women in Non-traditional Areas' for pastoral/counselling work.

The location of the courses is important, too. It should obviously be convenient for the students: an advantage about training organised in conjunction with the employer, particularly a large employer, is that there will probably be facilities available on-site; alternatively, it might be considered an advantage to be away from the workplace and from the pressures associated with it.

Arrangements also need to be made for disabled students: disabled access to the building and to the various facilities is just beginning to be thought of; less common is an acknowledgement of the needs of, say, students with impaired hearing or sight.

As far as time of day is concerned, it is self-evident that certain times are extremely inconvenient (for example, for people with domestic responsibilities). Attention also needs to be paid to people who get (paid) release from work to attend, but who may have to run the gauntlet of resentment from colleagues as well as having to fit the work left undone into the previous or following day. The GLC had the foresight to open a special 'central fund' to pay for, amongst other things, extra hours to do the 'cover' work for staff attending the courses.

A crèche, too, is something without which some

aspects of recurrent education will never get off
the ground, and ideally it is very close by, so
that parents can visit their children with the
minimum disruption to their studies. It should
not, however, be allowed to turn into some obscure,
reified facility at the end of a corridor: creche
workers should have the chance to make a contribution to the institution's educational philosophy.
The same may be said for all other support services
staff, such as portering, cleaning and catering
workers. Student unions also need better funding
in order to be able to assist individual students
in particular areas; perhaps more crucially, recurrent education students need formal representation
on the governing bodies of the institutions where
they study.

We all want trade union members to be encouraged to put recurrent education on their personal
agendas. However, trade unions themselves pay
little more than lip service, for the most part.
The Trades Union Congress, with its position papers
(e.g. Priorities in Continuing Education) and its
ill-fated Education Alliance, has failed to make
any wide-ranging impact mainly because the policy
has confined itself to arguing for more access to
education facilities instead of also re-thinking
the content and objectives of existing and potential courses (see also Action: Education; a TUC
Guide for Trade Unionists, TUC, May 1983).

There may be some mileage in the ideas underlying the Labour Party's 1983 General Election
pledge of a 'universal entitlement' to one year's
full-time education with full financial support for
everyone who is over the age of 18 and has not had
any full-time education since the age of 16 (see
Education after 18: Expansion without Change,
Labour Party, 1982). But all of this will be
nothing other than an unhappy cosmetic exercise
without the very toughest statutory backing for
working people to have time off work with no loss
of pay or any worsening of conditions of employment.

They say that nothing as important as education should be left to educationists; at all
events, recurrent education gains qualitatively by
being community-based: in this respect, local
organisations serving young people, the unemployed,
migrant communities and the like need to participate in the whole scheme. There would also be
considerable advantages to be derived from a link-

up between the LEA and such local state, public and national agencies as Departments of Social Services and the National Health Service.

For as long as the system is top-down, it will not make the desired-for impact on the shopfloor. For as long as recurrent education is to all intents and purposes directed by outsiders (no matter how clever and perceptive and well-intentioned we might be), it will continue to be viewed as something impenetrable or suspect, or just plain alien.

The slow appearance of workplace-based study groups, and of pioneering techniques such as distance learning, is truly exciting. We need to get into the business of creating the conditions in which the system can be handed over to the customers. Less an umbilical cord, more a Gordian Knot.

## References

ACACE 1982, Basic Skills, Leicester, Advisory Council for Adult and Continuing Education.
GLC 1986, Training for Change - The GLC's Equal Opportunities and Posititve Action Programme, London, Greater London Council.
LP 1982, Education after 18: Expansion without Change, London, The Labour Party.
TUC 1983, Action: Education, a TUC Guide for Trade Unionists, London, Trades Unions Congress.

## 21. EDUCATIONAL GUIDANCE SERVICES IN ACTION

Dorothy Eagleson and Mabel McGowan

## Northern Ireland's Place in History

Basically, 'guidance' in education is the presentation of knowledge, information and/ or advice to individuals or groups in a structured way so as to provide sufficient material upon which they may base choice or decisions. Counselling in education may be described as the interaction developing through the relationship between a counsellor and a person in a temporary state of indecision, confusion or distress, which helps that individual to make his own decision and choices, to resolve his confusion or cope with his distress in a personally realistic and meaningful way, having consideration for creative and practical needs and for the likely consequences of his behaviour.

(Hoxter 1981)

The theory and practice of vocational guidance go back to shortly after the First World War. By the nineteen sixties it was accepted by schools, colleges and universities that students should be encouraged to explore their future careers, and the Careers Service throughout the British Isles had developed to a degree which, while dependent on local interest, and the amount of financial support available, indicated that the need for a planned and sophisticated approach was generally accepted. Careers or vocational guidance subsumed a degree of educational guidance, since subject choice was obviously crucial, but it was only with the development of adult education provision and the concept of recurrent or continuing education

227

that the idea that anyone returning to study after an interval might need some help began to become part of educational thinking. For teachers of adults it was evident that lack of earlier <u>educational</u> guidance was often responsible for the number of mature students knocking on doors seeking information, and, very often, guidance about the opportunities open to them.

'Brokerage' agencies had been in existence in the United States for some years, educational institutions and voluntary providers in Europe were more informally responding to adult enquirers and good teachers of adults building a degree of guidance into their courses, but there was little in the way of a more planned approach. But in 1967, in Northern Ireland, the Council of Social Service agreed, at the request of the Clement Wilson Foundation (a charity which had already helped finance a number of vocational guidance projects in the UK) to act as the sponsoring body for what was initially called an Adult <u>Vocational</u> Guidance Service. This acknowledged the need identified by the Careers Service, which was receiving an increasing number of requests for information and guidance from adults to which it had neither time nor resources to respond adequately. However, it was soon evident that the majority of clients of the new Service were seeking educational guidance, at least initially: for many, a job or career depended on acquiring educational qualifications at various levels, and their original aims would often be modified in the light of educational experience.

Once the Service was renamed Educational Guidance Service for Adults a new constituency of clients came forward, including people with literacy problems, or learning difficulties, and others looking for interesting leisure pursuits or ways to spend retirement or to improve their ability to help their children, as well as those hoping to use their learning to enhance career prospects. By the early 1970s it was clear that the Service was meeting a real educational need.

In 1977 the first significant international move to put adult educational guidance on the continuing education agenda (prompted by the International Round Table for the Advancement of Counselling, which had for several years considered educational counselling topics at its biennial conferences), was made by UNESCO, which, with the University of Southern California, sponsored a

seminar with participants from all over the world
(Europe being represented by Northern Ireland and
Germany). They, working on a discussion document
written by Dr Paul Bertleson of UNESCO, produced a
Report (University of Southern California 1977)
which is still of first importance for anyone working in or interested in definitions, theory, practice and development of adult educational guidance.
This was followed by a special edition of the
International Review of Education (1977) which
chronicled recent developments.

The European Bureau of Adult Education organised a conference on Information Guidance and Counselling Services (EBAE 1981). Four years later in
Britain, the Venables Report (OU 1976) had stressed
the importance of guidance in adult education.
Following this there was some interest from Trades
Unions, universitites and a few politicians, and by
1980 about fifty Services were in existence in the
British Isles (many at least partly sponsored by
the Open University), though several initiated in
the seventies were only to survive for a short time
- a general hazard, as there was no firm national
base, often local goodwill rather than adequate
resources, and no secure funding.

A working group to explore needs and developments was set up by the Association of Recurrent
Education, which had stressed the needs of adults
for information and guidance since its inception in
1975. This lead eventually to the formation of the
National Association of Educational Guidance Services (NAEGS).

Despite the general acceptance of the need,
and the examples of what had been done by existing
Services, formal acknowledgement by Government came
only when at the 1984 ARE Conference the Under
Secretary of State, Peter Brooke, said:

> One of these topics which seems to us to
> merit further examination is the question of
> educational guidance and information for
> adults. Since the Advisory Council high-
> lighted the importance of this subject in
> their report 'Links to Learning' interest
> has tended to focus largely on the develop-
> ment of independent Educational Guidance
> Services for Adults of which there are now
> about 50. I greatly welcome these develop-
> ments and the establishment of the National
> Association which has recently been formed.

The National Institute of Adult Continuing Education had consistently promoted the need for Educational Guidance Services for Adults (EGSAs). Although the Government did not renew the remit for the Advisory Council for Adult and Continuing Education, which had demonstrated its interest by publishing two reports, Links to Learning and Case Studies in Educational Guidance for Adults, when the replacement Unit for the Development of Adult Continuing Education was established its first development group was given the task of preparing Helping Adults to Learn. This elicited a large number of responses, which were used in compiling the final report - The Challenge of Change (NIAE 1986). This makes recommendations for the development of educational guidance networks and the establishment or development of local units with the following functions:

- disseminating information about guidance and the network;
- management of information about learning opportunities;
- staff development for guidance workers in all agencies;
- monitoring the range and quality of the service;
- feedback to providers of learning opportunities;
- promotion of guidance, and of education and training;
- servicing of co-ordinating and managing bodies.

In addition to carrying out these co-ordinating and support functions it suggests 'we believe that the Unit should be a direct provider of the full range of guidance activities' and recommends a national unit to:

- gather and disseminate information about good practice in educational guidance for adults;
- provide consultancy support to local and regional guidance providers;
- advise central government on national educational guidance needs, and on ways of meeting them;
- develop and promote techniques for monitoring the quality of the service;

- co-ordinate, sponsor and contribute to the training of educational guidance workers;
- sponsor innovative work and research;
- raise public awareness of educational guidance;
- provide a forum for the agencies concerned with the development of educational guidance, at national, regional and local level.

The need for guidance has been emphasised by the establishment of a number of agencies concerned mainly with information on the provision for continuing education - Educational Counselling and Credit Transfer Information Service, PICKUP, the Open Tech, the Council for Educational Technology Learning Links project, aspects of the work of the Further Education Unit; all these point to the advantage of co-ordination and the kind of central unit suggested in The Challenge of Change.

From the perspective of the eighteen years of experience of the Northern Ireland Service, the brief historical summary given above - and much has been omitted - is both satisfactory and disappointing. It is satisfactory in that the importance of educational guidance for adults is now nationally and internationally recognised; disappointing in that it has taken nearly twenty years for this to happen and that so much good effort has in the meantime come to grief.

In Northern Ireland, the Service had its Government funding withdrawn when the Minister of Education of the day thought that such matters were more properly the business of the five Education & Library Boards (local education authorities), a belief not, apparently, shared by the Boards, only one of the five setting up a service, which closed in 1984. EGSA survived its difficulties because of pressure, local, national and international, from referrers, clients, voluntary organisations, and not least the Association for Recurrent Education, which lent its name and goodwill at a crucial moment, and whose then President, Gerry Fowler, made it a parliamentary issue. The Jackson Report (1979), produced by the committee set up by the Minister as a result of that pressure, made it clear that such Services were essential and should be developed (Appendix).

The basic recommendation that EGSA should continue was accepted by the Department of Education (Northern Ireland) and funding restored, but

despite continuing representations no further
development took place: this is particularly ironic
in that the Northern Ireland experience and expertise was recognised when the organiser was invited
to serve on the UDACE Development Group, charged
with discussing possible developments in England
and Wales. In March 1986, however, the Northern
Ireland Council for Continuing Education announced
an enquiry into local provision: the outcome will
not be known before the publication of the present
volume.

The Northern Ireland experience has left those
involved with certain convictions about educational
guidance services: the UNESCO report (1981) suggested that:

> a comprehensive centre ... may be operated
> by an existing adult education body, such as
> a national association, a university insti-
> tute, or some other central agency. How-
> ever, in some cases it will be desirable to
> establish such a centre as an independent
> information and counselling service for
> adults, maintaining close contact and co-
> operation with all adult education agencies
> but remaining administratively autonomous.

EGSA would assent to this: to be separate from
the providers and not under pressure from any
particular interest, and to be seen to be so by
referrers and clients, is essential, and also helps
to ensure guaranteed confidentiality. It is vital
to be part of a network, not only in the obvious
area of adult continuing education, but in that of
the social services, voluntary and statutory, and
to be recognised as an impartial information/advice
centre in the same way as Citizens' Advice Bureaux
and Law Centres, to take two examples. It is
equally vital that clients be aware that a Service
has an advocacy role, and that the local experience
of staff and their demonstrable professional competence should make suggestions about additional or
modified provision acceptable to the providers.

For the individual, access to objective tests,
which can reassure uncertain adults about their
academic potential or assess why someone is having
difficulty with reading, has been shown to be very
important, and the Northern Ireland Service believes such a facility is essential.

Finally, the importance of the information-giving role cannot be overstressed - it is vital that clients can be assured of being given accurate, complete, up-to-date and appropriate information; everything else depends on this, and the most experienced guidance workers can do considerable damage if they are not competent in information-giving. The question of counselling cannot be discussed here, but EGSA offers clients continuing support for those who wish it, and to do this effectively Services must have full-time staff, available when needed by clients, and with professional training.

EGSA now is an independent voluntary organisation, grant-aided by the Department of Education for Northern Ireland up to 90%, but having to find the rest of its income elsewhere, thereby ensuring its independence. This is achieved partly by providing and disseminating back-up material for television and radio programmes, which are becoming of increasing importance in adult education, and by offering a consultative service to several other organisations.

A vital part of the Service's acceptance is support from the local community, and the independence of its Management Committee, members of which are representative of, but do not directly represent, various educational and voluntary social service interests.

The UDACE discussion document suggested that 'if adults are to make the best use of these opportunities, in order to contribute to society (in paid or voluntary roles) and to lead satisfying lives, they need comprehensive information about what is available and guidance to help them to make appropriate choices'. One section has the heading A National Strategy. That this is now seen as an important matter of public discussion is in itself a satisfying outcome for the Association for Recurrent Education, whose concern for proper information and guidance to be available has been constant and pressing: within the next decade perhaps the expansion of Services will at least partially match the increasing needs of adult learners.

## Current Issues in the Practice of Adult Guidance

The following areas of good practice in EGCA organisation have emerged from discussion in the National Association of Educational Guidance Services (NAEGS):

1) Availability to all.
2) Impartiality.
3) Range of information provision.
4) Adequacy and source of funding.
5) Staff development.
6) Links with other agencies.

## Availability to all

This can be seen first in terms of _intent_ on the part of an EGSA. We welcome all sections of the community at every educational level as client enquirers, and participants in counselling interviews. This means men, women, unemployed, handicapped, elderly, ethnic group members, offenders in prison or on probation, long-term hospital patients, poor and homeless as well as those who may perhaps be classified as belonging to the so-called normal-average range. Any one of these may be seeking basic literacy or numeracy; or first tentative steps in 'return to learning', or assessed further education courses in specific study areas, or degree studies in higher education, often preceded by preparation to qualify for entry upon such course, or post-graduate or higher degree studies to meet a personal challenge or up-grade professional qualifications.

Many locational or timing factors may nullify the intent. A counselling base in an inaccessible location, or open at inappropriate times can be self-selective. Some city centre locations provide major parking problems and a rural setting may be totally inaccessible to the non-car owner. At the same time 'business' hours may exclude the employed whilst a polytechnic site location may scare away the illiterate.

Timing and placing of publicity are another aspect of the same issue. For this purpose inexpensive advertisement in a local free newspaper delivered weekly into all homes is useful. So too is a breaking-down of the public into a wide-ranging pattern of target groups; it may be best to reach the elderly through packs of leaflets in sub-post offices on pension days; the house-wife through contact slips at supermarket check-outs on Fridays and Saturdays; the reader through leaflets and posters at library counters. Such target-aiming produces a controlled response. Similarly, the 'drop-in shop' may pick up those who fight shy of completing a form, appending a signature and engaging in making and keeping an appointment.

## Impartiality

The word 'impartial' may bear more than one meaning, but 'not favouring one more than another' accommodates our objective and can walk hand-in-hand with the intention of availability to all. So Peter Jones, the unemployed baker who needs to move from addition to subtraction, to division from multiplication, is entitled to neither more nor less time than Dr Susan Grey, the immigrant without English educational qualifications, who seeks a change of career. Both have a background story to tell. Both have sunk pride or mustered courage in making a decision to come to us.

So then a good counsellor will have at his/her fingertips route directions to a numeracy tutor as well as to a careers guidance office and will him/herself be learning encouraging, supportive and calming behaviour towards the shy, the pessimistic, the self-deprecatory, the excitable and over-enthusiastic, and well-spoken, the clumsy and the unfortunate - to name but a few of the qualities and characteristics a counselling client may present. All this is a matter of human understanding and non-prejudicial response.

## Range of information provision

The aim is to have information available and at one's fingertips or to know where to find it. The alternative is the same as that open to the teacher who may disseminate his/her own knowledge and learning, or may teach the class how and where to find out for themselves. The first course is speedy and effective, to the limits of a teacher/counsellor's own awareness and learning. The second is slower, may require individual effort, and will teach development and use of initiative and open up realms beyond the facilitator's level of achievement.

The good counsellor will be able to use one or the other method well. He/she may be capable of both and ready to change the approach according to the circumstances. Such flexibility could be an important aspect of good practice.

We have studied one North of England service where the supply of wide-ranging information in tangible material form is incomparable - sectionalised, classified, multiple copies of everything and a member of staff available and approachable. This is to be admired. It is a system which can well be used in a library, specific counsellors responding to requests with push-button speed, accuracy and appropriate information on every step of the educational ladder.

We all try in our own ways to send a client away with a mutual smile, a selection of appropriate knowledge and guidance towards acquiring more, the opportunity to talk at home about it with wife or friend and the confidence to choose between alternatives, knowing he can come back and be welcomed in two or three weeks time, having made or being close to making his own decision. There is however no one right way to do it.

Course provision changes, because of both demand and resource availability. Keeping up with the pace of change is an information problem issue in itself. Is this perhaps one of the areas where we might gain by sharing the changing information between the services in a region? Some are currently engaged in setting up the machinery for carrying out such an exercise. Others, working on a national scale, plan to draw on the services of computer technology. We cannot however all yet draw upon such provision.

## Adequacy and source of funding

Differences in funding reflect variation in starting positions and in the degree of official utilisation. Few of us would claim adequate funding, yet most would be reticent if asked to produce a desired budget. What however do we need?

1) Staff.
2) Premises.
3) The apparatus and mechanism to carry communication.
4) Regular access to up-to-date literature on educational opportunity and provision for the not-so-young.
5) Loose cash to buy a stamp or a book, provide coffee or lunch for a formal guest, pay a subscription or meet an urgent need.

So who provides all these? A local education authority showing unusual eagerness to utilise the service? A college or polytechnic whether sharing the dream or recognising the value to itself of a student supply? The Manpower Services Commission,

with its own range of problems, tied to time
limits, and geared to the production of semi-
trained personnel for non-existent employment?
Counselling charges, rare, and difficult to harness
in par with impartiality and avaiability to all?
The begging-bowl, collecting a little from here and
some from there? (Skill in its handling may be
neither unproductive nor undignified, but the piper
may find himself playing a complex tune). Nowhere?
And does that inevitably mean insecurity, breakdown, or the use of volunteers? The freedom to
realise the dream is then in jeopardy.

## Staff development

The problem of staff development is closely
linked with questions of training, of who trains,
who needs training, who is prepared to list the
skills and the knowledge required, where and when
and for how long, of whether assessment should be
included, and of who pays.

Will adult education counselling sicken and
die whilst counsellors are engaged in training
counsellors or being trained? A non-rhetorical and
important question is this: 'Are the necessary
skills inborn or can they be learned?' Does education provide the answer? Is education drawing out
or leading out of what is present in embryo, and
will come to life in the hands of a skilful mid-
wife?

## Links with other agencies

We need a network of mutual support and co-
operation, to be able to dial the Careers Guidance
Officer with the client present and be able to open
easily with, 'Peter, it's Margaret. I have a
client here, can I put him on to you?' There is a
good chance then that the triangle will be productive.

Again, a few years ago there was much discussion about the 'advocacy role', and here the
network again facilitates. 'Robin, I have a young
man with a grant problem. How can we help him?
Listen ...'. That young man and his young family
will not starve whilst he learns.

Or, 'Mr Hughes, the Manager at the Job Centre
tells me he could place up to two dozen of his
unemployed if they could have a good quality crash
computer programming course provided for them and

completed by Christmas. Could you manage an Easter start with a good teacher? I can guarantee your numbers'. That Principal would sooner wait until September but all of us, he included, are learning to trust the other modes on the network. He will be proud of a healthy 6 month old class by September.

A nationwide carpet of accurate information provision about educational opportunities in the post-school years, available at every educational level and to all social classes of any creed, colour or political affiliation, is a dream which increasing numbers of guidance tutors are engaged in converting into reality. Those of us who are members of NAEGS are doing so with a missionary zeal. To date we have scattered rugs on the earth and flagstones, but here and there they are beginning to overlap and to simulate total carpet cover.

For the EGSAs need help, through recognition in our own areas that what we are attempting is right and good and worthwhile; through recognition on a national scale of the same values to be developed in the 'uncarpeted' areas; through grant-aid to our endeavours to improve our weaknesses and overcome our shortcomings. This will help us to attract others to co-operate in our work, either by joining us or by attaching their own concerns to the same networks for the benefit of every adult seeking post-school opportunities, whether formal classes or community activities, and using us to find what they seek if it exists or to work for its initiation if it does not.

## References

ACACE 1979, <u>Links to Learning</u>, Leicester, Advisory Council
for Adult and Continuing Education.

ACACE 1984, <u>Case Studies in Educational Guidance for Adults</u>,
Leicester, Advisory Council for Adult and Continuing
Education.

Butler, L. (ed) 1985, <u>Educational Guidance: A New Service
for Adult Learners</u> (2nd edn), Milton Keynes, The Open
University.

Charnley, A., Osborn, M., and Withnall, A., <u>Educational
Information, Advice, Guidance and Counselling for Adults</u>,
Review of Existing Research in Adult and Continuing Educa-
tion, Volume VI.

EBAE 1981, <u>Report: The Development of Information, Guidance
and Counselling Services</u>, European Bureau of Adult Education.

HMSO 1979, <u>Report of An Enquiry into Educational Guidance
for Adults in Northern Ireland</u>, (The Jackson Report),
Department of Education for Northern Ireland, London, Her
Majesty's Stationery Office.

Hoxter, H. 1981, <u>The Forms, Methods and Techniques of
Vocational and Educational Guidance</u>, International Case
Studies, Paris, United Nations Economic, Social and
Cultural Organisation (UNESCO).

International Review of Education 1977, Vol.XXIII, No. 4.

Ironside, D. 1981, <u>Models for Counselling Adult Learners</u>,
Toronto, Ontario Institute for Studies in Education.

Ironside, D. 1982, <u>Adult Learners in Three Countries:
Models for Counselling Services</u>, International Journal for
the Advancement of Counselling.

NIACE 1985, <u>Helping Adults to Learn</u>, Unit for the
Development of Adult Continuing Education, Leicester,
National Institute for Adult Continuing Education.

NIACE 1986, <u>The Challenge of Change</u>, Unit for the
Development of Adult Continuing Education, Leicester,
National Institute for Adult Continuing Education.

OU 1976, <u>Report of the Commitee on Continuing Education</u>,
(The Venables Report), Milton Keynes, The Open University.

University of Southern California 1977, <u>International
Symposium on Ways and Means of Strengthening Information
and Counselling Services for Adult Learners</u>, University of
Southern California.

Appendix

## Educational Guidance for Adults in Northern Ireland

Report of an Enquiry set up by Lord Melchett, Minister of State, 1979, London, HMSO, (Jackson Committee).

### Summary of Main Recommendations

### General

i) Educational guidance for adults should be accepted as a normal, necessary and permanent education service (para 88).

ii) The Department of Education's Estimates should make specific provision for the service in Northern Ireland (para 89).

iii) Plans should be made initially for a four-fold expansion of present adult education guidance facilities within a five-year period (paras 81,91).

iv) The service should be made accessible to adults in all parts of the Province and be organised as a network of fairly small units (paras 51,81).

v) There should be freedom to experiment with means of improving the service (paras 55, 73,74).

vi) There should be diversity of provision, giving an element of consumer choice, and not a service operated exclusively by area boards (paras 31,87).

vii) The service must be client-orientated and should cater for all adults aged 18 or over (paras 62,63).

viii) The service should maintain close contact with the Employment Service (para 71).

ix) Special attention should be given to areas in which the take-up of educational facilities generally is low and to the needs of disadvantaged or handicapped people (paras 47,52).

x) The normal running costs of the service should be met from public funds and clients should not be charged a fee (paras 68,85).

## 22. EDUCATION FOR ADULTS: A MULTI-CULTURAL DIMENSION

Jean Jackson

> Racism is not only a permanent structural, ideological and political feature of British Society, but it is also a permanent feature of our educational system in general.
>
> Chris Mullard, (1979)

Britain has traditionally been a multi-cultural society made up of diverse national cultures - English, Welsh, Scottish and Irish. Historically, 'settlers' from the Norman and Saxon periods and Jewish immigrants at the end of the last century and again with the Poles, Spaniards, Italians, Hungarians in the first half of this century along with others from the 'White' Commonwealth, have been absorbed into the society, or should they choose to do so, remained culturally distinct.

The change in the immigration pattern of black people (racially distinct groups) from the 'New' Commonwealth after the Second World War is the dimension that has brought the issue of multi-culturalism into sharp focus and their 'visibility' has made them vulnerable in personal and institutional terms.

The present ethnic composition of Britain is, as in many other contemporary societies, varied. That is, multi-cultural, multi-ethnic, multi-faith, multi-language.

## Policies

Throughout the world in countries where there are minorities and different racial mixtures within the national borders demanding or requiring political and educational recognition, Governments have adopted different policies. These policies can be categorized:

i) <u>Integration</u> as in America, France, Australia and in Canada, where immigrants are encouraged through language and education to integrate into mainstream society. Further, in the early 70s the Canadian Government appointed a Minister of State for Multi-culturalism, set up a Multi-culturalism Directorate and also the Canadian Charter of Rights and Freedom explicitly enshrining the rights and freedom against discrimination, based on national or ethnic origin, race, colour, religion, sex, age or physical or mental disability as part of the basic ethic of Canadian society.

ii) <u>Recognition</u> as in the Soviet Union, India and China where the various nationalities, cultures and languages are recognised and given equality of status within the constitution.

iii) <u>Unification</u> as a means of bringing together the various groups and peoples through the medium of a national language of instruction and where cultural pluralism, as in Singapore, is encouraged.

iv) There is also the <u>laissez-faire</u> or <u>non-recognition</u> or <u>ad-hoc</u> approach as in Britain where no official policy is adopted and where policy statements tend to be made by Government in response to problems and needs as and when they arise.

Although successive Governments since the 1950s have issued statements and legislation on race and immigration, the first major policy statement on education was made in 1966 by Roy Jenkins, who advocated a policy of 'equal opportunity, accompanied by cultural diversity, in an atmosphere of mutual trust'. This aim has yet to be realised in educational provision at all levels. Some steps have been taken, but they have not kept pace with the rapid demographic·and technological changes in society and problems continue to occur. The lack of an official policy, in a de-centralised system of education, leaves local education authorities (LEAs) to adopt and/or implement statements of policy according to their interpretation, local requirements and considerations. As a result, there is wide variation in the quality and direction of approaches across the country.

A survey in 1982 (Mullard, Bonnick and King, 1983) showed that 36 of the LEAS in the U.K. have issued policies. In the Inner London Education Authority (ILEA) (one of the fore-runners) the first policy statement (1977) and progress report (1979) were mainly about the school sectors and after consultations, in 1983, the authority published Vols. 1-5 of its Race, Sex and Class series of documents, of which Vols. 3, 4 and 5 are relevant to the post-school sector.

## Beyond ethno-centricity

The curriculum is 'a selection from the culture' (Lawson, 1973). In a multi-cultural society the question to be asked is - whose culture?

The ethnic and cultural diversity of British society has serious implications for education and the erosion of ethno-centricity from the school curriculum and all other sectors of the system should be a fundamental aim.

If we accept that an aim of education is to prepare children to live in the rapidly changing world of tomorrow, could we afford to maintain an education system that is based on an ethno-centric mentality and a curriculum that remains 'essentialist'? (Holmes, 1979). Is intellectual development another aim of education? Then surely, teachers have a responsibility to help and encourage the discovery of truth and movement beyond prejudice, ignorance and the notions of racial and cultural superiority which are re-inforced by a system of education whose foundation remains ethno-centric. Further, given the changes taking place in society and the inter-dependent world we now live in, 'usefulness' also becomes an important aim.

## Recurrent education

Since the late 1960s many educationists in OECD member countries have been putting forward 'Lifelong', 'Continuing', 'Permanent' or 'Recurrent' Education as the solution to the problem of the inadequacies of the educational systems.

This Association (see Mitchell, 1982) defines recurrent education as 'a comprehensive educational strategy including all levels of education provision'. Its essential characteristic is the distribution of educational opportunity throughout the life span of the individual as opposed to the traditional pattern of education provision in which the majority of formal education is experienced in

243

the first 25 years of life.

In a London Association for Comparative Education occasional paper, Kallen (1980) calls it a 'paradigm or an organisational principle ... a distribution of opportunities for learning over a person's life time in accordance with their needs and motivation'. He goes on to say 'it is not a panacea' ... but 'it holds promise ...'.

In Britain, despite the acknowledged inadequacies of and crisis in the present system of education, the repairs, additions, and adjustments that are continually being made to the front-end model are moving the system more to an adult continuing concept than a recurrent education concept.

The evidence continues to show that the British education system is failing black (and working class) children. The difficulties and experiences of ethnic minorities in the school system are well documented and more and more school leavers are looking to further and adult continuing education for courses which are of value to them, and would allow them to mix education and training with work.

## Multi-culturalism in adult/continuing education

### i) Multi-cultural/Ethnic Education

Despite the amount that has been written over the past decade about the subject, there is still no consensus on a definition for multi-cultural/ ethnic education. For me, multi-ethnic education suggests ideally, a form of education suitable for a population in which there are a number of diverse ethnic strands and where no ethnic strand is dominant and neither is any inferior. It pre-supposes the elimination of racist and similar tendencies in educational theory and it also assumes the development of awareness not only of diversity but the value of diversity and a determination to develop it.

The bulk of the literature on multi-cultural/ ethnic education addresses itself to the school sector, but much of it is equally applicable to the post-compulsory sector. Where described, approaches and courses are still 'peripheral', 'ad-hoc' and 'tacked on'. Steel bands, dressing up in national costumes, ethnic dance and cultural evenings are some of the activities put forward as good practice both in schools and in adult education.

## ii) Adult Education Objectives and Provision

In adult education, as well as in schools, the general response has been an attempt to meet language needs but relatively few resources have been devoted to meeting the other special needs. ACACE in the report, 'Basic Education for Adults' (1979) stated there is a 'tendency to stereotype the needs of the immigrant adult to basic English Language learning and to neglect other needs'. The Russell Report also warned against the 'adoption of a blanket approach to the needs of the disadvantaged' ('disadvantaged' as used in the Report).

The ILEA policy document Vol. 5 in the Race, Sex and Class series sets out the objectives of the work in further, higher and community education as follows:

> The Authority recognises that every aspect of the education which it provides must fully reflect the multi-ethnic character of London's population, if it is to be equally accessible to, and effective for, the whole population. It is also un-equivocally opposed to racism and racial discrimination. Every aspect of the Authority's work needs to be examined in order both to eliminate racial discrimination and the effects of racisim and to promote effective multi-ethnic education.

Provision in adult education for ethnic minorities has focused mainly on English as a Second Language (ESL). ESL provision/schemes were developed in response to the arrival of the East African Asians in Britain in the late 1960s. This group presented adult education with a challenge in terms of language teaching, and provision for rapid acquisition of language skills was perceived as a 'panacea'. Many saw language barriers as the real obstacle to progress and assimilation into British society.

Over the past two decades, the model of assimilation has gradually been discarded and changes in the degree of 'integration' are reflected in current thinking and provision. Students are actively encouraged to 'use' ESL classes as a springboard to mainstream adult and further education.

Ethnic minority adults are looking to adult

education to provide courses leading to basic skill acquisition, English, numeracy, access and pre-access courses. Apart from adult education, there are the further education colleges and the poly-technics in the post-school sector and all in all, the changes, provision and curricula to meet ethnic minority needs have been largely piecemeal, ad-hoc and fragmental.

The Further Education Unit (FEU) Interim Report (September, 1985) states:

> It is the ordinary adult worker who normally finds it the most difficult to get into the existing structure of vocational qualifica-tions ... the problems and limitations are well known and the sheer complexity of the system is daunting to those who are uncer-tain of what they could be doing and of their ability to do it.

In the case of ethnic minorities, these are further compounded by language difficulties, dis-crimination and low educational achievements.

The adult education sector is often the most accessible part of the education service for minor-ities and its responsive tradition makes it an obvious vehicle for some of the solutions being proposed to meet the adult population needs; yet it remains relatively under-used. Adult education could be the bridge to other forms of education not only for the ethnic minority groups but for the ethnic majority as well. It could offer an alter-native route, a second chance, and it could also be a way in which a reconciliation between the divi-sions and demands of non-vocational and vocational courses can be effected.

At a time when technology is making those who are unskilled and unemployed almost unemployable and when the increasing complexity of social organisation requires rising personal standards of competence in response to change, a more comprehen-sive institutional framework needs to be developed to assess and analyse the varied and wide needs of the adult population in general and the ethnic minorities in particular.

Equally, in continuing discussion on the issues of paid education leave, distant and inde-pendent learning, adult/vocational training, and access, the implication for and the needs of minor-ity groups cannot be ignored.

## Teacher Education

Since 1972, the major focus of research activities at the UNESCO Institute of Education have been Lifelong Education and its implication for schools, including teacher training.

Teacher training and attitude are important in any system of education but they become crucial in a continuing/recurrent system of education for a multi-cultural/ethnic society. A 1973 Report of a Select Committee of the House of Commons noted that students should be made aware that, wherever they teach, they will be doing so in a multi-cultural society. It also proposed specialist courses in race and community relations at Colleges of Education. A decade later, Watkins (1984) points to a survey he conducted which shows:

> at best an unsatisfactory picture regarding the preparation of teachers for working in a multi-ethnic society and at worst an alarming ostrich-like lack of interest.

He goes on to say:

> however much there might be changes in text books and ethno-centric curricula, there is unlikely to be much real improvement in the classroom until changes have begun to take place in teacher education institutes.

Craft and Atkins (1985) write:

> nowhere in England and Wales can a graduate in ethnic minority community languages obtain an appropriate training for teaching.

Despite the many policy documents, reports and recommendations, the evidence shows that initial teacher training institutions have remained relatively inactive and reluctant to respond to the needs of schools and society. In the past, changes in the education system have taken long periods to work themselves into practice. Can such leisurely perspectives be afforded?

Some action is required by the Department of Education and Science (DES) and/or the validating universities/agencies to ensure that teachers are equipped to work in the real world.

The 1981 Home Affairs Committee of the House

recommended that every initial teacher training course should be examined by the Council for National Academic Awards to see that it accurately reflects the society in which those who follow the course will be working. It also proposed that all teachers should have at least some initial special-ised training to enable them to perform effectively in a multi-racial classroom.

Again, the focus is on the school, but it is all equally applicable to teachers in the post-compulsory sector, as they too, determine the quality, scope and style of the multi-ethnic educa-tion available to pupils and students in their classrooms. Support for tutors and resources to help tutors to attend in-service training (INSET) must be given.

## Conclusion

In any discussion on education for a diverse, multi-cultural or multi-ethnic society, racism and institutional racism are important issues. Like 'multi-cultural society' and 'multi-ethnic curricu-lum' the term means different things to different people. Where there is agreement is on how it is practised. Racism is not only overt malicious acts of discrimination, but also the deep, subtle preju-dices held and exercised against black people. This 'inferential racism' (Hall, .1980) is mani-fested beyond relationships, infecting policies and institutions.

In terms of educational policies, as already stated earlier in this essay, the DES maintains its policy of 'no policy', but many LEAs have formu-lated local policies, which in a decentralised system, are subject to interpretation by the heads/principals/teachers for implementation in their classrooms. The DES contents itself with giving funds and advice, and the House of Commons with Select Committee Reports, while avoiding the cen-tral issues of race and racism. Comparatively, this is in sharp contrast to the interventionist policies in Canada and the USA.

Cultural diversity is a fact of life in British society and education in this context can-not continue to ignore the issue of race.

The notion of assimilation in the 1960s has given way to integration and cultural pluralism, again a concept that is vague and difficult to define but can be used by dominant groups in society to maintain the status quo and their power position; thus continuing the 'malignant relationship' which is based on a tacit agreement of power/powerless; strong/weak; independent/dependent; helper/helpless.

## References

A Policy for Equality, Vol. 3, ILEA, Race, Sex and Class Series, 1983. Anti-Racist Statement and Guidelines, Vol. 4, ILEA, Race, Sex and Class Series, 1983.

A Strategy for the Basic Education of Adults, ACACE, 1979, para. 24.

Craft, M. and Atkins, M., Teacher Education and Linguistic Diversity: A National Survey, Educational Review, Vol. 37, No. 2, 1985.

FEU Response to the Review of Vocational Education: Interim Report, para. 5, September 1985.

Hall, S., Teaching Race, Multi-racial Education, Vol. 9, No. 1.

Holmes, Brian, (ed) International Guide to Education Systems, IBE/UNESCO, 1979.

Kallen, D., London Association for Comparative Education, Occasional Paper No. 2, 1980.

Lawson, Dennis, Social Change, Education Theory and Curriculum Planning, University of London Press, 1973.

Little, A., Willey, R., Gundara, J., Adult Education and the Black Communities, ACACE, para 23, 1982.

Lynch, James, Human Rights, Racism and the Multi-cultural Curriculum, Educational Review, Vol. 37, No. 2, 1985.

Mitchell, Harry, A Recurrent Education Framework - the Newcastle-upon-Tyne Model, Discussion Paper No. 9, ARE, January 1982.

Mullard, Chris, Racism in Society and Schools: History, Policy and Practice, Occasional Paper, No. 1, University of London Institute of Education, 1979.

Mullard, C., Bonnick, L. and King, B., Racial Policy and Practice: a letter survey; London Race-Relations Policy and Practice Research Unit, 1983.

Multi-Ethnic Education, Joint Report of the Schools and the Further and Higher Education Sub-Committee, November 1977 (ILEA 269).

Multi-Ethnic Education - Progress Report, Joint Report of the Schools and FHE Sub-Committee, June 1979 (ILEA 9196).

Multi-Ethnic Education in Further, Higher and Community Education, Vol. 5, ILEA, Race, Sex and Class Series, 1984.

Watkins, Keith, Training Teachers in the U.K. for a Multicultural Society. The Rhetoric and the Reality, Journal of Multi-lingual and Multi-cultural Development, Vol. 5, No. 5, 1984, January 1982.

## 23. RECURRENT EDUCATION AND ADULT BASIC EDUCATION: A PRACTITIONER'S VIEW

A.D. McMahon

A few years ago, students started coming back to Adult Basic Education (ABE) groups:

When I was here before, I didn't know I'd need the maths.

I needed something to do on Monday mornings now that I'm not working. What have you got?

(These and later quotations are from students in Bradford who have over the years contributed to the practice of ABE through the revelation of their own insights).

Students are using provision recurrently. At that time, it was useful to know that recurrence is part of a view of how education systems ought to work. Adult Basic Education began to see the need to expect repeat use, instead of trying to assemble a tidy package of communication, numeracy and literacy skills that would last students their lives long. A banking concept of ABE is as misleading for adults as it is for children in school. Furthermore,

... a narrow concentration on skills, whether in the three Rs or in so-called 'life-skills', may be seriously misdirected if by that term is meant cognitive and enactive achievements or behavioural objectives externally defined. The starting-point and the guidelines must be found in the potential students' own view of themselves.
(Charnley and Jones, 1979)

Many people in ABE would observe that progress, too, is a matter to be judged by learners:

> I copied out the book. They told me not to,
> but I did. A few weeks later, my wife said,
> 'You're not looking at the book'. I
> realised that I used to do it word for word,
> now I do it five words at a time.

## Designing for recurrency

Expecting to respond to student goals as they
return implies different learning structures and
curricula from those most of us knew as students.
For ABE, designing for recurrency is a struggle
that changes every year, partly because practitioners and participants share an absolute view of
learning, one based on success or failure. Relative success and its satisfactions, the fuels for
future learning, remain as hard to identify and to
validate as ever. Success depends on what happens
in learners' lives and on how their experience has
taught them to judge it.

As illustrated below, people find it easier to
return to ABE if the provision is open in style and
broad-based in content, if their former experience
of learning suited them, and if their own goals
determine what they study:

> If I get this business off the ground, I'll
> have to keep the books. I've got this book
> on accounting. Can we work on it?

> I look around the room and see what other
> people are doing and I say to myself, 'I've
> done that!'

> When I went to the group, I thought 'What
> the hell's this?' It was actually learning
> to think how to write half a page. Before,
> when I was with the home tutor, I told her
> that I wanted to read. I wasn't bothered
> about the writing. She used to slip some
> in, though -- days of the week, things like
> that. I knew how to write, but didn't
> write, and I couldn't read it if I did write
> it down.

This list and set of examples make designing
for recurrency seem much simpler than it is in

practice. Learning basic skills and finding ways
to use them in everyday life is a long and uncom-
fortable process. What educationists call 'the
demands of adult life' create questions to which
there are no educational answers. People who are
learning change their goals as they learn. Success
can go unrecognised, simply because people who've
learned tend to forget that they've done it:

> Oh, I could always read (from a student who
> had come as a non-reader). What I really
> need is the writing.

And there are times when what goes on in ABE
is just not good enough:

> I went to the class for a while. She kept
> asking me what I wanted to work on. I said
> 'Your're the teacher, you tell me'.

Nevertheless, as recurrent systems get built,
the experience ABE has had in dealing with repeated
use may prove valuable. For example, unhurried
receiving of newcomers is essential. Time for chat
that may become counselling is important. Everyone's view of what's on offer must be clear and
often updated -- other learners are often the best
presenters of this information. Whatever planning
system there is must be able to accommodate new
learning requirements quickly and smoothly.
Changes stemming from users' views of what's going
on must be incorporated into provision, and be seen
to affect it.

Recurrency presents powerful arguments for
creating stable, long-term, visible ABE schemes,
because people will use them over and over, as
their learning requirements change. This also can
give ABE an intelligible status -- that of access
provision. In practice ABE as access means entry
to further education (FE), and FE, though changing,
is as yet largely unsuitable for mature students in
style, teaching method, support provision, bridging
and preparatory courses. This view gives yet
another function to access ABE -- that of advice,
support and counselling, if only at the start of
what one student called the

> limboland. You've got all those new skills
> and you can't put them into practice. I was
> thinking 'God, what have I done?'

More difficult to talk about is access, not to courses, but to whatever users invent for themselves. In ABE, students have produced books and newspapers, organised events, run courses, started small businesses, formed pressure groups and community organisations. Perhaps it's only in unspecialised parts of the education service that this kind of flexibility is possible. Some accommodation to this kind of educational invention will have to be made if the recurrent education system is going to work.

## Deterring recurrency

In 'new' areas of work, the relatively low status of organisers and teachers keeps them from information about what's going on in the world outside their own provision. ABE isn't alone in suffering from innovation at the bottom being misunderstood elsewhere. Scale helps to solve this problem, though labour-intensive ABE can rarely hope to accumulate the student hours to gain department or unit status, and thus control over its own work. ABE shares with universities its low tutor/student ratio: perhaps it should also share their interest in, and funding for, research.

Diversification -- provision for mentally handicapped, for people who don't speak English, combined with fulltime Manpower Services Commission (MSC) courses for teenagers, examinations, Open Tech facilities, special project money (travellers, mentally disturbed, etc.) -- is one way to get big enough to get the information, management training and voice in policy-making necessary to develop ABE. Other community educators seem justified in maintaining their separateness from these mishmashes of educational disadvantage. Every new source of funding affects ABE provision, sometimes unpredictably.

External realities fencing in adult education, FE and voluntary groups -- all of which host ABE -- put pressure on ABE to develop. Development from inside, from student requirements, is, in theory and practice, likely to be useful to future students and to a future coherent educational system. ABE must make difficult decisions about how much of its organising power it devotes to attracting support; using its experience to help build a local recurrent education system can often seem less of a priority.

One of the attractions of the comprehensive
movement for secondary schools was its potential
flexibility. Schools as microcosms of the adult
community outside could respond to new learning
requirements thrown up by those communities. However well this works for children, a comprehensive
recurrent education system that includes adults
seems a long way away, even in access terms:

I went to the Job Centre and told them what
I'd learned, and he said, 'You want something practical then'. I went back four
times, and I began to believe him, and
thought I'd train to be a cook. Not everybody would have gone back four times. They
finally told me about (the local advice
service for adults). They sent me somewhere
else, who told me about the mature students'
course.

The local alliances among colleges, extramural
departments, community schools, education advice
services, local authority adult education departments and voluntary community education units more
often circumscribe educational spheres of influence
than help potential users get in and around. After
all, a student transferred is student hours lost.

## Ways ahead

ABE practitioners, like everyone else in AE,
balance student goals with available funding, the
requirements of its many administrators settings,
the necessity for educational alliances and whatever information it can get about what education in
the future should look like.
Vocabulary, as usual, both helps and stands in
the way when thinking about ABE and recurrent
education. The  verbal shorthand for that future
education system -- continuing education, recurrent
education, lifelong learning, éducation permanente
-- has itself spawned a literature and debates to
which it is worth attending. 'Recurrency',
'access', 'comprehensiveness' all assist ABE practitioners to see how to plan to help people to
learn. Churlish though it may seem, such discussions often remain with those paid to think in
universitites and higher education departments, who
carry out their briefing responsibilities by mounting in-service training and publishing in journals

outside the ambit of those who need the information, just as surely as they need to know what the next funding source for ABE is likely to be.

For the systemically simple-minded, it is easier to discuss whether the future system is usable by its clienteles. A usable education system pays attention to its links, so that those coming to it for the first time, and those inside it, can tell where they are going. Space to speculate, whatever 'course' an adult is following, seems another of these minimal requirements. 'Usable' also means flexible enough to change as learning requirements change. One good way to hear what educational requirements are going to be is by listening to adult users.

Learner autonomy, student empowerment, community control and self-directed learning are all ways of talking about listening to what people want and structuring to make sure they get it. So far, student places on course committees and academic boards, special user groups in local centres, even the Education Centres Association and National Students' Union (for literacy students) leave something to be desired when it comes to learners taking control. It is as if educationists have not yet understood that the learning system we are building will look radically different from the one we came from, and will change constantly. We need what adult students know about the usefulness of learning in the worlds they deal with every day, and we will be short-sighted if we don't begin to build in ways which ensure those opinions are elicited, discussed, refined, presented as proposals and carried out. Changes from within, understandable enough, bear less legitimacy than what comes from outside -- planning for an adaptable technological labour force, for example.

The abolition of the Advisory Council for Adult and Continuing Education paves the way for a new body with 'development' a prominent part of its title and its brief. The educational policies of political parties matter, and sensible participants in educational systems will use what they hear from party education spokesmen to try to establish a usable education system for the future, something of the shape of which may be implied in this statement from a spelling student:

> Everyone is responsible for his own learning. You have to do it yourself. You can

look at numbers and they go together -- one and one is two. Words don't go together like that, and to find out how they fit, it's no good asking someone who can do it. My ten-year-old daughter can spell anything you want, but she can't tell me how she does it. People who can do it can't tell you how. They've forgotten. Maybe someone who has just gone through it, would be able to tell you, because he'd remember. I think these people could help others to learn.

## References

Charnley, A.H. and Jones, H.A. (1979), The Concept of Success in Adult Literacy, ALBSU, London.

# 24.  SECOND CHANCE PROGRAMMES

Linden West

## Introduction

The literature of recurrent education has sometimes suffered from two major and related shortcomings. First, whilst the polemic against the existing educational system has been strong, the literature has been vague about how the aims and values of recurrency should be translated into actual provision. Secondly, recurrent education has occasionally been presented as merely a set of organisational principles and technical arrangements which, it is claimed, will help to redistribute opportunity by making education and training more widely available throughout life. I assume that many recurrent educators are also interested in the detail of content and methodology to enable education to become more meaningful to a wider range of people.

It is time that the debate moved on to specifics and I believe the experience of Second Chance can help on this. Central to both Second Chance and recurrent education is a set of similar values. These include the importance of securing personal autonomy within learning and beyond; the nurturing of critical, independent thinking and defining learning in a context of personal development and self-realisation. We need to know more about attempts to express these in actual programmes. Second Chance has also been primarily directed towards adults gaining least from conventional schooling, higher and further education. To understand its development may help in the search for greater equality in the distribution of educational resources. Second Chance has much to say about the organisation of adult education, the role of the teacher and the nature of the curriculum for those at the margins of our society.

I use the term Second Chance to describe a particular form of provision developed by some Districts of the Workers' Educational Association (WEAS) and university Extramural Departments.

I am not referring to the wide range of return-to-learn courses which have been developed in recent years. There is as yet no adequate empirical research into these. My experience is of developing Second Chance in a particular sense and of directing a research project into its meaning for students. I believe that the research indicates that Second Chance works for some of the most educationally underprivileged. There is much of value in these programmes to inform wider policy development and the organisation of other educational opportunities.

## Second Chance - The Experience So Far

The first Second Chance course began in Liverpool in the mid-1970s. It developed from adult educationalists' involvement with groups of community activists during rent strikes and community campaigns. A series of short courses and informal educational activity generated a demand for more 'wide-ranging' and 'analytical' treatment of 'working class issues'. This took the form of a 20-week course, held on one day a week, devoted to a study of Merseyside and Britain's social and economic development. A little later writers' workshops were added whilst individual tutorials were introduced to remedy educational deficiency and lack of confidence. Students were mainly activists in the trade union movement or community groups and the day release scheme was used for those in full-time employment (Yarnitt, 1983).

This pattern was repeated in other places, particularly Southampton, although courses there developed a particular orientation. There was a strong feminist basis to some Southampton courses and they were often directed exclusively at what were described as working class women (Thompson, 1983). Both the Liverpool and Southampton schemes had a similar ethos and design. Content was regarded as important as well as process within learning. Learning was more than simply a matter of people functioning more effectively together - it was a means of acquiring a greater social/political awareness and analytical skills to interpret and explain personal and social experience and, if necessary, to act to change it. Detailed attention was paid to the development of study skills - writing, reading, numeracy, organisation of time, use of libraries - these were incorporated into the work of the group as well as individual tutorials. Homework was an essential element and a period of residential education was added as a way of consolidating collective and individual learning and group cohesion.

There had been a lengthy debate in the WEA's Berks, Bucks & Oxon District in the early 1980s about what the District should do to promote working class adult education. The increasing scale of unemployment and social inequality was set against limited resources for development work. Money had been channelled into a range of initiatives - courses at Unemployed Workers' Centres, Welfare Rights courses on council estates, 'Teach-Ins' for community activists - none of which seemed sufficient to meet the learning needs of participants. There was much frenetic activity but little sense of coherent purpose of design. Second Chance provided a way forward for the District. If educational deficiency was to be tackled seriously, time and resources were needed to enable this to happen. It was better to provide a relatively small number of high quality educational opportunities than attempt to be all things to all people.

The first courses began in Milton Keynes in 1984 and were subsequently extended to Oxford. They had the following aims and objectives:

## Aims of the course

1. To increase students' self-confidence.
2. To help students develop critical, independent thinking.
3. To help students to see themselves in relation to others whose views may differ from theirs, and to recognise others' ideas.
4. To help students express themselves more clearly and creatively.
5. To help students develop their own control over their own lives.

## Objectives

By the end of the course <u>students should have the following knowledge</u>:

1. Know how to study more effectively, know own strengths and weaknesses in regard to studying, know how to use time more effectively.
2. Know about a variety of techniques they might use to improve reading, notetaking, etc.
3. Know which books, aids are available to help improve study skills.
4. Know something of how writers, speakers can mislead.

## Students should be able to perform the following skills

1. Organise a weekly study schedule and stick to it.
2. Write more confidently.
3. Take notes from books, TV/films, speakers, meetings - critically.
4. Prepare and present orally an opinion/argument to a group.
5. Find information from library, town hall, etc.
6. Begin to understand and read material presented as graphs and statistics.
7. Begin to distinguish between 'straight' and 'crooked' thinking.

## Students should develop the following attitudes

1. Be more confident about improving their learning.
2. Enjoy learning.
3. Be co-operative, not competitive about learning. Be willing to question their own and others' views.

Initally, course content developed around the history, economy and sociology of the New Town of Milton Keynes. However, students wanted to explore themes beyond their own locality and topics such as education, the family and the media came to form the core curriculum for most Second Chance courses. The topics allowed tutors and students to exploit personal and group experience as a source of evidence and a means to enliven academic concepts - for example, the function of social institutions such as schooling or the family. School experiences could be uncovered through group discussion and writing; links could be made with people living at other times and in different places via the use of historical autobiography or literature. Feelings of personal and social failure and rejection could be generalised into patterns which raised doubts about explanations based on individual inadequacy.

The District had carefully targeted its courses towards those most disadvantaged by conventional provision. Courses were free and child-care facilities were always available. Specific attempts were made to recruit from the ethnic minority communities and working class women whilst subsequent efforts have been directed towards the long-term male unemployed manual worker. There was no problem in recruitment (apart from within the last group) and courses could have been filled many times over.

It was obvious from the beginning that the District's capacity to provide such courses was constrained by limited staffing and financial resources. Success presented a massive dilemma. The attempt to establish Second Chance coincided with reductions in grant-aid to the WEA from the Department of Education and Science and LEAs. Other sources of income and support had to be uncovered if the programme was to develop. One step towards this was to establish a credible research programme into the effect of the courses on students as well as to experiment with new methods of evaluating the quality of what was being provided. The District combined with Oxford University Department for External Studies to establish a research project focused on student experience of Second Chance and the extent to which the courses provided a dynamic towards continued learning or other forms of social participation over a period of time. The two agencies also collaborated to devise a scheme of evaluation, exploiting group discussion and individual questionnaires, which systematically examined the components of the course - group meetings, individual tutorials and the residential - as well as specific elements of content and method within them. The research and evaluation have enhanced the clearer understanding of Second Chance and of how general aims such as increasing student control in learning, the nurturing of critical, independent thinking and the concern to place learning in a context of wider personal development find practical expression. (WEA BB&O District, Oxford University Department for External Studies, 1985).

The research has underlined how important tutors are in translating these general goals into successful practice. Teaching is not to be devalued in Second Chance - in the sense of tutors providing a framework to link experience with social theory and an environment in which groups function well whilst not neglecting individuals. Increased student control in learning, critical awareness and personal growth depend on careful planning and attention to detail. It is instructive to analyse more specifically the tutor's role in securing broad objectives such as these.

There is little doubt that attempts to develop a more student-centred dynamic are fraught with difficulty. Tutors have employed a variety of methods to maximise participation and democratise decision making. Unfortunately, students can feel intimidated in small groups as well as larger ones - in some instances even more so. They become anxious about revealing aspects of personal history. Other students can appear to be domineering and destructive. Students may feel insecure or confused when conventional expectations, culled from school experience, are not met: 'It's your job to teach us!' Students may demand highly conventional types of assessment - homework should be marked and graded, punctuation and spelling corrected. When students are asked to contribute towards deciding content and methods, there can be feelings that tutors really know what should be done and they are trying to hide it. Students can be uncertain, despite constant efforts by the tutors, that they can choose topics that relate to their own experience or lives because they continue to see education as something apart from their normal lives. Students become frustrated and sometimes angry with sessions which involve learning skills they do not associate with education. They may be asked to present a case or summarise what someone else has said to them but it takes time to recognise the importance of the skills they have used or what they have learned. Group decisions over content can be especially perplexing. Students may have accepted a tutor's suggestion but may find themselves having a choice only to be placed in a minority. Other students quickly learn the tutors' jargon or what they think is of interest to tutors and when asked about their own views use the tutors' terms and ideas - they are telling the tutors what they think the tutors want to hear.

The tutors' perspective on these processes is also interesting. Tutors are sometimes divided and uncertain about ways to develop greater student control over learning. Some tutors accept that student independence is paradoxically dependent on them providing a clear framework of content and method in which learning skills and confidence can be nurtured. Other tutors see themselves as less directive and more responsive to student demand. In practice, though, they often feel forced to exercise more control in the group than they would like. For example, successful groups depend on accepted groundrules - of who speaks and when, of the need to listen and to give space to all participants - but this takes time to develop. Tutors can feel that they are forced to assert these rules fairly constantly as an alternative to confusion and frustration. Groups can take a long time to establish a collective responsibility.

Similarly, tutors can find that responsiveness to student demand can lead to dissatisfaction among students and incoherence in content - a compromise between group members can produce general frustration: 'Why didn't you just choose a topic for us?' The research has indicated that tutors are not always aware of how instrumental they are in shaping group decisions. For example, when 3 or 4 workshops are offered at a residential, tutors can unwittingly manoeuvre students into even-numbered groups or communicate by gesture or tone what they really think is important. Clearly, the process of extending control to students is in practice beset with contradiction and frustration. A paradox may be that increasing participant control in learning depends on tutors exercising responsibility to reconcile coherence and responsiveness in content and to introduce methods which enable a gradual sharing of power.

The development of critical awareness and independence of thought in students is also a complex process. Students begin with a deficit view of education in which tutors know best and students should merely learn. They are passive recipients of other people's knowledge. In part, this reticence can be broken by the struggle for more participatory, responsive forms of learning discussed above.

In part, it may depend on the extent to which tutors convey the habit of critical orientation towards their own ideas and experience. But it also depends on the extent to which the abstractions of critical awareness and logical thinking are deconstructed into specific and discrete stages which can be learned and applied. A good example of this is in a study skills exercise devoted to 'straight and crooked' thinking which was originally developed in the Liverpool scheme (Edwards, 1985). Students are introduced to devices which are often used by speakers or writers to mislead or propagandise and then asked to detect them in other pieces of writing. For example, the use of 'persuader words' such as 'obviously', 'clearly', 'surely', or 'as everyone knows'. Emotive language may be employed - 'these militants have the economy by the throat': 'militant' is used to convey images of people whose aim is to destroy something of value whilst the image of 'have the economy by the throat' is one of a strong, brutal, aggressor against a helpless victim. The use and misuse of analogy and metaphor is also developed: 'So to separate a child from its natural parents is akin to murder - the branches cannot survive without their roots'. The power of the analogy makes it difficult to challenge the assertion. A metaphor such as the 'ship of state' may assume a common interest among social groups which is not self-evident. Distinctions between empirically grounded and testable statements ('The sun is shining') and attitudinal statements ('You're a reactionary swine!') are useful and produce lively discussion. Similarly, syllogism - logical argument developed from a false premise - can unlock a range of assumptions and beliefs: 'Premise One: Immigrants are lazy and sly; premise two: Tariq is an immigrant; conclusion: Therefore Tariq is lazy and sly'. These examples illustrate that the barriers to clear thinking, informed reading and critical listening can be identified, broken down into components and exploited to examine one's own beliefs, attitudes and opinions. The success of this is in large part a function of good teaching - in the sense of clear exposition, intelligent examples and devising the means to test one's own as well as other people's statements. Critical, independent thought is nurtured by good teaching.

The literature of Second Chance places learning within a framework of personal growth.

Learning is not seen as an isolated, disconnected mastery of technical skills or a consumption of knowledge. It is a process of becoming more self-aware, socially conscious and assertive. It is a way of giving life to the positive, questioning and reflective dimensions of personality. Many students on Second Chance progress in this way but their experience is confused and contradictory. Personal anxiety, relational strain and social unease may result from personal re-evaluation:

'My husband, our relationship became quite strained. I think he felt threatened because I was on this course'.

'Yes - friends who drop in for coffee - I feel their gossip and coffee sessions are boring. I want to fill my day with more fulfilling things...'

'...in some ways I feel to have grown apart from some relatives. Perhaps I think I am getting ideas above my station, so I don't say much about what I am involved in'.

'I am more frustrated with my life-style. I need other interests, other than work and my family' (WEA, BB&O District, 1985).

For some students, Second Chance is an attempt to resolve personal difficulty and anxiety. For others, it is to reaffirm a capacity for growth which has already begun. The experiences which produce this and the pedagogic consequences which stem from it are fraught with danger. To some extent the need to reflect on origins and destinations is catered for in the individual tutorials, although most tutors stress their role as educators rather than therapists. Some tutors have encouraged participants to reveal aspects of experience which have been hurtful and destructive. This can be tortuous since many participants, particularly working class women, have been the victims of personal violence or abuse. Discussion on one course began to uncover common experiences of family violence and incest which were psychologically distressing and destabilising. In this case tutors allowed the discussion to develop, confident that the group could handle it. Some participants felt disturbed and frightened. Some retreated, others opened up, finding comfort and support in shared revelation. The tutors justified this excursion into group therapy on the grounds that Second Chance existed to enable personal experience to be reinterpreted and re-evaluated in a positive way. If experience has been hurtful and bruising and has provoked guilt and self-denigration, all the more reason to unlock and share it.

Other tutors are more concerned to lay down narrower parameters in their work - the intensely personal and psychologically dysfunctional are for therapists not them. In practice, such distinctions are difficult to draw; personal experience cannot be neatly compartmentalised into the appropriate and inappropriate. For most members of the women's course, the shared revelation of abuse powerfully reinforced the group's cohesion and motivation to learn. Participants on Second Chance have been damaged or made to feel inconsequential and a prerequisite of growth is for this to be acknowledged and remedied. Tutors carry a responsibility to exercise judgement - to draw firm guidelines or to allow the group to handle the complicated and hurtful. The practice of using participant experience as a source of evidence is not easy when the students have been deeply damaged by it. Its successful exploitation will depend on attributes of group leadership, self-awareness and discrimination exercised in course planning and individual sessions. Lack of care can undermine the momentum towards positively reinterpreting the past and future possibilities.

In general Second Chance students define themselves as being more in control of what is happening to them, more socially aware and confident after a course than before. In-depth interviews and standard questionnaires have revealed feelings of purposefulness, higher self-esteem and well-being after courses have finished. Most students have chosen some other form of continuing education or training, or are more socially and politically active. These feelings may of course dissipate over time - how far Second Chance has provided a sufficient dynamic is unknown and will be the subject of a longitudinal study. At present, the evidence indicates that Second Chance works for most students. It therefore provides a model worthy of wider replication and a basis of experience to inform the development of recurrent education.

## Second Chance and Recurrent Education - Some Concluding Thoughts

The inspiration behind Second Chance and some of the values of recurrent education are very similar. Personal autonomy has been regarded as central to the purpose of recurrent education (Harris, 1974). This would include autonomy within learning and beyond. In the first case the ideal is that the learner has gained knowledge and understanding to enable him/her to pursue further knowledge and that s/he is better able to conceive and achieve ends which s/he values. In the second, it would include the exercise of informed choices at a personal and social level. In part this may depend on control over material resources but it is primarily concerned with the individual gaining some sense of control over personal and social events, often in co-operation with others. It is a choice between being an object of other people's decisions or a subject actively defining and influencing the course of events. Its realisation assumes a degree of social and personal awareness as well as confidence and skill to interpret events and to act upon them. Learning is also placed at the core of human realisation; the spirit of inquiry, of seeking to interpret and explore, to make sense of self and context is at the heart of human fulfilment and psychological equilibrium. Finally, recurrent educators have been concerned to secure greater equality of access to educational resources as opposed to the elitism of existing institutions and the divison of society into educational 'haves' and 'have nots'.

I have tried to show that some of these values are given positive expression in Second Chance. This experience can be used to enrich the debate. In particular, Second Chance highlights the weakness and vagueness of some approaches to educational development with particular reference to the organisation of educational opportunities, the role of the teacher and the nature of the curriculum.

I believe that recurrent education has suffered from an obsession with de-institutionalising education and developing alternatives such as learning webs or directories. Educational bureaucracies are said to control and distort what is done. I would not suggest that the management of public resources of this kind should be left as it is, but there may be a danger of discarding both the wheat and chaff. Second Chance has worked because it is able to draw on the material and human resources of established agencies; careful attention has been paid to the mechanisms through which learning can be enhanced (the class, the tutorial and the residential) and a curriculum through which people can develop confidence, skills and knowledge. Neither does Second Chance depreciate teaching in the sense of communicating knowledge beyond the experience of the group and planning ways in which knowledge and experience can best be exploited. Much academic knowledge may be tainted by the socially determined beliefs of those who have constructed it, but this is no reason to debar people from becoming familiar with competing social theories, in part through imaginative teaching. Teaching is more than facilitating learning - the latter can be achieved by simply providing premises and resources. Mere facilitation can involve an abrogation of responsibility in which individuals lose direction and purpose. It is difficult enough to make sense of social and psychological theory, without abandoning tutors who can inspire and enlighten.

Second Chance should be considered to be good recurrent education in practice - 'good' in the sense of ridding recurrent education of some of its vagueness and conceptual obsessions as well as being grounded in the experience of working class adults. It has provided forms of progressive learning to those most in need and should be more widely known and available in the struggle to establish the recurrent idea.

## References

Edwards, J. (1985), Learning Together: a Study Skills Handbook, WEA West Lancs and Cheshire, Liverpool.

Harris, A. (1974), Autonomy in Houghton, V. and Richardson, K., Recurrent Education, Ward Lock Educational, London.

Thompson, J. (1983), Learning Liberation: Women's Response to Men's Education, Croom Helm, London.

Workers' Educational Association (1985), Berks, Bucks & Oxon District, Second Chance to Learn Research Project First Report, Oxford.

Yarnitt, M. (1983), Origins and Dilemmas, Second Chance to Learn, Second Chance National Conference, 11-17 November, 1983.

THE OPEN UNIVERSITY: RETROSPECT AND PROSPECT
IN RECURRENT EDUCATION

Nick Small

## Theme

The Open University (O.U.) originated in ambiguity and this has informed its purpose and its practice. The result is that it functions as an institution of recurrent education without always recognising or realising this, and so its policy-making and discussion is not ceaselessly dominated by values of recurrent education; its main financial provider, the government, does not consciously treat it as devoted entirely to recurrent education.

## Retrospect

The origins of the Open University, though they can be read back to the 1920s, are usually attributed to a speech by Harold Wilson in Glasgow in 1963, and more practically to a White Paper, 'A University of the Air', Cmnd. 2922, of February 1966. This based its case on arguments for use of the mass media, emphasising technical progress and how one person could lecture to thousands, leading to 'an imaginative use of teaching techniques and teacher/student relationships'. The White Paper gave the University the three-fold task of 'the improvement of educational, cultural and professional standards generally'.

Strong support led to rapid development, with 1971 being the first year of teaching. The speedy establishment of the Open University is attributed to the enterprise and the commitment of Jennie Lee, and a body of opinion that saw the O.U. as offering a second chance to those unable to proceed to a university education at the usual age in Britain, around 17-21.

The ambiguity of origin provides the opportunity to argue that the O.U. was not founded on social equity considerations alone. Was the O.U. a standard institution of higher education based on multi-media systems, i.e. different in method, but otherwise similar in content and practice to the rest of the sector? Or was its primary function compensatory in educational terms, with a special focus on those social groups and classes in the population that (for whatever reason) engaged in higher education in disproportionately low numbers?

The Open University attempted to exploit both aspects. They are not necessarily mutually inconsistent, but the thread of ambiguity led on into the purpose of the institution. Was it providing university education or adult education? The answer seems simple: university education for adults. The British university tradition, however, is founded on research and teaching in institutions where students under the age of 21 are the main cohort. The O.U. response in its early years was to emphasise its own commitment to the university tradition of scholarship by focusing almost entirely on the creation of excellently produced undergraduate courses. The great amount of energy and resource that has gone into student support (mainly by way of the staff in the thirteen regional offices) - in terms of preparation for study, educational guidance and counselling and the growth of expertise in correspondence tuition among the part-time tutoring staff - was not anticipated in the very early stages. Student needs and demands forced themselves on to the institution, have been acknowledged, and systems of student support have been created. A wholly part-time over-21 undergraduate population taught mainly by correspondence has been recognised as having different educational needs (in kind, as it were, as well as in degree), from the hitherto more usual full-time under 21 student population. Both formal and informal research by staff of the O.U. developed knowledge of an area to which little attention (compared to the education of under-21 year olds) had hitherto been paid. University education for adults in this context is a different proposition. Ensuring that O.U. qualitifations are accepted as comparable to those of equivalent institutions maintains the tension of producing courses recognised academically elsewhere but appropriate for an older, experienced but educationally heterogeneous student group. The academic emphasis predominated in the early years.

The O.U. practice contained further ambiguities. Anyone over 21 could apply irrespective of educational background and experience for one of the five foundation courses (or, as time went by, to an increasing range of higher level courses within what became known as the associate student programme). Not all applicants could be admitted, quotas being necessary by course and region in some instances. Educationally, the courses tend to inflexibility and rigidity in the pacing of the teaching: the multi-media elements, to be well integrated, generally assume and require student conformity to a predetermined pattern of study. There is little or no room for student negotiation, though mediation by tutors, and by other student support systems, can alleviate or soften the impact of baldly delivered material. The distance education format is predominantly one-way, and the word 'delivery' is appropriate. Courses are produced with a greater or lesser idea of the level of interest, education and experience of potential students in the minds of the group (or course team) who produce the course. Getting agreement on writing level in the course team can lead to extensive debate as one aspect of course creation that can often be an abrasive experience. The positive side is that 'delivery' or method is a constant and serious issue; along with high standards of presentation, this has established the reputation of the O.U. as course and materials provider.

The O.U. Planning Committee in 1969 stated that 'education generally and higher education in particular is, at one and the same time, a necessary condition of a modern technological society and a defence against its abuses'. This neatly illustrated the conflict between a mass provision (or standard types and levels, irrespective of student variation) and the individual student. The student in a distant education system was reckoned to be working on his or her own, in isolation. Tutorial support offered some limited compensation.

Through the 1970s, interest in other kinds of course provision developed, usually of a short, non-credit nature for specified groups who were encouraged to study as a group activity. This was an acknowledgement of one of the Charter's objects 'to promote the educational well-being of the community generally'. All O.U. provision can be

defined as recurrent or continuing education, but
for internal purposes and to distinguish certain
courses (and sources of funding) from the mainstream undergraduate provision, there is a Centre
for Continuing Education which has sections producing short courses and study packs in professional and vocational areas. These areas in the
mid-1980s are: Community Education, Health and
Social Welfare, Management Education, Personal and
Cultural Education, Professional Development in
Education, and Scientific and Technological Updating. They are intended to be self-financing.

The prompting for this extension of provision
away from degree courses was formalised by the
Report of the Committee on Continuing Education,
chaired by the late Sir Peter Venables, which
reported in December 1976. Its seminal thinking
was influential far beyond the bounds of this one
institution in the case it made for and consequently the encouragement given to a national
council for continuing education, a national educational advisory service for adults, positive discrimination in fee awards, the promotion of paid
educational leave, the integrated development and
use of library services, and so forth. Some of the
early ambivalences of the O.U. position had been
recognised, and general (not institutional) changes
were proposed. The O.U. was pressing issues that
would ease the way for adult members of the population as a whole towards participation in education.
It was acknowledging its role as a spokesperson for
the constituency from which it drew its students,
not just the students themselves.

## The statistical melange

This is a brief coda on the O.U. pattern of
study, and the number of courses and of those
studying them. The academic year runs for about 32
weeks from February to October, with assessment
usually on a 50:50 basis of course work and exam.
Degrees are awarded on completion of six credits
(eight for an honours degree). Each credit requires up to 400 hours of study (200 hours for a
half-credit), about 12 hours and 6 hours per week
respectively. The main form of study is by correspondence texts (say, 65%) supported by one-week
summer schools on almost a third of the courses,
home experiment kits for about half the students,
television and radio programmes (which account for

perhaps 10% of the learning material), etc. (Personal contact can be up to 15%, written or practical work 10%.) In 1986, there were about 64,000 students studying 125 undergraduate courses, a further 10,000 students taking post foundation courses as associate students and around 20,000 individuals taking short courses; and 900 post-graduates. Annual applications number over 40,000 with 20,000 admitted in 1986 (a figure decided, as in practice is the fee, by the Department of Education and Science). (56,000 applied for places in 1986, including nearly 15,000 previously unsuccessful applicants; nearly half of those admitted to foundation courses for the degree are previous applicants.) Normally, about 36% of new students lack minimum university entry requirements. In addition to 125 undergraduate courses, there are 200 Continuing Education courses and packs. Since 1973, 69,000 people have graduated.

Virtually all materials are available for public purchase, so courses are subject to general as well as academic gaze. This applies most obviously to television (over 27 hours of broadcasts weekly in 1985) and to radio (6 hours). The BBC/OU Production Centre produced 233 - 300 radio and audio casette programmes in 1985, and 200 television programmes (many of them for video cassette distribution), with several million viewers each year for the networked items.

The recurrent grant to the O.U. is paid direct by the DES (i.e. it does not go through the University Grants Committee), and in the mid-1980s is around £59 million. DES has indicated that it will remain at this figure 1985-87, i.e. assuming a more severe fall than was experienced in the early 1980s. The student contribution through fees has risen as a proportion of university income from nearly 14% in 1980 to almost 21% in 1985, and could increase further. (A full credit undergraduate course fee approached £150 in 1986, with the residential summer school week costing nearly £100.)

Because students study part-time at home, and remain in employment, thus contributing to the economy, the cost per graduate is naturally less than where students are resident and study full-time.

Undergraduates are admitted by way of a foundation course. Around 1980, there was a 53:47% split, Arts/Social Science:Maths/Science/Technology. Government has provided some special funding to assist a reversal of this. By the late 1980s a majority of students will be admitted to science-based courses. In 1987, on an intake of 22,000, the Arts:Science split falls to 51:49.

Students under 21 are now admitted though demand is small - 1.4% of the 1986 intake being under 21. The median age of new undergraduate students has for some years been consistently around 32 or 33 years, i.e. when family and job commitments (70-80% are in paid employment) put conventional full-time higher education virtually out of the question.

## Prospect

The achievement of the Open University is considerable. It has established correspondence study as a generally acknowledged, 'high-profile' means of learning, not a provision either confined to certain professional qualifications, or of last resort. It has shown that strong student motivation can overcome limited educational background. The O.U. pattern of part-time provision has been emulated by other institutions offering courses to older students. Though these are of a mainly 'face-to-face' nature, many institutions and groups of colleges are offering 'open learning' courses (though the term lacks a commonly agreed definition). In 1973, the Russell Committee felt that

> the example of the Open University is likely to bring into prominence the need for similar forms of provision at other levels and in non-academic fields which could benefit from being serviced by modest analogues of the Open University.

(DES, 1973)

This has not happened, though the influence of the O.U. (no doubt also benefiting from the spirit of the time) has encouraged or inspired a multiplicity of initiatives to extend educational provision and support services to a wider adult constituency. This may even extend to the Open Tech, a part of the Manpower Services Commission's New Training Initiative; this is a series of programmes devised on a modular basis (not an institution) developing and applying 'new methods of learning' which 'can make training available much more widely, readily and flexibly' (DoEmp., 1985).

In the mid-1980s, education feels itself in crisis, with falling rolls and contracting resources. Higher education faces its particular crisis and dilemma of a 'public face set towards mass higher education, with a private face bowing to the older elitist traditions' (Van der Eyken, 1973). The government's view in the mid 1980s is not to extend the age participation index on entry to higher education of around 14% for those under 21; the index for those aged 22-25 is projected as 0.5%, and for those over 25 (based on the 25-34 year old population) 0.25% (DES, 1984). This does in fact constitute 'a significantly increased number of mature full-time students'; and there is some increase in part-time provision proposed, and also a mix of full-time and part-time study (DES, 1985). Despite the trebling of higher education provision over the last twenty years, and a high proportion of entrants over 21 in public sector higher education, Britain's remains a very undereducated population. There will be work of a compensatory sort for any Open University well into the future.

Government has recognised this, and has seen the remedy at least in part as an emphasis on training for industrial change. Institutionally, the O.U. 'will continue to be the main provider of part-time higher education by distance methods'. Its existence, once questioned, seems assured. Collaboration with the 'UGC and the NAB [for these terms, see Glossary] and directly between the Open University and other institutions to ensure the most effective use of resources in delivering higher education to a dispersed student population' is the government's programme for the future of the O.U. (DES, 1985). The Open University faces its own financial crisis in the mid-1980s. Its accounting structure is peculiar in that there are heavy course development costs before students enrol. Running costs are then comparatively low, requiring high numbers to justify the initial investment. Reduced funding over several years means difficulties in preserving mainstream work, and little encouragement for marginal or new developments. Nevertheless, efforts are being made to produce taught higher degree programmes, and advanced and professional diplomas, for example. The likelihood is that government funds for special programmes will lead much more to centrally-controlled not institutionally-controlled courses and materials provision.

## Conclusion

Returning to the first of the ambiguities mentioned at the beginning, whether the emphasis should be on technical opportunity or social equity, it appears that government is opting for the former. Whether the economic problems of society can be resolved discretely on the basis of economic policy; whether education can of itself rectify social and economic problems; or whether social policy is the key element within which economic and educational policies are formed; are issues that are not addressed in any national debate. The suspicion of philosophical discussion allied to pragmatic and incremental policy-making remains part of British tradition.

There may be general agreement that adults are a major resource and investment. Agreement is less likely on how to interpret and act on that statement. The Open University is the major institution in higher education offering a form of recurrent education. It could offer a wide range of provision with that purpose, widely defined, specifically at the forefront of policy. Its achievements to date have been considerable; its existence and example have been a great encouragement to many other institutions and individuals both in Britain and abroad; it has greatly encouraged others in relevant aspects of recurrent education it could not itself pursue; but ambivalence about its role and purpose, and external circumstances, have prevented its fullest possible contribution to the creation of a system of recurrent education in this country.

## Afterword

Two Open University colleagues, commenting on this article had contrasting reactions to it. One felt the author had been insufficiently harsh in his strictures and criticisms. The opportunity given to the Open University to promote a recurrent education strategy had at best been fumbled, with chances missed. The other colleague thought the major contribution made by the O.U. had been undervalued. The institution has shown that it is possible to study to an advanced level (given the right conditions and support) whatever the age (assuming reasonable health) and in spite of the fact that school experience did not indicate any great ability. Some 70% of the 5,200 part-time tutorial staff work in other educational institutions, and many must have been influenced to a greater or lesser degree by experience of this massive open learning system, and undergone staff development programmes - some carry-over to their other work seems inevitable.

The O.U. in its more reflective moments, does perceive of itself as a harbinger of change, and does offer potential for a fundamental re-ordering of the educational system in the direction of recurrent education. In terms of equity, the social and occupational range of O.U. students is very wide, with a national mature student survey showing that one in two O.U. graduates had 'blue collar' fathers, compared to one in five in conventional universities (quoted in the O.U. response to Cmnd. 9524). The theme of ambiguity referred to earlier continues with the development of improved, expanding and cheaper information technology that could have implications for increased participation so long as the potential educational benefits are given priority.

The government's Green Paper 'The Development of Higher Education into the 1990s' (Cmnd. 9524, May 1985) is discussed in this volume by Fowler. That document is supportive of some extension of part-time study and the role of distance learning - some compensation in an otherwise limited paper. The order of change for a radical policy shift that recurrent education requires is not approached. The O.U. response reminds government of the research surveys that indicate demand amongst adults for a part-time first degree of the order of 3% - one million. A serious strategy would address this matter. In the mid-1980s, the Open University has shown what is possible - like so much in education, the reality is still far behind the potential.

## References

Department of Employment (1985), Employment: the Challenge for the Nation, Cmnd. 9474, London, HMSO.

Department of Education and Science (1966), A University of the Air, Cmnd. 2922, London, HMSO.

Department of Education and Science (1973), Adult Education: A Plan for Development (The Russell Report), London, HMSO.

Department of Education and Science (1984), Demand for higher education in Great Britain, 1984-2000, Report on Education No. 100.

Department of Education and Science (1985), The Development of Higher Education into the 1990s, Cmnd. 9524, London, HMSO.

Open University (1969), Report of the Planning Committee to the Secretary of State for Education and Science.

Open University Charter (1969).

Open University (1976), Report of the Committee on Continuing Education.

Open University Students' Association (January 1986), Development of Higher Education into the 1990s. A Response by the Open University Students Association.

Open University (1986), Into the 1990s The role of the Open University in the national provision of part-time higher education. A commentary on Cmnd. 9524 The Development of Higher Education into the 1990s.

Van der Eyken, W. (1973) in Tunstall, J., (ed), The Open University Opens, London

# 26. UNIVERSITY ADULT EDUCATION: WHAT PROSPECTS?

Brian Groombridge

The situation is full of promise, for society, for the Universities and for adult education as a special genre of continuing education. There are reasons to doubt whether, in Britain at least, this promise will be realised, even though 'continuing education' is in fashion again and universities are expected to contribute to it.

Alastair D. Crombie, returning to Britain as an observer after a decade working in Australia, puts it well in The Demise of the Liberal Tradition (University of Leeds, 1983). His essay is entitled 'Does university adult education in Britain have a future?' He accepts that this title may seem odd, given the renaissance of interest in the education of adults worldwide: 'to be in adult education today is to live in exciting times' (p.49). And yet - 'in times of rapid change and sweeping transformation, an illustrious past is no guarantee of a secure future, and may even become an impediment when basic assumptions need to be re-examined. This is as true for the universities themselves as it is for their extra-mural or adult education departments' (p.50).

The basic assumptions that need re-examining in this case concern the nature and function of universities and the relationship between universities and the society of which they are a part. The future of university adult education as a specific issue depends on the answers to two large questions: What are universities for? How prepared is Britain to reform the compact and understanding between the state, the universitities and society at large? There are few signs as yet that many universities are seriously interested in these questions.

In broad brush terms, there are three classical answers to the question: what are universities for? These answers are loosely associated with geographical regions, sufficiently to justify such labels as (A) the European mainland or Continental view; (B) the North American view; and (C) the British view. According to (A), universities are essentially for research, but also for the maintenance of an intellectual culture and for teaching an elite of young people, to meet future commitments. On this view, adult education, even the education of adults, is not university business. That rejection may be expressed aristocratically or in democratic terms. Rectors of mid-European universities who say that for their institutions to do adult education would be like using race horses to draw ploughs, give unequivocal expression tò the Continental tradition (aristocratic version). The democratic objection to adult education as a university purpose is associated historically with the Grundtvigian assessment of universities as epitomising the dead hand of academe. On this view, adult education is too important to be left to them. N.F.S. Gruntdvig, the founding genius both of modern Denmark and of Danish adult education, saw universities as part of the problem, not as part of the solution - democracy needed awakened and enlightened citizens, but hierarchically-minded universities, with their abstract learning, were an oppressive force, not a liberating one.

According to (B), the North American view, universities are for research, for teaching, and for public service. Public service may take a variety of forms, but it usually includes adult education, extension work, and continuing education with professional and vocational objectives.

Although universities in Britain have had a formal commitment to adult education for over a century, view (C), the British view, was not securely established until after the Second World War (if 'secure' is the right word, since the commitment is beginning to look shaky again). Writing in 1948, the then chairman of the University Grants Committee (UGC), Sir Walter Moberly, was not afraid (unlike some of his successors) to relate 'The Crisis in the University' to the moral and political crisis in the world. He criticized universities for being half-hearted about extra-mural work. They should either get out of it or do it properly. He was in favour of doing it properly:

> to withdraw - or, as university teachers so
> often do - to regard extra-mural work as
> only a casual and marginal activity, would
> be calamitous and retrograde. The alterna-
> tive is to take it more seriously.
>
> (Moberly, 1949, p.259)

What happened was that the universities, or at
least those with extra-mural departments, provided
an academic contribution to the general service of
adult education in partnership with local education
authorities and the Workers Educational Association
(WEA). This partnership was underwritten by direct
grants to the universities from the Department of
Education and Science through the so-called 'Responsible Body' regulations. Hence, on view (C):
universities are for research, for teaching, and
for a very specific genre of adult education characterised by a particular kind of curruculum, and
an ethos which it shared, more or less, with its
partners in the field. Universities were once also
for cultural maintenance (production of the
clerisy) and for imperial management, and part of
the universities' current malaise stems from uncertainty about what are the modern equivalents of
those social functions. The unease of their extra-
mural departments, on the other hand, comes not
only from this deep uncertainty about the relationship between the university and society, but also
from uncertainty about the relationship between
such departments and their parent universities.

In recent decades, universities have behaved
as though it was self-evident and generally accepted that their service to society consisted solely
in their research and teaching. Society - through
governments of every hue, supported by an audibly
indifferent electorate - has treated universities
as a self-indulgent and over-priced inheritance
from a more prosperous past. To be fair, this
breakdown of confidence is by no means a purely
British ailment. The prevalence of it is analysed
in a study from the Organisation for Economic Co-
operation and Development (OECD, The University and
the Community, 1982). It quotes the Rector of Mons
(Belgium), who could be speaking from almost any
OECD Member country:

> The university feels it is not well liked by
> society, and society feels it is not well
> served by the university (p.23).

British universities urgently need to adopt a Europeanised version of model B: they should recognise, and welcome, public service, community-related roles, including commitments to adult and continuing education, and they should do so for their intellectual health, their moral well-being, their cultural relevance, and their political survival. The transformation of 'extra-mural' work and the broadening of 'continuing education', and the concomitant adaptation of departments, centres and units, must proceed as part of a larger strategy.

I shall now assume that Britain does find ways of dealing satisfactorily with these large matters. What would then be the universities' commitment to adult and continuing education, to mature students generally, and to society at large? It would take at least the following six forms:

1. <u>Adult Education, reconceived in contemporary terms</u>

When Olof Palme was assassinated on 1 March 1986, the world lost not only its greatest internationalist: it also lost a prime minister with a profound conviction about adult education: it was an indispensable component of a mature and modern democracy. 'Sweden' he would say 'is a study circle democracy'. No British government has ever come within miles of this understanding. The late and now much missed Tory, Edward Boyle, as Secretary of State for Education, believed in the long-term residential colleges, such as Ruskin and Hillcroft; creating the Open University was Labour Prime Minister Sir Harold Wilson's finest single achievement (his view as well as mine), thereby making a major reform in higher education which also did something for the status of adult education and mature students in general. For the rest, the perception of adult education as bingo for the middle classes has pervaded almost all policy, and even some of the practice, for almost half a century. University academics who examine extra-mural students on diploma courses in archaeology, conservation, literature, geology, and many other subjects, and Her Majesty's Inspectors who look at non-award bearing courses run by the university departments, know the falsity of that image. They recognise that much of the work is in every sense worthy of a university.

It has, however, suffered from a weakness, in that while university adult education has been conspicuously part of adult education ('RB' work in association with the Local Education Authorities, the WEA and others), it has also been perceived as only marginally part of the university. University departments of adult education should both assert their own values more confidently and raise their game. Personal development remains of cardinal importance: adult education (including the universities but beyond them) is almost the only sector which gives priority to the growth of individuals over the classifying and controlling requirements of systems and institutions. Yet the university element in this sector must not only contribute to the personal development and satisfaction of a few hundred thousand students, it must also play a much more overt, high-profile role in democratic dialogue and social reform, within the context of a European polity, however defined, and a planet at risk. University knowledge as a whole must be more accessible for these larger purposes.

## 2. Access to Higher Education

A good deal has been written about access to higher education but the use of university adult education courses and facilities to improve access for mature people to degree and postgraduate work remains at a fairly rudimentary level. The scheduling of adult education courses is inconvenient for most people; links with the public sector through Open Colleges and in other ways are patchy as between one place and another; degree courses are not always structured so that advantage can be taken of previous experience and qualifications; mature students get more encouragement in prospectuses than they once did, but their 'entrance' still tends to be regarded as 'special'. Moreover, the teaching is still, for the most part, on campus. It is not provided, as in the United States and elsewhere, where people work, nor are there, as yet, many alternatives to the now expensive, once 'Open' University.

## 3. Other Forms of Continuing Education

University adult education is (uneasily) part of higher education. It is undoubtedly part of continuing education, comprehensively defined (as

by Venables, ACACE and the UGC). A great deal of
university adult education is of vocational significance and overlaps with PEVE (post-experience
vocational education), a truth often obscured by
the fallacious antithesis: liberal/vocational.
'Liberal' relates to style and philosophical
justification; 'vocational' relates to specific
labour market purposes. People who study for an
extra-mural course on ecology and conservation may
and do go on to higher education in an aspect of
the subject; or change their jobs; or become better
informed and more active citizens, or simply have
their understanding enlarged.

4.   Dialogue work

It is obvious that many of the world's difficulties stem not altogether from sheer ignorance or
perversity, but from a general inability to use the
knowledge that already exists. People and society
face issues, whereas universities have only subjects and disciplines. Straight academic or professional up-dating is needed, but inter-professional work, cross-cultural work, appropriately
undertaken by universities (as by polytechnics and
other institutions, of course) goes some way to
overcome the mental compartmentalisation and the
administrative departmentalism which promote inef-
ficiency and undermine rational, democratic management. Museum curators need to learn from geolo-
gists; architects, site managers, urban planners
and builders from each other; para-medics from
medics and vice-versa, as well as from patients.
There is a sense in which we are all partially
qualified now, and we need to find new ways of
pooling our knowledge and intelligence. The educational implications of that require a particular
form of adult/continuing education for which the
experience of university adult education departments makes them peculiarly suitable.

5.   Community Consultancy

Knowledge transfer does not have to take the
form of courses, or to presuppose a relationship,
still less a one-way relationship, of teachers and
taught. The familiar relationship between the
university and the National Health Service (NHS) is
more complex, for example, as is the more recent
notion of Science Parks. Several Land Grant

universities in the United States exemplify a range
of public service roles, such as community consultancy, and the provision of information and advice,
which cannot be reduced simply to continuing education specifically construed. There is a moment in
the OU/BBC television programme about the University of Wisconsin (made for course E355, the Education of Adults), where a Wisconsin citizen, facing
some practical dilemma, says 'I'd better call the
University'. The University of Helsinki, through
its Centre for Research and Training at Lahti, has
demonstrated, in a wide range of modes, the significance of the University's knowledge for economic
and social regeneration in Finland. Specifically,
it has helped individuals change careers, industrial enterprises to recover their profitability,
communities to develop, and regions to experience
economic regeneration. Departments of adult education can be instrumental in enabling universities
to perform this function.

6.  <u>Second Order Work (development of theories,
    research, operational development, training
    the trainers)</u>.

Adult/continuing education is not only a
family of activities - it is also a field of study
in its own right. Many universities in Britain
(Glasgow, Leeds, Nottingham, Manchester, Southampton, Surrey and others) now make a significant
contribution to that study through a range of award
and non-award bearing courses, to degree level and
beyond, and through research. As I write, informal
discussions are going on in London which may lead
to setting up a University-wide consortium of
institutions promoting the systematic, multi-disci-
plinary study of adult learning - at several levels
- individual, group, organisational, societal and
global.

It is not at all apparent that the universities' commitment to adult and continuing education,
and to mature students generally, will embrace this
diversity. Policy formation in this area is rudimentary. At present, governments and university
politicians themselves fail sufficiently to distinguish the various forms and functions of continuing education (adult, recurrent, complementary,
supplementary and so forth) and their thinking
about resources reduces to the single, undifferen-

tiated maxim that it must pay for itself. As to the role of departments of adult education in this situation, once again Crombie puts it well. There is much that is maddening in his essay (quoted above), but the 'critical transformation' he recommends is urgent and essential:

> from a situation in which adult education is the exclusive responsibility of a single specialised part that is for this purpose extruded from the university, to one in which it is a generalised function of the university as a whole, under the leadership and management of those with distinctive competence in such work (p.89).

It remains to be seen whether and which universities have the will, the energy and the vision to undertake such a transformation.

## References

Crombie, A.D., The Demise of the Liberal Tradition: two essays on the future of British University adult education, University of Leeds, 1983.

Moberly, Sir Walter, The Crisis in the University, SCM Press, London, 1949.

Organisation for Economic Cooperation and Development, The University and the Community, Centre for Educational Research and Innovation, OECD, Paris, 1982.

27.  THE THIRD AGE

David Wood

> After  the first age of childhood and  youth
> and the second of active  employment,  there
> follows the third age of active retirement.
> (Prospectus  of the University of the  Third
> Age (U3A))

## The Nineteen Seventies

Most  published writing on lifelong or  recurrent  education  throughout the seventies made  no
more  than a passing reference to education  provision for older people  (e.g. Faure 1972, Houghton &
Richardson 1974,  ACACE 1979, and even ACACE 1982.)
It was recognised that older people were a significant  and  increasing segment of the adult  population;  their  particular  needs  might  be  met  by
reduced fees,  by day-time provision and by classes
in  homes  and  hospitals.  A  minority  had  been
catered for in short pre-retirement courses,  which
usually  dealt with money and health  problems  and
recommended activity in retirement.  When educators
have  a negative view of ageing,  lifelong learning
to  them  lacks  importance and becomes  a  way  of
simply  helping  elderly people to adapt to  a  bad
situation.  (Coppard 1981)
The  1979 World Yearbook of Education  'Recurrent Education and Lifelong Learning' (Schuller and
Megarry 1979) has no special chapter on the  education  of the elderly and the topic merits only  two
mentions  in the index.  Although the Yearbook had
an American Consultant Editor, only one chapter was
contributed by an American writer.  'Strategies for
Lifelong Learning' (Himmelstrup, Robinson & Fielden
1981)  which was a symposium of views  from  Europe
and  the  USA  gave a whole  chapter  to  'Lifelong

Learning and the Elderly'. One outcome of an industrialised and wealthy society is an increasing population of socially confident elders. It was not surprising that gerontology, the scientific study of ageing, should emerge and develop fastest in the United States. By 1970 a graduate programme in 'educational gerontology' had been established in the University of Michigan (Glendenning 1983). Meanwhile the market orientation of American colleges had stimulated them to offer vacation courses to an expanding and not unwealthy retired population. The 'Elder Hostel' movement was surprised to find a strong demand for intellectual and 'credit' courses as well as 'hobbies' courses. Simultaneously the 'Gray Panthers' were becoming a powerful political force fighting against age discrimination particularly in the professional labour market.

Meanwhile in France the 1968 Law on the Direction of Higher Education gave universtities the obligation 'to provide for the organisation of lifelong education'. The 'Université du Troisième Age' was established in Toulouse in 1973. The development of U3As in France and other countries has been extensive, very varied in form and content and at the moment is not well documented (Reeve 1980; Withnall, Charnley & Osborn 1980).

## The Nineteen Eighties

In 1981 a gathering of adult educators, gerontologists, age-concerned charities and others concerned with the elderly launched 'The Forum on the Rights of Elderly People to Education' (F.R.E.E.) to act as a clearing house for information, to publish a quarterly information bulletin and to organise occasional conferences. The 1985 conference, for instance, discussed 'Spanning the Generation Gap' including significantly the contributions the old can make to the young.

Also in the early eighties a number of semi-popular books were published, e.g. 'Older Learners' (Johnston & Phillipson 1983) and 'Age is opportunity: education and older people' (Midwinter 1982).

In 1984 after two years planning, the University of the Third Age (U3A) was formally constituted and by spring 1986 boasted 115 groups and apporoximately 7,000 members (Third Age, No. 8). The British U3A is a loose federation of self-help groups practising a variety of learning/studying processes ranging from traditional but unpaid teaching to learning exchanges, as advocated by Illich. Local groups range from memberships in tens to hundreds and from activities which are little different from some luncheon clubs to highly organised educational programmes. The U3A demands and offers no qualifications; its most university-like quality is a declared interest in research, especially research into the needs and potential of the elderly.

It must be emphasised that the main provision of education for the retired is still, as it has been for decades, local authority, Workers Education Association and university adult education classes, especially those which take place in the day-time. Such education is not normally age-related and is vulnerable to economic squeeze. Midwinter considers that 'the British elderly are just the worst schooled of any developed nation ... Now less than 2% of those retired and those retiring seem to be involved in any formal learning activity', and yet the irony is that they were the generation 'who, during their working lives, subsidised the most gigantic educational bonanza in our history' (Midwinter 1982, pp.6-7).

## The Nineteen Nineties

Psychologists used to believe that they could measure mental abilities and that these were relatively fixed for each individual; these abilities would increase till young adulthood and then slowly decline. In recent decades these views have been challenged with respect to both the young and the old. It is not argued that there are no changes in abilities, e.g. recollection of the location of one's spectacles or somebody's name, but that 'There is human potential for intellectual development from infancy through old age' (Allman 1982). It is also argued that 'Many aspects of psychological development depend very much upon the interaction of the individual with the culture he lives in, and changes in the behaviour of an individual over his life course may be more affected by changes in the culture he lives in than by changes in his body' (Woodruff and Birren 1975).

Some social theorists express similar points of view arguing against society's 'marginalisation' of the post-work population. For instance, it is argued that 'the dependence of the elderly is being manufactured socially and that its severity is unnecessary' and that the dependency is being deepened by 'the imposition, and acceptance of, earlier retirement; the legitimation of low income; the denial of rights to self-determination in institutions' (Townsend 1981).

The objects of the British U3A include:

FIRST,  to educate British society at large in the facts of its present age constitution and of its permanent situation in respect of ageing.

SECOND, to assail the dogma of intellectual decline with age and make those in their later years aware of their intellectual, cultural and aesthetic potentialities.

SIXTH,  to undertake investigations into the process of ageing in society, and especially on the condition of the elderly in Britain and the means of improvement.

If the U3A carries forward these objects, it will constitute a campaign for a form of purposeful recurrent education which may help to re-define status-awarding work and redistribute work, education and leisure throughout an individual's lifetime. The Third Age will merge back into the Second Age.

This will not be a straight-forward task. Each cohort (those born in a certain year or decade) will have different life experiences and different expectations; each group, whether based on social class, religion, place of origin, work or family experience, will have different expectations. U3A may become just a cultural club for those who call themsleves 'pensioners'. It may be just an addition to the plethora of educational institutions; it may, however, become a catalyst contributing to bringing the immense potential of the 'marginalised' Third Age population to self-awareness and thereby social action. Education is about the formation of future society.

## References

Allman, P. (1982), Adult Development: An Overview of Recent Research, Nottingham University (xeroxed).

Advisory Council for Adult and Continuing Education (1979), Towards Continuing Education: A Discussion Paper, ACACE, Leicester.

Advisory Council for Adult and Continuing Education (1982), Continuing Education: From Policies to Practice, ACACE, Leicester.

Coppard, L.C., Lifelong learning and the elderly in Himmelstrup et al (1981).

Faure, E. et al (1972), Learning to be - The world of education today and tomorrow, UNESCO, Paris.

F.R.E.E. Information Bulletin, Bernard Sunley House, 60 Pitcairn Road, Mitcham, Surrey CR4 3LL.

Glendenning, F. (1983), Educational Gerontology: A Review of American and British Development, International Journal of Lifelong Education Vol. 2, No. 1, pp.63-82.

Himmelstrup, P., Robinson, J., and Fielden, D. (1981), Strategies for Lifelong Learning, A symposium of views from Europe and the USA, Esbjerg: published jointly by the University Centre of South Jutland, Denmark, and the Association for Recurrent Education.

Houghton, V. and Richardson, K. (1974), Recurrent Education: A Plea for Lifelong Learning, published by Ward Lock Educational in conjunction with the Association for Recurrent Education.

Johnston, S. and Phillipson, C. (1983), Older Learners: the Challenge to Adult Education, Help the Aged Education Department, London.

Midwinter, E. (1982), Age is opportunity: education and older people, Centre for Policy on Ageing, London.

O.E.C.D. (1973), Recurrent Education: A Strategy for Lifelong Learning, Paris.

Reeve, J. (1980) The Universities of the Third Age - An experience in educational provision for the retired and elders, London. University Diploma Thesis. Unpublished, but available on loan from the Centre for Policy on Ageing.

Townsend, P. (1981), The Structured Dependency of the Elderly: A Creation of Social Policy in the Twentieth Century, Ageing and Society Vol 1, Pt. 1.

The University of the Third Age, 6 Parkside Gardens, London, SW19 5EY.

Withnall, A., Charnley, A., and Osborn, M. (1980), Review of Existing Research in Adult and Continuing Education, Vol.II The Elderly, NIAE, Leicester.

Woodruff, D.S. & Birren, J.E. (1975), Ageing - Scientific Perspectives and Social Issues, D. Van Nostrand Co, New York.

# 28. THE DEVELOPMENT OF RECURRENT EDUCATION IN SWEDEN

Karl-Axel Nilsson

This chapter is based on the transcript of a lecture given by Dr Nilsson at ARE's 1984 annual conference at Sheffield Polytechnic.

In presenting it the Editors are assuming that the reader has some background knowledge of Sweden as a large Scandinavian country with a relatively small population which in little over one hundred years has evolved from an agrarian society into what is often regarded as a post industrial stage, with an export led economy sustained by less than one third of the labour force and enviably high levels of productivity associated (until very recently) with almost perfect industrial relations. Private corporations account for 85% of Swedish industry with cooperatives and public enterprises sharing the rest. In comparison with most industrial countries Sweden has placed more emphasis on maintaining a high level of employment than on keeping down prices. This has produced major budget problems and Sweden is acknowledged to be among the highest taxed nations. Unemployment, however, has not exceeded 3% since 1940.

Education in Sweden has been systematically reformed at all levels since the early 1950s. This process has been dominated by the Social Democratic Party which has had power for much of the last fifty years. Its consistently stated purpose in educational reform has been to make the system and process more democratic.

Private schools are very few in Sweden and virtually everyone goes to the local nine year comprehensive school from 7 to 16. The great majority go on to an integrated upper secondary school - in effect a tertiary college though often on several sites. This is described as a 'school for everyone' and is intended to open the way to a very wide span of higher studies for those wishing to continue their education. There is an obvious generation gap in Swedish education and adults finding their basic education insufficient can study the same courses as the school population in municipal adult education. Traditional adult education circles are a long established feature of Swedish life, often with strong trade union connections. Typically more than three million persons take part each year out of a population of 8.3 million (1981).

In 1977 Sweden officially adopted the concept of recurrent education as the basis for all of its post-school provision.

Detail on all aspects of Swedish education and society can be obtained free from: The Swedish Institute, Kungstradgarden, PO Box 7434, S-10391, Stockholm. The Institute's Fact Sheet 'Higher Education' was used as background reading to Dr Nilsson's lecture.

****** 

In Sweden the traditional category of students enter higher education shortly after completing their schooling. Swedish universities and colleges base their admissions on average marks from the Gymnasieskola or upper secondary school, to which over 90% of 16 year-olds go after nine years of compulsory school (Grundskola). Students opting for gainful employment at 18 plus can improve their credits. Supplementary points are awarded for between 15 months and 3 years employment. This 'recurrent' group now outnumbers the traditional category among applicants for most study programmes. Apart from the new group being older and having acquired experience of working life, there is no reason to dramatise the difference between the two groups. The possibilities of using work experience points to offset deficiencies of upper secondary school achievement have come to be very limited. One need only mention that two-thirds of recent applicants have had maximum work experience points or none at all. People in Sweden, however, are also offered a third way into higher education which frees them from the restrictions of their school marks. Instead the basic requirement here is that the applicant must be at least 25 years old and must have acquired at least 4 years' work experience. This is the so-called 25:4 rule and has acquired some international fame.

I would like to emphasise that this third category constitutes a minority of students compared with the first two. The 25:4 rule can of course be utilised both by applicants with different school marks and by applicants who have never attended upper secondary school at all. We do not know the exact size of this latter group, because people are not obliged to append good or bad marks to their application papers. We know that this group is very small. Of the new students admitted to study programmes at Swedish universities in 1982, only 720 persons or 3.8% had not appended any secondary school certificates.

With the latter two groups in mind, one can roughly assess the Swedish system of recurrent education by considering those who successfully apply for higher education after age 21. Even when the reform came into operation in 1977, just over half the applicants were at least this age. The mature students were prepared for the reform, because it had been preceded by several years' experimentation. Their educational interest has proved permanent and the number of applicants has risen ever since the reform came into force. University and college capacity for recurrent education, however, has not kept pace with the demand. Consequently the proportion of older students actually commencing their higher education has declined throughout the period under consideration. In recent years, moreover, various measures have been taken to increase the admission of young students and thus limit the number of mature students. Two years ago, for example, the Government decided that 30% of places in each study programme were to be reserved for students whose upper secondary school leaving certificates were not more than three years old. The focus of attention in Sweden at present is on the problems of young people. Percentage admissions for this category have declined still more steeply. Every new academic year is preceded by a discussion of this in the editorials and correspondence columns of our newspapers, relating the educational demand of the younger generation to the existence of recurrent education. The debaters appear already to have forgotten the developments which led to the changes in the Swedish educational system during the 1970s.

Fifteen years have now passed since we began seriously discussing the introduction of a system of recurrent education in Sweden. I experienced the background in a very tangible manner at my own university in Lund. Allow me, then, to return to this building one evening in September in the turbulent year of 1968. The students of Paris occupied the limelight that year, but surges of protest were also noticeable even on the fringes of Europe. Young people's demonstrations were aimed at capitalism and the war in Vietnam, but everyday discussions were more concerned with the shortcomings of their teaching. It was above all the students at faculties of social sciences and arts who queried the content of teaching in view of current social developments. Our university was suffering from growing pains. We had not been able to cope with the tremendous growth in the number of students. In 1960 Lund University had 5,000 students, but by 1968 this figure had passed the 20,000 mark.

The building belongs to the Academic Association. This particular evening a banquet is in progress in the great hall on the second floor. The Swedish Prime Minister, Tage Erlander, is guest of honour. He is visiting the city to open our teaching hospital which is still the largest in the country. It towers like a giant - and also as a symbol of the megapolitan thinking of the 1960s - above the city's medieval cathedral.

The honoured guests were not, however, the only people who turned up at the Academic Association that evening. An unusually large number of students also appeared. On the first floor there was a classical student cafe called Athens, long since closed because of its enormous proportions. As the banquet proceeded on the second floor, the first floor filled up with students. The banquet speeches on the second floor came in for competition from revolutionary speeches on the ground floor. The building had been occupied by thousands of students and no less a person than the Prime Minister was their prisoner. Elsewhere in the world this would have been regarded as a highly dramatic event. Tage Erlander, however, was not particularly worried. Instead of calling out the police and army, he went down to the student cafe, got hold of a microphone and made an impromptu speech. He spoke a great deal that evening about the development of Swedish democracy, but also about the situation at our universities. The aggressive mood abated and the first applause came when Tage Erlander admitted that conditions at our universities would have to be changed. He ended his speech by announcing that the Government would appoint the 1968 Education Commission to try to put things right. Nobody then raised any objections when Tage Erlander announced his intention of going home to bed. The revolution was over and we reverted to ordinary Swedish debate and legislated reform. Both in Sweden and abroad, the 1968 Education Commission came to be known as U 68.

The very next year, the new U 68 Commission presented its first ideas on the subject of recurrent education. These ideas were a response to the Commission's main task of tackling the unrestrained growth of higher education. It had become necessary on economic grounds to restrict the numbers of new students admitted. This was a highly controversial measure and could only be justified politically if the young persons excluded from university were given a second chance later on in life. This resulted in a system whereby admission capacity is determined annually by the Government, after a consideration of student demand and a review of job opportunities in consultation with employers and unions.

Now in the eighties, we are once more faced with rising demand for higher education, due partly to a bulge in the young population. Recurrent education was originally intended as a means of countering such problems by increasing mobility between education and vocational activity. Clearly the need for such mobility is heightened in a period of structural change in production and restraints in educational expenditures.

Students today are far more adaptable than students of my generation. Examples of this can be seen if we consider the 55,000 persons who applied for the 19,000 available places in the autumn term of 1982. The low percentage admission rate reflects this change of attitude. One finds that many of the applicants had alternative opportunities which proved more attractive than the offers which most of them actually received from the university or college. Before the 19,000 places could be filled, offers were actually made to 45,000 of the applicants!

But these figures also conceal an element of mobility in the education system; particularly in the traditional student categories, it is still common practice to change study programmes or in some other way work out one's own salvation in the education system. The original idea of recurrent education was that students should also be able to alternate between employment and education within a study programme. U 68 presented organisational models whereby students would enter employment after one or two years' basic studies in higher education. After a period of gainful employment they would then be given the opportunity for more advanced and specialised studies. In this way it would be possible to support a process of long-term adjustment to the labour market. Vocational competence could be successively renewed and innovations and technical progress transmitted to the community at large. This, of course, is a far more sophisticated form of recurrent education than we have actually been able to achieve.

When speaking of the work experience which nowadays often precedes higher education, we include all employment regardless of its relevance to the field of studies. A system of higher education interspersed with gainful employment presupposes an advanced co-ordination between the various sectors of higher education studies and different branches of employment. Co-ordination of this kind simply cannot be brought about overnight, merely by structural changes in the education system. Changes are also needed in the organisation of working life, and in attitudes - especially within the universities. These have been slow to occur and the political determination to introduce a more advanced system of recurrent education diminished when the growing pains of the 1960s appeared to heal of their own accord.

The politicians had been disturbed, not only by the rebellious tendencies at the universities but by the problems which would be transmitted to the community at large by the threat of unemployment among the rapidly growing numbers of highly educated young persons. The danger of this unemployment was probably exaggerated. One should remember that Sweden in the 1960s still had a lower ratio of graduates in its workforce than comparable industrialised countries. The labour market proved to have good capacity for absorbing graduates. Much the same also applies to the austere labour market of the 1980s. Graduate unemployment is still below 1.5%. Young people, however, reacted

vehemently to the employment forecasts. Throughout
the 1970s, the proportion going on to higher education declined from year to year. Thus even before
the higher education reform, a growing potential
demand had been established for recurrent education. This is one reason why the interest shown by
mature students in the new higher education opportunities proves to be an abiding phenomenon.

Ironically at the same time as interest in
recurrent education diminished politically, those
in higher education were growing more positive
about the idea - paradoxically enough, for the same
reason. The principal motive force was the
presence of numerous young lecturers from the
expansive period who were now faced with unemployment as a result of the declining student population. The possibilities of compensating this by
recruiting mature students gave them an incentive,
just as the social debate of the 1960s had given
them arguments for challenging existing university
activities. It ought to be possible, they maintained, for our knowledge and resources to be used
and marketed better in view of the growing and
changing educational needs of the community. It
was now that we acquired courses not only in
political science but also in public health and
medical administration. Languages also came to
include a number of new specialised English courses
for economists, engineers et al. Chemists discovered that a course in chemical health hazards
was needed for safety representatives and so on.
All this, proceeding alongside the regular study
programmes led to the creation of a parallel system
of separate and individual courses. Most students
can both select separate courses from the regular
programmes and study new, specialised courses.
Whereas the idea of an organised intermediate leaving system proved utopian it was now hoped that a
'temporary utopia' could be achieved by means of a
system of individual courses.

It was intended that students would have
greater liberty in building up their own study
programmes and would be able to alternate more
easily between employment and educational activity.
Our students were to be able to return to higher
education several times and renew their knowledge
by means of individual courses. Under the 25:4
rule, new social groups of adults would be offered
further education and would be able to enter higher
education without any long-term commitments.

In practice, the programme of studies at Lund University includes about 500 different individual courses, most of them 10-20 weeks' studies. 200 courses are open to newcomers. These particular courses, naturally, are especially interesting to working people who want to enter higher education. Significantly this too is the sector of university education where adjustments to the needs of working life has primarily been achieved. One can of course choose to study full time or part time. Classes are frequently held in the evenings.

The connection between the declining number of young students and the introduction of the system of individual courses can now clearly be seen from course returns. To begin with more than 80% of the individual courses were concerned with the social sciences and humanities. These two fields had suffered the greatest losses of young students and were therefore in the best practical position to adapt to the new market. In reality, therefore, individual courses can be used as a substitute for an intermediate leaving qualification only in a limited part of the university. In recent years, new courses have been developed, for example, concerning information technology, biotechnology and developments in medical science.

These courses, however, are primarily intended for graduates wishing to renew their qualifications. The general tendency has been for growing emphasis to be put on the role of individual courses as further education for graduates. During the 1980s, the University for example has taken over responsibility for the training of school personnel. Teachers now return regularly to the University to attend short extension training courses.

The system of individual courses can be summarised like this: forty per cent of the students admitted to universities and colleges take individual courses. These students are older than the students following traditional study programmes. Only one-third are under 25, and another third are already 35 years old. The oldest group, 70% have degrees already. It is not particularly common for people to use the system of individual courses as a means of putting together a longer programme of education. Only a small percentage take full degrees by combining individual courses.

In reviewing the impact of recurrent education in Sweden we should also consider the results

obtained by students following regular study programmes. In the short programmes, training pre-
school teachers, nurses, etc., practically all
students have taken degrees after three years.
Turning to the longer, traditional programmes of
university studies, we discover a completely different picture after five years. A large proportion of students following social science and arts
programmes drop out before graduating. Even among
engineers and scientists it has become increasingly
common for a progressively longer period of time to
elapse before graduation.

These changes are usually explained in terms
of poor initial qualifications, the inadequacies of
teaching and so on. But it is hard to believe that
short-term and long-term programmes differ so con-
siderably in these respects. In reality, among
employers the content of studies has begun to over-
shadow the degree concept. In attractive technical
fields, capable technologists are frequently
recruited before they graduate. Sometimes part of
a study programme combined with a specialised individual course can possess more market value than an
actual degree. Intermediate qualification is
beginning to materialise in a more varied and individualised manner than was envisaged by U 68.
There is nothing new about this. If anything the
data indicate that this situation has evolved gradually throughout the 15 or 20-year period to which
I am referring. Thus nowadays most students engage
in some form of recurrent education.

The Swedish education reform in the 1970s was
a manifestation of this development. The administrative rules aimed at supporting recurrent education were framed at a particular point in our
history. The shortcomings of the system can also
be attributed to past circumstances.

During the sixties there was much discussion
of the ways in which Swedish universities seemed
closed to the influences of society and economic
enterprise. Today the university gates are wide
open. Regular contacts between universities and
the employment sector are producing an interaction
which can respond more flexibly to the specific
conditions of different educational and occupational fields. In this way recurrent education can
begin to be designed with more variety and local
relevance. Developments of this kind are now in
progress. But above all I believe that the role of
the university in continuing the education of those

who are well educated already will increase even further. This will partly result from the polarisation between the poorly educated and very highly educated sectors of employment which is a consequence of the ongoing automation and computerisation of production and administration. There is great confidence today in the ability of the well-educated élite to get Sweden out of its current economic crisis. So the authorities are now issuing instructions to the effect that courses must be concentrated more on education which can benefit our export industry. Fifteen years ago anything of this kind would have been considered a threat to university liberties. But there are also other voices.

One day I met a group of workers attending a part time course in environmental problems. They had decided to do their project work in the field of noise problems. One of our experts at the university was the main reason for that choice. He had measured noise at their workplace and contradicted their demands for a better working environment. They did not trust the expert's findings however and now wanted to learn how to do their own noise measurements. Eventually, they presented a paper in which they proved that the expert had been wrong. Quite simply, he had lacked their knowledge concerning the parts of the production process and the points in time where problems of noise occurred. Their essay on the subject was a constructive combination of scientific knowledge and practical experience. It is by looking at recurrent education as an encounter between practically generated and research-based knowledge that we can idientify its qualities for the future development of society.

We have just emerged from a period dominated by problems of quantitative balance and are entering a period concerned with problems of qualitative balance. Sweden needs an intelligentsia of international status. But it is equally important that each and every one of us should genuinely know that our personal and professional knowledge has a bearing on a common future. It is a dangerous tendency when the knowledge possessed by the majority is held in contempt by a powerful minority. The guiding star of Swedish educational policy has long been to create a wide fund of common knowledge and understanding on which to base the development of democracy. To remain true to this we need recurrent education.

# 29. RENEWING THE AGENDA IN AUSTRALIA

Chris Duke

The recurrent education concept has enjoyed higher salience in Australia than in most countries outside Scandinavia since its appearance in the context of OECD's round of country papers which followed the Organisation's original 'clarifying report' (OECD, 1973; Duke, 1974). It found its way rapidly into the lexicon of education commission and committee reports which are a feature of modern Australian educational administration - and perhaps of its policy-making, though the link between ideas and action is problematic. The report which led to the creation of the Technical and Further Education (TAFE) Commission (later Council), and an attempt to alter TAFE's Cinderella status, took a particularly bold stance, based on recurrent education, and a decade later writers are going back to the Kangan report as the most visionary yet practical of this report series (Kangan, 1974). Successive reports of three different Commissions which merged in the later seventies to become the Commonwealth Tertiary Education Commission (CTEC), like CTEC in its subsequent annual and triennial reports, have frequently alluded to recurrent education as an appropriate strategy, and it also featured in the terms of reference of the Williams Report deriving from a major Committee of Inquiry into Education and Training, though the result has been called a lost opportunity (Williams, 1979; Sommerlad, 1980). Recurrent education practices are also more evident in Australian post-secondary education than in the comparable sector in Britain - a fact which had led some apologists inaccurately to claim that a recurrent education system is in being. It is much easier to re-enter the formal education system in later life than in Britain, and to pursue

302

studies on a more flexible, spasmodic or part-time basis. External studies were sufficiently widely established in the early seventies that a 'Committee on Open University', for example, recommended building on this multi-institutional openness rather than creating a distinct UK-style Open University. The Australian National University is not atypical in having in most years somewhat more than a third of its students studying part-time, and half or more of all its students not having come straight through 'front-end-loaded' from school - students, that is, in the recurrent education mode. On the other hand Australia has its full share of segmentary departmentalism in policy-making (education separate from training; social welfare, labour market planning and education separate from one another; health, immigration, Aboriginal affairs and other functions struggling to liaise through interdepartmental committees and to win or retain resources from the financial and control departments in a somewhat fragmented and piecemeal way.

In this context, and with the multiple problems of recession, and unfamiliar high and persisting unemployment settling in Australia several years later than in the North, the Centre for Continuing Education (CCE) staff at the Australian National University judged it timely to take a new initiative, in 1983. A series of consultations and working parties late that year and early the next led to the publication and wide dissemination, especially among educational policy-makers and administrators in Australia, of a 'statement of intent' (CCE, 1984). <u>Recurrent Education for Australia</u> recalled the central values and purposes of the concept, referring especially to the OECD 1973 report, and argued that the new circumstances which faced the country required that RE be put back on the agenda of policy-makers and, if possible, brought to the active consideration of those in other social policy-making sectors. This short paper merely alludes to that statement, and reflects upon the attempt to reactivate a flagging debate in new circumstances. The paper itself, and subsequent documents indicating the progress of the programme, may be obtained from the Australian National University's Centre for Continuing Education (PO Box 4, ACT 2601, Australia).

The statement foreshadowed a series of research and linked policy studies predicated on an

Renewing the Agenda in Australia

urgent need to reconsider the place of education in
Australia in the new era of very rapid change.
Recommendations should be generated for implementation within and beyond formal education institutions. The project was committed to system change
and reallocation of resources, rather than creating
a parallel alternative system. Four core values
were identified as a basis for the programme, and
related to the OECD 'clarifying report': avoiding a
sterile dichotomy between the individual and
society (and between education and training);
equity (with a question about any possible role for
education as a redistributive mechanism); the
special features of adults' learning; and the
balance and mix of education, work and leisure
throughout the lifespan (a question critically
addressed by Colin Bell of the Centre for Employment Initiatives in London, in a conference on
national economic development and recurrent education in Perth, Western Australia, in September
1985). The Statement suggested that drift and a
crisis in public confidence would continue to
blight education without some clear policy ration-
ale, such as RE appeared to provide. The paper
sought, in the span of a dozen pages, to be lively
yet reassuring, practical though not pedestrian.
Thus it set out eight examples of criticisms
attractive to sceptics, and commented briefly on
each, and gave four examples of tasks for the
future of Australia, each of which had to treat RE
as a central consideration: industrial and economic
reconstruction towards high technology; reallocation of employment opportunities and the benefits
accruing therefrom; an Asian and multicultural
future; and reconstruction of the Welfare State.
It also alluded to the social conflict likely to
derive from a laissez faire drift into a society
highly polarised in education and information.
Apart from the proposal to seek a synthesis between
individual and societal purposes (less innocent
than it may sound) the Statement was most explicit
in taking a stand against full employment as the
only desirable future. It suggested, indeed, that
present policies to get people into paid employment
at any price should be modified: both to move
people from unsatisfying into satisfying paid
employment or formal education; and to move them
from unsatisfying paid employment to satisfying
non-paid employment (see Robertson, 1985). Admittedly, in the two years since this was dissemin

304

ated, it has become less difficult to allude to alternatives to full employment, save among candidates at election time. It is however a tactical question whether such an admission and proposition will alienate those whom a practical, policy-oriented document is intended to entice.

The remainder of the Statement set out a focus for the programme for a period of five years at the least, and listed the tasks which the central group in the National University and federal capital felt it their opportunity and obligation to attempt. This included questioning, analysing and promoting discussion about the different factors favouring, and obstacles to shift towards recurrence in education system-wide: party and bureaucratic policies and commitments; community and media attitudes and preferences; the Australian federal system; economic circumstances and assumptions about education; and culture, tradition and established practice. The programme was intended to clarify issues and create a new agenda, identifying the right questions being tougher, often, than getting the answers. Alternative scenarios, solutions and implications should be developed collaboratively with community and policy-makers for their consideration. Some immediate steps were set out as a form of commitment, together with several modes of dialogue and dissemination foreshadowed in the Statement and in other papers at that time. The Statement concluded with a list of subject areas in which the core group itself, as the node in a national network, expected to make contributions. These ranged from technological change through industrial democracy, paid educational leave and multicultural education to youth policy and adaptation to life-span changes. The idea was to make some mutual public compact as well as to convey the breadth of 'recurrent education policy studies'; it was indeed acknowledged during the formative sessions of the core group that if, say, 'technological change' had been chosen instead of 'recurrent education', one would still have derived a lens through which to examine the many interlocking elements of modern society. Interconnectedness, interdisciplinarity, were at the core of modern policy-making for a complex society.

Nearly two years later, it is still too early to judge whether this attempt at renewal of agenda is proving successful, though there can be no disputing that it is timely. The Australian federal situation, and the peculiar advantages of a Canberra location, mean that direct analogy is unhelpful. However, some aspects of this initiative could usefully provoke thought in Britain and other comparable nations.

The Statement seems to rescue 'recurrent education' from the scrapheap of fashionable ephemera to which too many new terms 'educational' are deservedly assigned with the passing seasons, reasserting its core meaning and distinguishing it for instance from continuing education as a form of provision. It seeks to push it out beyond the education departments and ministries to the attention of those administering, and planning for, other social policy departments, to insist that departmentalism is a sure recipe for failure in planning for post-industrial society. It gently challenges the utility of the 'work ethic' as currently deployed, and hints at a need to reconsider (not reject) individualism in the neo-barbaric days that have followed the glorious indulgent years of continuous growth and full employment. It acknowledges the need to rethink many basic assumptions, recognising the difficulty of doing this and the dynamic inertia which educational institutions display along with other kinds of bureaucracies. It inclines towards the counter-intuitive, challenging for instance the view that even with high youth unemployment, increased retention into upper secondary and tertiary education is a good thing (Smith, 1986). At a time when it is becoming common in Britain to talk of the two-year YTS as presenting compulsory education to eighteen, the argument is worth examining.

What has the programme actually achieved? And what problems have been encountered along the way? Although two central members of the group have unexpectedly left since the Statement was disseminated, it is still worth addressing these questions briefly, albeit in an interim and nonjudgemental way. The initial dissemination of the Statement attracted a wide and generally highly favourable response, mainly from people in educational administration, policy-making and research. The only critical response was from several readers sceptical of institutional education generally, who saw the programme as locked into institutional self-serving. The core group in the university department concerned, with a similar number of co-workers from elsewhere and a wider group of associates, has used a newsletter to distribute news, put interested correspondents in different parts of the country in touch with one another, and seek reactions. A network of recurrent education researchers, activists and other proponents has thus been initiated. A 'roadshow' has also visited several cities, conducting participative seminars in different settings to gather information, test opinion and promote concepts of recurrent education. Some of these have been freestanding events; more commonly they are associated with visits for other purposes, or added in to existing national conferences, for example of adult educators. Several working papers have been drafted and disseminated, or placed for publication. One 288-page volume comprising papers on the school curriculum, retention, and the economics of recurrent education, appears early in 1986 (Smith et al, 1986) and a second is intended later the same year, with a core concept document to follow perhaps a year later. The group has also submitted evidence verbally and in writing to major national inquiries, for instance into training and into technological change, and in these and other ways has raised the profile of recurrent education as a policy option in many, mainly educational rather than wider, quarters.

As to problems, and leaving aside those peculiar to the particular situation and membership, the largest is perhaps that of strategy: to whom is the work addressed, how are different groups and institutions involved, what is the best balance as between data collection, conceptualisation, dialogue, proselytising, disseminating, etc.? Behind this lurk questions, assumptions, prejudices and instinctual preferences about how change occurs, what policy-making really is, and so what policy-oriented studies are and how, if at all, they may influence policy-making and practice. In a subject and with a group infused with values and oriented towards action, these are hard enough to handle even with complete clarity and consensus within the group. In fact, and naturally enough, such consensus does not extend beyond a general orientation, a belief in equity, participation, diversity of provision, student-centredness, etc. Given the chameleonlike qualities of the recurrent education philosophy and concept, the RE programme also becomes a battleground for whatever differences of value and priority may inhere within the group. Thus utopianism and pragmatism coexist uneasily.

The truly radical nature of RE is agreed by all,
and incrementalism eschewed; yet there is a desire
to effect real reform rather than merely to strike
postures or fashion elegant prose. The programme
is about recurrent education for lifelong learning,
yet frustration with the conservatism of educational institutions drives some to an anarchist and
anti-institutional stance. The process however
brings into focus a serious debate about voucher
funding as a means of empowerment, despite the risk
that this will bring the whole programme into dis-
repute. Within the group, and spilling over
periodically in public 'roadshow' and conference
presentations, there is a struggle to hold the
balance as education to enhance learning - and
extending educational resources to other kinds of
potentially and already educative institutions like
the workplace, the family and community groups is
advocated rather than simply abandoning 'education'
for recurrent learning. Such a road leads to turning the back on all formal education, including the
vast public investment in the education enterprise,
and on the inequalities of access and outcome which
those espousing recurrent education seek to
address.

If the 'RE roadshow' is in constant danger of
being hijacked to serve one or another worthy but
different cause, at any rate, so long as the internal dialogue is also a constructive and accessible
one, which does not discredit the whole programme
and concept, this can be a healthy source of tension. An impression, rather than a conclusion so
early in the day, is that the Australian RE programme, launched by the statement of intent of May
1984, has brought RE back into many people's con-
sciousness, and encouraged a number to look at
their work and role, from this - as it seems -
extremely relevant perspective. At the least, it
may be claimed that the concept is being rescued
from being written off as an indulgence of the more
affluent and easy late sixties; for, as the group
has insisted, the force of the RE argument is
increased rather than diminished by the economic,
and social, circumstances of the eighties. It is
hard to avoid the conclusion that the same applies
with equal force to Britain although the economic
and social circumstances are different in some
respects; the term has never won even the nominal
and official acceptance allowed it in Australia,
and the means of promotion and dissemination have

to be different in so different a political and cultural system.

References

Centre for Continuing Education (1984), Recurrent education for Australia, CCE, ANU: Canberra.
Duke, C. (1974), Recurrent education - policy and development in OECD member countries: Australia, OECD: Paris.
Duke, C. (ed) (1978), RE 77: trends, tensions and trade-offs. Report of a national seminar on recurrent education, AGPS: Canberra.
Kangan, M. (chairman) (1974), TAFE in Australia. Report on needs in training and further education, Australian Committee on Technical and Further Education AGPS: Canberra.
OECD (1973), Recurrent education: a strategy for lifelong learning, OECD: Paris.
Robertson, J. (1985), Future Work. Jobs, self-employment and leisure after the industrial age, Gower: Aldershot.
Smith, B.W. (1986), Keep them in school? Retention and all that, in Smith (1986).
Smith, B.W. et al (1986), Recurrent education: a revived agenda, Croom Helm: Sydney and London.
Sommerlad, E. (1980), Williams and recurrent education - a lost opportunity? Studies in Continuing Education 5, 26-42, Adelaide.
Williams B. (chairman) (1979), Education, training and employment. Report of committee of inquiry into education, training and employment, AGPS: Canberra.

# BIOGRAPHICAL NOTES ON AUTHORS AND EDITORS

**Allan AINSWORTH** is Group Personnel Manager of John Player & Sons and has wide experience of personnel management in both public and private industry. He is currently chairman of the Schools Panel of the Confederation of British Industry, a member of its Education and Training Committee and of the Schools Curriculum Development Committee.

**Philip BARNARD** is at present a Development Officer at the Further Education Unit (FEU) with responsibility for work in the adult education area. Before joining the FEU he worked in the adult education service in Hertfordshire, and with the Inner London Education Authority. The views he expresses in his contribution are of course his own, but not necessarily those of the FEU.

**Andrew BENNETT**, the M.P. for Denton and Reddish, speaks for the Labour Party in the House of Commons on further and higher education.

**Tim BRIGHOUSE**, the Education Officer of Oxfordshire, was once a teacher in grammar and in secondary modern schools, and held administrative posts in the education service in Worcestershire, Huntingdonshire, and Inner London.

**Alan CHARNLEY** is Associate Director of the National Institute of Adult Continuing Education, responsible for the Research, Library/Data Base and Information Sections of the Institute.

**Michael CUNNINGHAM** is a full-time official of the National Union of Public Employees (NUPE) in London, who has taken a special interest in post-school education and in the negotiation of paid time-off for NUPE members to undertake training. His books include trade unionists' guides to fringe benefits and to occupational health and safety.

**Carol DALGLISH**, the Director of the State Mill Centre, Rochdale since 1984, was previously Head of the Continuing Education Unit at the West Sussex Institute of Higher Education and adviser to the West Sussex LEA on adult basic education. She has written on illiteracy among offenders, and on adult education in Hong Kong and chairs ARE in 1987.

310

**Chris DUKE**, foundation Professor of Continuing Education at the University of Warwick from 1985, was similarly foundation Director of Continuing Education in the Australian National University, 1969-85. He is the editor of the International Journal of University Adult Education, and the author of many studies of adult, continuing, nonformal and recurrent education in both industrialised and Third World societies.

**Dorothy E. EAGLESON**, the Organiser/Counsellor for the Educational guidance Service for Adults, Belfast (the first service of its kind in Europe, started in 1966), is also a member of the Unit for the Development of Adult Continuing Education's group on educational guidance, and president of the National Association of Education Guidance Services.

**John FIELD** moved recently from the Northern College to the Department of Continuing Education of the University of Warwick. He is author of Education for a Tolerable Society: Working Class Education in the Dearne Valley, 1918-1945, and he is active in the Workers' Educational Association.

**Gerry FOWLER**, the Rector of North East London Polytechnic since 1982, was three times Minister of State for Education and Science in Labour Governments, as well as holding other ministerial appointments. Formerly Professor of Education at the Open University, he has twice been president of the Association for Recurrent Education, was the founding Chairman of Youthaid, and is a Vice-President of the Society for Research into Higher Education.

**Colin GRIFFIN**, a tutor at Hillcroft College, is also a tutor in adult education for the Open University, and for London University Department of Extra-mural Studies. He is an Associate Lecturer in the Department of Educational Studies at the University of Surrey. His work on Curriculum Theory in Adult and Lifelong Education was published by Croom Helm in 1983.

**Brian GROOMBRIDGE**, Director, Department of Extra Mural Studies (since 1976) and Professor of Adult Education (since 1979), University of London, is a former adult education student, tutor, centre principal, researcher, pioneer of educational television, and Head of Education at the Independent Broadcasting Authority. Books include "Television and the People" (1972) and (with Jennifer Rogers) "Right to Learn" (1976).

**Keith HAMPSON**, the Conservative M.P. for Leeds North-West, was from 1967-74 a lecturer in American Studies at Edinburgh University. A former personal assistant to the Rt. Hon. Edward Heath, he was in succession, from 1976-84, Opposition Spokesman on further and higher education, and Parliamentary Private Secretary to first the Minister for

Local Government and then the Secretary of State for Defence. He is a Vice-President of the Workers' Educational Association.

**Phil HODKINSON** is Head of Sixth Form at Estover Comprehensive School, Plymouth. Having previously coordinated one of the pilot Certificate in Pre-Vocational Education (CPVE) schemes in Bedfordshire, he is now coordinator of Estover's scheme, which is part of the West Devon CPVE consortium.

**Geoffrey HOLLAND,** the Director of Manpower Services Commission (MSC) since 1981, is a career civil servant, who was seconded from the Department of Employment to the MSC upon its inception in 1973. He was first Head of Planning at the Commission, and then Director of Special Programmes. He has written widely on manpower, education and training, and management.

**Jean JACKSON** is Lecturer in Charge of an English as a Second language department in the ILEA Adult Education sector. Her research base is post-compulsory education in England and Wales and the United States with special reference to non advanced further education.

**George LOW** is editor of Education magazine, on whose staff he has worked for 12 years. Before that he was senior editor in the Open University Faculty of Educational Studies. He was a founder member of the Association for Recurrent Education and chairman in 1983. He is vice-chairman of the Education Correspondents Group.

**Mabel McGOWAN** has operated an Educational Counselling Service for Adults in Yorkshire for ten years, guiding some six thousand people into levels of study ranging from basic literacy to higher degrees. Recently retired from full-time employment in higher education; she remains a part-time staff member of the Open University, Director of Wakefield U3A, and still operates her counselling service.

**Naomi Sargant McINTOSH** had polytechnic experience before she became Senior Lecturer, then Professor, in Educational Technology at the Open University, of which she was ultimately Pro-Vice-Chancellor. She left the University to become Commissioning Editor at Channel Four television, her present post. She has written widely.

**Mandy McMAHON** lectures in Continuing Education at Bradford and Ilkley Community College. She has done survey research, small network studies and literacy work in the Americas, and currently is at once participating in and studying team management in adult education. She is Treasurer of the Association for Recurrent Education.

**Roger MERCER,** Principal Lecturer in Education Management at Sheffield City Polytechnic, once taught in secondary schools and then in initial teacher education. He chaired the Association for Recurrent Education in 1986.

**Frank MOLYNEUX** was a lecturer, and is now an associate lecturer, at Nottingham University, where he specialises in Comparative Education, and is involved in Ray Morgan's research. He is a founder member and past chairman of the Association for Recurrent Education, and became its President in 1985.

**Karl-Axel NILSSON** is a senior member of the Planning and Budget Division of Lund University, with a particular interest in the impact on universities of Sweden's recurrent education policy.

**Nick SMALL,** who is a staff tutor, School of Education, for the Open University in Yorkshire, had his initial education in Britain, but then trained as a teacher in Uganda and first taught in a secondary school in Tanzania. He has taught in a Leicestershire community college, and in continuing education in the University of Zambia.

**Anne SOFER** chairs the Social Democratic Party (SDP) Education and Training Policy Group. She was until 1986 SDP member of the Greater London Council and the Inner London Education Authority for St. Pancras North, and is a regular columnist in 'The Times'.

**Michael STEPHENS** has been the Robert Peers Professor of Adult Education at Nottingham University since 1974. Formerly a Research Fellow at Johns Hopkins, and Visiting Professor at Harvard and Visiting Fellow at Yale Universities, he has written and edited numerous books and articles on post-school education.

**Arthur STOCK** is Director of the National Institute for Adult Continuing Education, and Secretary to the Management Committees of the Institute's satellite organisations ALBSU and UDACE (see Glossary for these terms), to its REPLAN Committee and its Wales Committee.

**John TAYLOR,** a former lecturer in adult education at Edinburgh University, was first Director of the Scottish Institute of Adult Education and then Secretary of the Advisory Council for Adult and Continuing Education. He is now at the Open University, helping as Senior Liaison Officer to develop the Educational Counselling and Credit Transfer Information Service (ECCTIS).

**Linden WEST,** District Secretary of the Workers' Educational Association's Berks, Bucks and Oxon District, had previously headed the Adult Basic Education Unit of Lothian Regional Council, and has worked in universities and for LEAs. His special interest is the development of educational opportunities for working class people.

**David WOOD** ended his salaried life as Head of Education at Leicester Polytechnic, having taught in schools and colleges after army service from 1940 to 1946. Retiring in 1979, he remains as active as before, as Secretary of the Nottingham U3A branch.

**Maureen WOODHALL,** a lecturer at the University of London Institute of Education, has published widely on the economics and finance of education, her most recent book (with G. Psacharopoulos) being <u>Education for Development</u> (OUP, 1985). She has been a consultant to the Open University, OECD, UNESCO, and the World Bank.

# INDEX

# Index